ODYSSEY UNCHARTED

A World War II Childhood Adventure and
Education Wrapped in mid-20th Century History

by

FLEMMING HEILMANN

TELEMACHUS PRESS

This is the autobiographical memoir of C. Flemming Heilmann. While it is intended to be accurate, the events, accounts and descriptions used are subject to the author's memory and perspective. The author recognizes that some dialog may not be complete and that other persons mentioned herein may have a different perspective on the events, accounts and descriptions used in this book. The author intended no harm to any persons living or dead in creating this memoir.

ODYSSEY UNCHARTED

Cover designed by Telemachus Press, LLC

Cover art:
Copyright © iStock_528554136_HadelProductions
Copyright © Dreamstime_862675
Copyright © Dreamstime_7303068
Copyright © Dreamstime_11034739

Published by Telemachus Press, LLC
http://www.telemachuspress.com

Telemachus Press, LLC
7652 Sawmill Road, Suite 304
Dublin OH 43016

ISBN: 978-1-945330-29-2 (eBook)
ISBN: 978-1-945330-30-8 (Paperback)

Library of Congress Control Number: 2017944627

Subject: BIOGRAPHY AND AUTOBOGRAPHY / PERSONAL MEMOIRS

10 9 8 7 6 5 4 3 2 1

Version 2017.06.29

To my father,
Poul Bent Heilmann

Acknowledgements

Odyssey Uncharted is my first attempt at writing more than an article here, a travelogue there. Since embarking on this yarn based on childhood and teenage memories some years ago, the narrative has changed in several ways, including the period of my life addressed, the commentary on contemporary world events and sociopolitical trends along with my perception and prioritization of the important lessons I learned from my itinerant early life. Consequently, there have been dozens of people who have helped me in different ways. I cannot name them all, but that doesn't mean that I am less than grateful to every one of them.

However, there are people who have had especially deep insight and have been useful, kind, encouraging, patient and generous with their time. Of these, Judy Heilmann has the right to have all those adjectives applied to her role as advisor and critic-in-chief. Hana Lane, Catherine Breen, Maureen Judge and the Westport Writers Workshop have all given time, disparate ideas and good advice.

At Telemachus Press, my editor Karen Lieberman's role was absolutely pivotal, Steve Himes—with tolerance of my sorry IT limitations—made sure the process moved forward and MaryAnn Nocco then pulled the pieces together in production.

I am deeply grateful and thank them all.

Flemming Heilmann
Rowayton, Connecticut, June 2017

Chapters

ODYSSEY UNCHARTED

A World War II Childhood Adventure and
Education Wrapped in mid-20th Century History

Chapter I

Fortress Singapore

" … the worst disaster and largest capitulation in British history."
Winston S. Churchill

A FEARFUL, TEARFUL farewell in a monsoon deluge. My weeping mother, *Mor* (Danish for mom), my big brother John clearly distressed, and I myself at age five quite confused and frightened, all three of us completely saturated on the deck of the evacuation vessel. We were watching the small dark silhouette of *Far* (as Danish kids call their dads) melt into the gray monsoon cascade obscuring the quayside as the ship inched silently sideways from the dock, its lines being cast off, and then slipping out into murky Singapore Harbor like a retreating ghost stealthily disappearing into its own shadowy nowhere.

This is a true and indelible memory among my very earliest childhood recollections.

The very memories are difficult to pinpoint and define, because one never knows which of them might have been instilled by the anecdotes of parents or by images in old photo albums, and which of them are truly pulled from the bottom of the jumbled pile of remembered childhood crises and excitements. In my own case, the nether reaches of that pile are all Malay images: memories drawn from my first five years, spent in Perak on a rubber plantation called Jendarata Estate. It was the headquarters of a Danish-owned enterprise encompassing five plantation properties, literally chopped out of the tropical lowland jungle at the foot of the Malay Peninsula's mountainous spine, which runs from the Thai border to the southern sultanate of Johor just north of Singapore. Here the rubber trees, oil, and coconut palms were planted by the thousands along the northern bank of the slothful Bernam River separating the sultanates of Selangor and Perak as it meanders in slow motion across the steamy flats toward the Straits of Malacca.

I also remember my very best Malay playmate, Fatimah, with crystal clarity. I adored her unreservedly and she remains a vivid picture in my mind seventy-five years later. Immaculate glowing-gold complexion, huge ebony-black eyes in which you could not tell pupil from iris, immense curling lashes, finely chiseled nose and sculpted lips, smiley dimples, and shimmering blue-black hair falling softly in waves to the small of her back. We played together incessantly with her dolls, gorgeously dressed in miniature *sarongs* and silk *baju tutops* of stunning color, just as she would herself be dressed on *Hari Suci*, sacred Muslim days. We played the games of five-year-olds anywhere in the world, communicating freely in the simple Malay of children. It was my preferred language, ahead of the Danish and English spoken by my parents and European adults in the world around me.

Again with unbridled affection, I recall my tight relationship with Fatimah's father, our *syce* or driver, Abdul bin Rahman. Abdul welcomed me into the bosom of Malay Muslim values and traditions. Whenever he wasn't busy driving the big black shiny 1936 Buick for my parents, he would happily sit for hours, relaxed on his haunches, coaching me in Malay mores, Islam's five core principles, its rules, and good Muslim manners, including what foods were off limits and how to eat with only my left hand. Abdul was my gentle Malay mentor, a small, wiry, soft-spoken man with high cheekbones and a broad brow below his carefully combed-back black hair, visible only when he was not wearing his *songkok*. I could never negotiate enough time with Fatimah and Abdul.

From infancy I was assigned to the fussing care of my Chinese *amah*, who preferred to have me play at home inside the bungalow or in the garden, where in *Mor's* sight she could display her hovering attention to my every need, real or concocted, and so justify her employment. Every white child and the children of wealthy Chinese had an *amah*. The majority of them were recent immigrants or expatriates from China's largest province of Guangdong, also known as Canton. Typically they would send most of their earnings home to their families, as their cost of living in Malaya was virtually covered by their employers, who provided lodging, meals, medical attention when needed, and complete sets of new clothing every Chinese New Year (including the mandatory black silky pants and white button-up cotton tunics, which were the trade uniform of *amahs*). They did not have a formal trade union as such, but they organized welfare associations to which they paid a modest subscription and elected leaders by ballot. These groups would rent a whole floor of a local shop house, typically a town house with a retail establishment on the ground floor and residential space above, where they would gather on their days off to gossip and relax, and they would use the space for storage of prized possessions acquired in Malaya and treasured memorabilia, which they had brought with them from China. These women were entrusted with the basic raising and well-being of thousands upon thousands of European and Chinese children, while their mothers enjoyed ample free time for tea parties, social pastimes, card games, and gossip at the club. *Amahs* dramatically lightened moms' burden of mothering throughout colonial Malaya. They could also have considerable influence over a child's early learning processes and values. My own *amah* would often talk of the need to work hard because hard work brought opportunity to make progress and to become wealthy:

"Amah tell you, Flemmin,' you work hard, it make lucky,"
she would say, "and lucky make you rich man! When you

are big, when you are rich daddy, I come take care your children. Flemmin', I tell you, work hard!"

Another indelible memory is that of "Uncle Gillah" (*gillah* is Malay for crazy) the wild Danish bachelor in charge of one of the plantation divisions, who in his Tiger Moth would buzz our Jendarata bungalow and parachute our birthday and Christmas presents onto the front lawn of the large garden, taking care not to have the precious package land in the crown of the huge Banyan tree at its center. This is a genuine memory, not the product of repeated anecdote.

It is more doubtful that I truly recollect the king cobra, which made itself comfortably at home coiled up in my cot one night at bedtime. That story was told and embellished so often by *Mor* at family gatherings over the next fifty years, I have no way of knowing. However, the story goes on to relate how *Far* shot the cobra and destroyed its nest, which was eventually found between my bedroom's floorboards and the ceiling of the dining room below. In my mind's eye, I still see the thieving monkeys, leaping from branch to branch, swinging tree to tree to strip the back garden of papaya, mangoes, bananas, and crimson rambutans. All sorts including Gibbons, Macaques, and Silver Leafed monkeys. I still hear the staccato chatter and excited screeching of the primates.

I still dream of that quiet, pampered, plantation childhood with ever-hovering *Amah* treating me like a delicate piece of Meissner porcelain—a collage of disconnected scenes from that placid tropical daily routine. The large, rambling bungalow (all white people's houses were "bungalows" in Malaya, as were the homes of rich Chinese *towkays* or merchants, whether the house had one or two stories). It was built to capture every hint of a breeze, with a deep shadowy porch encompassing the whole house on both levels; no glass, but permanent mosquito netting stretched across each window frame downstairs; and upstairs fine cotton netting suspended from the ceiling to the four corner posts of each bed and down to the floor, as there were no windows in the sleeping quarters. The *chichows*, tiny green lizards, clinging to the walls at night. *Far,* feigning conspiracy, whispered as he taught me to cause the little critters to drop their tails in shock reaction to the crack of clapped hands or the stomp of a leather sole on the polished red tile of the floor. *Far* dispelled my initial tears of horror by assuring me that their tails would grow right back, which indeed they did in a couple of days, ready for the next round of my dad's fun and games.

Sauntering strolls around the expansive rectangular *padang*—Malay equivalent of an English village green—in heavy late-afternoon heat, while *Amah* exchanged her stream of gossip in lilting Cantonese with passing women in baggy black cotton pants and white blouses buttoned at the throat. If I stepped off the road, *Amah* would command me to stay out of the *lalang,* the long grassy weeds where a cobra might well be lurking. Scorpions were also a threat if they were disturbed, as they arched their tail segments, venomous stingers primed to strike.

The garden was dominated by a beautiful giant banyan, which has forever been my personal symbol of that Malayan childhood. An ancient, sturdy trunk in the middle of the expansive front lawn supporting a wide parasol crown and drooping limbs from which occasional tentacles reached back down to the ground, striking new roots in the soil. The banyan was home to exotic technicolor birds, green doves or *punai,* and the common yellow-vented bulbul who would signal the arrival of every single sunrise within a minute or two of 6:45, continuing its repetitious call to action for about ten minutes until his daily duty was done. Mynas with yellow face masks, black-and-yellow sunbirds and melodious Oriental magpies, for some reason dubbed *Prosperity Birds* by the Chinese.

An artist's work in Malaya called for a palette loaded with every hue and shade. The country's flora, fauna and human life produced constant explosions of startling color bursting from flowers, fruits, butterflies, birds or snakes of every ilk; more colors radiating from saris, sarongs, and turbans of the Sikhs.

Europeans in crisply starched white shirts and slacks or calf-length skirts grunting and squealing their way through mixed doubles, sweat jumping from their brows and hot pink cheeks. Off court, others would await their turn as they cheered a good shot or confirmed a line call while sipping their iced lemon-barley water. The pale yellow four o'clock sun would cast blue shadows, lengthening quickly as they warned of approaching short-lived dusk. *Chocras*, little Tamil ball boys, scurried around to retrieve errant tennis balls like busy squirrels gathering nuts. They rejoiced in the 10 Malay cents each earned for ninety minutes of busy work.

Children's tea parties were as refined as the delicately sliced cucumber sandwiches prepared for the adults. Heftier jam sandwiches sans crust for the kids. Ice cream, chilled sago with dark rich molasses known as *gullah malacca*, doting mummies with their cups of steaming tea, and of course, hovering *amahs*. European women chatting while knitting white balaclavas and mittens for the heroic Finnish freedom fighters thousands of miles away, skiing around in distant Nordic woods draped in white camouflage of bed sheets, sniping at barbaric Bolsheviks. Colonial ladies of Malaya helped save Finland and the planet from those bloodthirsty Slav invaders from the Russian steppes.

Endless thousands of dark green rubber trees stood smartly at attention in ruler-straight rows like a tropical battalion of guardsmen block-ing the advance of the pressing jungle. The white NCO chevron patterns carved into the tree trunks by rubber tappers added to their military bearing. By contrast, the scruffy sprawling oil palms offered shelter and nourishment to evil slithering snakes and plump, scampering rats.

Rubber still dominated the Malay plantation industry in the 1930s, but was already losing ground to oil palms as chemically produced alternatives displaced rubber and latex in making tires, and the demand for vegetable oils for food products, soap, and cosmetics escalated. Coconuts, on the other hand, have never yielded their role in the Malayan plantation industry, nor their picturesque place in the lowland landscape and along fairytale tropical shorelines. Easy access to their husky fruit enhanced many of the dishes offered at *Mor's* curry lunches or *tiffins*, and gave Tamil laborers convenient access to juice for brewing *samsu*, their party libation and source of comfort and mirth.

All of a sudden, the late afternoon's thin sunlight would fade and then surrender to the precipitous descent of a blue-black velvet curtain, as if a chandelier were deliberately darkened on a dimmer-switch, allowing but a few minutes of heat-fevered dusk. High-density darkness, heralded first by a unison burst of cicadas lying in wait for the exact, predetermined moment. Minutes into the darkness a shattering cacophony of wide-awake noises, which would then persist through the dead of night until the horizon allowed dawn's early grey to lift the blue-black velvet curtain again. The impenetrable black of night was pierced only by the dizzy, darting white glow of a million fireflies. Isolated, always breathless, moments of silence and drama would be prompted by the blood-curdling strike of some prowling predator hitting its nocturnal quarry.

Playmates at the Plantation School, where employees' young children of all Malaya's races received a simple but solid start in English, reading, writing, and arithmetic, at first learning by rote and group recital, or by singing monotone chants in unison like little Buddhist monks or oriental Gregorians. That was the modus operandi, and it worked well to prepare them for local schools. Discipline reigned and facilitated a natural appetite for learning

Wherever there were people, blue smoke would suspend a thousand distinct scents, aromas and smells, now perfumed by flowers, now spiced by *kampong* or Malay village cooking, then acrid from the burning of buffalo dung or waste, or just plain old woody from ever glowing communal fires; but the smoke was always turquoise blue. On the hottest airless days bereft of breeze, when not a single palm frond would stir, the stagnant smoke would hang dead-still, a ghostly wisp suspended over flimsy stilted *kampong* huts with woven reed or *attap* roofs. A whole day could pass before the air again stirred enough to nudge the spent smoke away, only to be promptly replaced by gentle billows from the smoldering village embers awakened by the breeze. Dreamy wafts of scent from exotic fruits, whiffs of a hundred different curries cooking, incense drifting from joss sticks in a nearby Buddhist or Hindu temple, smells of fresh buffalo dung, the stink of newly cut durian fruit, sickly-sweet steam clouds from a palm-oil refinery, sour steaming vapor from a latex-curing plant. Interpretive smells of Malaya.

Mor would regularly invite the company's half dozen bachelor planters for Sunday *tiffin,* an elaborate curry lunch, involving servants in crisp white cotton uniforms and silly little white Nehru hats, extending to white gloves and red sashes across their chests for visiting VIPs and special occasions. A couple of pink gins or gin 'n tonics would precede the feast. Blistering *curry-nasi,* the Malay meal of steamed white and yellow rice, and an oft changing variety of curried fish, chicken and beef, sinuous *ikan kring* or dried fish, salty prawns known as *udang,* crispy deep-fried Indian *poppadums* and floppy *chapattis* both of which are Indian varieties of bread, mango chutney and scorching chili or *sambal*—all quenched by cold Tiger Beer. Red spiny rambutan, equally juicy lichee, papaya, mango, and other exotic fruit and dessert of *pisang goring*—fried banana—and ice cream, or perhaps *gullah Malacca* on a kind of ice-cold sago pudding to cool the tongue and palate.

Dipping a pinkie finger in my mother's solitary evening tipple of Harvey's Bristol Cream just before bed time; *Far's* not-so-solitary *stengahs,* meaning half soda water without ice and half Johnny Walker Red. Good old Cantonese *Cookie,* who was in charge of the kitchen and considered himself a chef, made little Chinese and other Asian cocktail snacks called *makan kichil,* literally meaning small food in Malay. *Mor* taught him to prepare the odd Danish dish according to the availability of ingredients. Cookie was competent and reliable, but addicted to a daily visit to his local opium den somewhere in the employee housing complex, where he would go for his "siesta" every day, as soon as lunch had been cleared away.

Apart from Cookie and *Amah,* the domestic staff consisted of Condaya the Telegu houseboy and gardener and a *tukan ayer* or the water bearer, both of whom were Tamils. They all lived in the roomy whitewashed servants' quarters on the far side of a kitchen courtyard at the back of the bungalow.

Hindu funeral processions, escorted by pulsating percussion groups and a couple of wailing Indian *nadaswaram* reed instruments, dozens of white-robed and turbaned pall bearers, women ululating and moaning, mounds of fragrant flower petals inundating the coffin to be interred on a consecrated burial lot at the end of the service road leading into the dark green rubber trees.

Slow moving Malay men in earth colored sarongs and white cotton shirts, occasionally with a ceremonial k*ris*—an ornate dagger—tucked in at the waist in response to a *fatwa*, some wearing the round white skullcap, proud symbol of the revered *Hajj* or a pilgrimage to Mecca. The women wore cheerfully colored and patterned sarongs and *bajus* or blouses, covering their heads only with simple scarves in those earlier colonial days before stricter orthodox Islamic practice took hold.

Pounding thunder, detonating sheets and spears of lightning, gusts of wind propelling cascades of raindrops the size of marbles. Huge post-storm puddles teeming with busy tadpoles; sticky-green frogs with ugly warts on slimy backs, sucking in gulps of steamy air in the post-deluge sunlight. Midday heat so intense the air seemed to vibrate in the shimmering white light, which cooked the earth. Skin itching from the rash of prickly heat, floppy cotton sunhats, clammy sweat-soaked shirts. Bilious attacks with fever and diarrhea, malaria and dysentery. *Mor's* cure-all antidote of castor oil poured into an egg cup of lukewarm, preserved orange juice. Billions of ever-present, ever-whining mosquitoes. Millions of brown and gray moths, hundreds of spectacular multicolored butterflies flaunting their décor and, as darkness fell, the dizzy dance of mesmerizing fireflies. The "Ice House Lorry" from Teluk Anson arriving twice a week, sputtering, creaking and straining under its crushing load of quarter-ton oblong slabs of ice to help preserve household perishables for a day or two, keep the butter solid, and the bottled beer cool. It also supplied the plantation ice house, a less than foolproof repository for local medicine supplies, which had to be protected from the heat.

Torpid *kampongs* along the banks of the opaque café-au-lait Bernam River oozing along its slothful path, giving home to child-snatching crocodiles as it made its lazy way west across Perak's fertile alluvial flatland. The ever-threatening jungle forcing riparian Malay villagers into reluctant action with *parangs* (very sharp wide-bladed knives) and *chunkils,* agricultural hoes, chopping away to beat it back and allowing them breathing room to tend their modest rice paddies, vegetable crops and banana palms. Women cooking rice and fish or chicken over ever-glowing embers between the *attap*-thatched huts perched on stilts. Little rural markets where hustling Chinese shopkeepers or itinerant vendors haggled loudly over the last cent for a pound of rice, bags of *ikan kring* or *udang*, pineapples, passion fruit, durian, a bolt of white cotton, three yards of brilliant silk or a pair of lacquered chopsticks.

Far, whose given names were Poul Bent, was known as PB to those friends and associates who didn't call him Mr. Heilmann or *Tuan,* Malay for Mr. or Sir, figured large in the landscape. In his starched white safari shirt, knee-length shorts, white cotton knee-stockings and polished black shoes, he would march resolutely across the *padang*—the large rectangular expanse of lawn around which houses and other estate buildings were deployed—to his office in the slanting light of morning, just minutes after the hurried sunrise. The administrative offices shared a building with the plantation's clubhouse, where the white *mems* or madams and *tuans* gossiped in woven reed or *ratan* chairs, sipping lemonade and barley water or tea. *Stengahs* and Pimm's or pink gins would take over later when the day's work was done. Ladies playing mah jong or bridge, interrupted regularly for chatter and gossip sessions.

Some of these many memories are derived from family anecdotes and photo albums, but most are vivid recollections drawn from early childhood realities. I certainly have no personal recollection of big brother John crashing into me on his bike as he rounded the bamboo hedge at the end of the bungalow's driveway. The impact sent both *Amah* and me literally hurtling through air to a hard landing a few yards up the road. The estate doctor was called in to confirm that nothing was broken and that *Amah* was not concussed. The story has it that I was left with a debilitating stutter for a month or so.

Then there was the story about me and Roman Catholics. John had, from the age of six, been sent to boarding school at a little Roman Catholic convent in the cooler climate of Cameron Highlands. So, at the age of nearly five I wanted to know what "Catholic" meant. My mother, with her infinite Lutheran tolerance and readiness to embrace all things Christian, defined and explained in diplomatic tones:

> "God can be served in many different ways, Flemming," she told me, "and the Catholics, who are very nice people, do some things differently and have some special rules. Their priests and nuns are not allowed to marry and have families, and they wear unusual clothes. They are allowed to eat meat six days a week, but only fish on Fridays. You know, other people like the Jews and Muslims, don't eat pork at all. Catholics go to confession every week to tell their priest whenever they have been naughty, and they go to something called mass every day to pray in church, where they use special smoke and holy water, and tinkle-bells—all to please God. And they do something called genuflecting and crossing themselves in front of the altar," she explained as she illustrated the maneuvers in a kind of curtsy, while making horizontal and vertical hand movements across her ample bosom, "just like this!"

Her explanation, as the story relates, prompted a prolonged and troubled silence on my part as I left her bedroom to ponder. After some time I returned to give vent to my concern:

"I don't like that Catholic stuff, *Mor*! Why does John have
to go to that kind of strange school? I don't want to go
there when I am six. Please, *Mor*, I don't want to be a
Catholic, I would rather just be a Dane."

Those early sentiments endured despite the enormous respect I
developed over the years for Jesuit education around the world. Jesuit
schools have brought enlightenment and progress to so many isolated and
needy communities around the world over several centuries.

The undying personal memory of the anxiety experienced as Malaya
faced imminent invasion by the Japanese is still crystal clear: leaving my
father behind as we were dispatched to an unknown destination in
Australia, the departure with *Mor* and brother John from Singapore Harbor
on board the evacuation vessel *M/V Boissevain* on a dark drenching
monsoon day remains sharply etched in my mind.

~~~~

Life in Malaya, not to mention the daily news, had for months been
dominated by stories of Japanese military aggression to the north, the
occupation of parts of China, attacks on French Indochina, and menacing
threats to Britain's colonial possessions. The Colonial authorities in Malaya
never came close to admitting substantive danger. The government
resorted to naïve propaganda and bombast, which was supposed to
reassure the population that all was well in the eastern reaches of His
Majesty's far flung Empire. *Far*, however, did not buy into the British party
line, sensing that a Japanese invasion of the Malay Peninsula was in fact a
very real and imminent threat. *Mor* had observantly noted an escalation in
the number of Japanese people in hotels and restaurants in Ipoh and Kuala
Lumpur. There were visiting Japanese businessmen, miners and journalists
all over the place. The Colonial regime tried pathetically to calm nerves

through 1940 by solemnly repeating that the Empire of the Rising Sun was no match for that of His Imperial Majesty King George VI, and that the Japanese were "safely contained" by the omnipotent Royal Navy deployed to the north and east of Singapore in the China Sea.

"Fortress Singapore is absolutely invulnerable," the news broadcasts assured us.

"The Royal Navy rules the Indian Ocean, the South China Sea and the western Pacific. The Royal Air Force provides cover wherever needed and vigilant reconnaissance from above."

"The RAF's Singapore and Johore bases secure ownership of the air from Bangkok to Batavia. The Army and colonial police forces control every inch of the Malay Peninsula and Borneo, from Kelantan to Sarawak."

"Wild rumors are to be ignored. They are unpatriotic and distracting," directed His Majesty's government via the airwaves from Kuala Lumpur and Singapore.

Behind the broadcaster's voice, the Band of the Coldstream Guards could be heard in the background, playing "Rule Britannia" and "There'll always be an England."

In the planters' community of Perak, PB was never quite accepted by the more blimpish of the Brits and, because of his skepticism, even less so as the war threat escalated. He did, of course, have a funny accent, and Europe was being ravaged by the Germans; so a "kraut" name like Heilmann was hardly an asset, nor was his clearly expressed judgment concerning Malaya's readiness for war. The Brits rarely called him by his "outlandish" Danish name, preferring PB. His forthright attitude and disregard of social rank didn't always fit, and it was known that Denmark's government was not exactly heroic in its stand against Hitler's threats. *Far's* approach to his job was uncommonly energetic and pragmatic. For example, he had long expressed non-conforming views on the planting industry's labor relations and employment conditions. His management style certainly differed from entrenched local practices, and he rarely bought the colonial party line.

> "God knows where he went to school," said Simon Spencer-Worthington in the Teluk Anson club bar. "We have to assume the poor chap went to some village outfit in the boonies of rural Denmark."

> "Strange little country he comes from! Doesn't have the clout of Holland, or even Belgium, does it! Danes know a bit about ships, rearing pigs, and dairy farming, I'm told, but that doesn't do him much good right here in Teluk Anson, eh? We're not exactly deep into the bacon or cheese business here, are we, old boy?"

> "Poor old Hamlet Heilmann! Something's rotten in the state of Denmark all right, and he's certainly got it arse about face here in Malaya. Never had the benefit of our Empire experience and background, of course!"

After Malaysian independence in 1957, Teluk Anson was renamed Teluk Intan, meaning Bay of Diamonds. The old name was in honor of Sir Archibald Edward Harbord Anson, first Lieutenant-Governor of Penang under British rule. After the British hand-over, Anson was no longer an appropriate hero for whom a good Malaysian market town could be named under the Malaysian *bumi putera* (sons of the earth) mantra.

At the Club, over too many pink gins or *stengah*s, the British propaganda was translated into planters' inane bar-room ramblings:

> "Listen old boy, the Japs only have aeroplanes made of varnished *papier mache*," said Godfrey Winterbotham. "Sod it! There's absolutely nothing to fret about! I know the French are messing up in Europe and Indochina, but we are British, after all. Different kettle of fish, dear chap!"

The reality was that brand new Japanese Zero fighters were to outnumber and outperform the Royal Airforce's obsolescent Brewster Buffaloes, leaving the British ground forces totally defenseless without air cover, as virtually all the RAF's planes were eventually destroyed in their hangars or on the tarmac aprons of their airbases before Singapore fell.

> "The bloody Jap navy is simply no match for *HMS Repulse* or the *Prince of Wales*—and then we have all our other men o' war lying off Singapore. Totally in charge of the South China Sea. They'll have no problem protecting Malaya— and the rest of the world for that matter—from those little yellow slit-eyed buggers. And they can, of course, only get at Malaya from the China Sea via Singapore. No other darn way to take this country on, old boy. Safe as a bloody bank, we are!" declared Humphrey Sandys-Wynch.

> "It's quite impossible for the Nips to get at our backs by air, you know, nor by land! The Siamese jungle to the north does that for us. With the China Sea nicely covered from Hong Kong to Singapore, the Navy's protecting our flanks, my dear chap—we're in excellent hands," said Jock MacTavish, "So, cheers, chaps! Bottoms up!"

In fact, General Tomoyuki Yamashita, the Japanese commanding officer running the war in Southeast Asia, had meticulously planned the surprise landing on the northern Malaya beaches of Kelantan, and every detail was precisely prepared months before, plotted and charted by civilian advance men—the Japanese visitors *Mor* had noticed in hotels and restaurants. The Nippon spy network had in truth done a meticulous job, right under the noses of the colonial government.

> "The Japs just won't know what the hell hit 'em if they try any monkey tricks on Singapore. You just wait and see! They'll scarper at the very first skirmish. Between 'em, the Royal Navy and the RAF will have those little yellow bastards for breakfast. Fuck Tojo, fuck the bloody emperor and fuck his rising sun, too!"

> "Japan's a pretty backward nation, you know. Crude, they are—I'd say bloody medieval. All they know about is Sumo wrestling and making swords, but that's all about fat fellows, samurai and that sort of stuff, not about modern war. And they have strange eating habits, I tell you! That's why they're all midgets and bow-legged. Weak bones! They can't even feed themselves properly. They eat too much rice and uncooked fish. Primitive lot, they are! So, there's naught to worry about, old cock! Keep your pecker up, old boy!"

And so the chatter and braggadocio went on. PB became a less frequent presence at the club, choosing to have his end-of-the-day *stengahs* in more carefully selected company. *Mor* and *Far* spent more time with good friends among the senior people of leading British plantation and trading companies like Harrison Crosfields, Sime Darby and Guthries, as well as some ranking colonial service officers.

The Malayan colonial government was populated by very different categories of civil servant. The top echelon generally consisted of bright people, well educated and urbane, usually with impeccable manners. The British Empire was still enjoying its heyday, and thousands of Britain's *upper crust* who had not chosen careers at home took challenging exams to join the senior ranks of the colonial service in leadership positions, where they often did valuable work on behalf of the Empire and its subjects in many different parts of the world from Hong Kong to Lagos. On the other hand, the lower ranks, including many DO's or district officers were often less educated, leaving them insecure in the colonial environment, where their station in life tended to outstrip whatever perch they might have climbed to back in the UK. These more junior servants of the realm could be overly preoccupied with the pedigree, as they all wanted to claim *upper crust* status or be seen by their peer group to have it. Vocabulary and given accents classified some as *"Non-U,"* suggesting they were not upper crust. Collectively, however, the British Colonial Service, which governed huge territories around the globe, was a far better colonist than its French, German, Belgian, Spanish, Italian or Portuguese counterparts. Its legacy was to leave behind much stronger educational and judicial systems and better infrastructures from which the local population could benefit, if they so chose. The colonial Brits were also solidly loyal to the Crown and extraordinarily incorruptible, unlike their counterparts from the European continent. If only their indigenous successors and rulers in Africa and Asia had emulated them in this respect, billions of people would be a lot better off today.

The irony in 1940 was that the British Colonial Service, while spinning this web of naïve drivel about the strength of the military forces, was at the same time broadcasting offers of free passage to women and children on chartered evacuation vessels from Singapore to safe territory in India, Australia or New Zealand. From their Whitehall home base, the British government was busily contracting with owners of passenger liners and smaller vessels anywhere they could be found, irrespective of flag or registration, as long as they were not of the enemy Axis. The objective was to provide safe evacuation for hundreds of women and thousands of children. Many had boarded these vessels in Shanghai and Hong Kong as the Japanese threatened British strongholds. All of them called on Singapore en route. Dozens of the ships that set course for the UK ended up in Australia, having been forced to turn around and head south again as the North Atlantic had become increasingly perilous. The mighty German Navy, starting in 1940, wrought its U-boat terror on civilian shipping, just as they had in World War I. These evacuation ships generally steamed for Freemantle, Western Australia's largest port serving Perth, or to Darwin. The majority of evacuation vessels from Southeast Asia, however, headed straight for Australia from Fortress Singapore, landing their precious cargo safely in Brisbane, Sidney, or occasionally in Melbourne.

The family had lived in Malaya through the 1930s because *Far* had made his career there with Copenhagen-based United Plantations Limited, a group of five Danish-owned properties, which grew rubber trees, oil and coconut palms, and produced latex, palm oil and coconut products, or copra. The Danish company was founded before World War I as cultivated, commercially grown rubber was being promoted by the British colonial government. Rubber was not native to Malaya, but originated in Brazil's rainforests, where British botanists "stole" 70,000 seeds that were sent to the Kew Botanical Gardens in England. A fraction of them germinated and were forwarded to the colonies in Southeast Asia. Another source of rubber at the time was the French Congo.

The United Plantations properties were located along the banks of the Bernam River, the boundary between the sultanates of Perak and Selangor. Furthest downriver, nearest the Straits of Malacca, was Kuala Bernam (*kuala* meaning river mouth); and way upriver, not far from the foothills of the Cameron Highlands, was Ulu Bernam. The word *ulu* signaled that the place was close to the river's source. At one time they also invested in tea, experimenting with crops on beautiful plantations rolling over the misty hills high in the Cameron Highlands. Jendarata Estate was the biggest property and home to UP's Malayan headquarters, some ten miles from Teluk Anson. Travelling between the estates meant either very long boat rides up and down the wildly meandering Bernam with its oxbow twists and turns, or quick ten to fifteen minute plane rides. Every property had simple grass or dirt airstrips to accommodate small planes like Tiger Moths, piloted by the planters themselves.

~~~~

Poul Bent was the younger of twin boys, by half an hour, born on a mid-size farm in Denmark, in 1901. According to Danish practice and lore of the time, his older brother by thirty minutes inherited the farm. All the family's liquid resources, and multiple loans secured by the farm, had been spent on the training and education of the twins' much older sister. Ellen had, from a very young age, shown extraordinary musical talent, especially for the piano. In fact, she must have been quite an exceptional pianist. She had spent three months as a pupil of the great Arthur Schnabel in Berlin during the summer of 1936, at the peak of his fame as one of the world's very top pianists. Ellen then had a successful debut in 1938 at the renowned Odd Fellow Palace in Copenhagen before contracting an aggressive, racing cancer from which she died within months in her mid-forties. When PB came to the end of his teens as World War I ended, there was no spare cash and no farming career open to him at home, so it was made clear that he was to move right along and make a living elsewhere. Far did just that, with a clear realization that his academic qualifications were meager, and that his narrow reservoir of skills and knowledge lay in agriculture, gleaned through his childhood and teen years working on the farm. According to history as related by the family, he took the train to Copenhagen where he could stay with relatives and launch his job search. He apparently used that era's equivalent of the Copenhagen telephone directory to seek out names of companies and employers with connections to, or actually engaged in agriculture or forestry. One of these companies was United Plantations, or UP, in which he discovered there were some distant cousins involved. This was how PB started his transformation from a modestly educated son of a farmer in rural east Jutland to a career pioneer in groundbreaking agricultural initiatives in distant undeveloped countries. He was selected and employed as a trainee planter (then commonly known as cadets) in Southeast Asia, building on his experience of growing things out of the ground. He was not impeded by the fact that he was a young man of pragmatic intelligence, courage, iron will—and he had little fear of taking considered risk. He did not shrink from the voyage half way around the world and taking a plunge into the unknown. He was going to make the best of the opportunity, sink or swim.

A planter's work in Malaya was no cakewalk. It was an especially tough daily routine for rookie planters and young managers on the smaller estates. The usual elementary conveniences and comforts provided by urban employers were not always there to alleviate the hardships of life at the edge of the tropical jungle. Rising at four-thirty to be ready for muster, the *coolies'* roll call by lamp light at five o'clock. Directing labor to the day's first workplace before the morning mist trapped by the trees could melt away, the dense canopy dripping from over head, the ground dank under foot as snakes slithered out of the way and the mosquitoes attacked. Explaining the foremen's—*mandors'* or *kanganis'*—marching orders. Kickstarting the actual rubber tapping and palm fruit harvesting. Opening the morning shift at the latex-curing and oil-extraction plants. Supervising the recording clerks—*keranis*—in the field. Back to the bungalow for a quick breakfast at nine-thirty. Clear the desk at the office by eleven, check out the latex or palm fruit weigh-ins at the processing plants, plot the acreage yields from the areas being tapped or harvested. Back for lunch at one o'clock. A one-hour *lie off* or siesta. Another round through the fieldwork locations, solving problems on the fly. Back to the office to complete the day's paperwork until darkness fell abruptly two or three minutes either side of six o'clock, depending on the time of year. Only then could the planter say *sudah habis*—all done—and make his way to the bungalow for a cold shower and his first relaxing *stengah* of the evening with his feet up. This pace was maintained five-and-a-half days a week through two o'clock on Saturday afternoons.

Tapping rubber requires more skill than harvesting palm fruit, and some judgment, too. Armed with special grooving tools and knives, the tapper cuts V-shaped channels through tree bark, from which white latex oozes into collection cups suspended at the lowest point of the V. The tapper moves onto the next tree when the latex flow slows to a near stop, signaling exhaustion of that particular tapping. The process leaves repeated tapping grooves which form chevron-type markings like the insignia of a military non-commissioned officer. All this work is performed in Malaya's heavy, incessant humidity and pounding heat. Flaming sun or drenching monsoon torrents. The anopheles mosquito always lurking. Malaria, dysentery and scrub typhus always threatening, especially on the estates where health and hygiene were not given the Danish management's high priority. Apart from the abbreviated weekends, planters' downtime was limited to two free days per month, four days over the Christmas holiday, and four at *Hari Raya,* the big annual Islamic holiday marking the end of Ramadan with feasts of multiple curries and *rendang*, a spicy meat dish. *Hari Raya* is the most important of Malay holidays, when Muslim families gather as Americans do for Thanksgiving, but with a faith-based, benign Islam's emphasis on philanthropy, forgiveness, and good neighborliness.

Far had to learn to speak effective Malay, Tamil, and Hokkien, a Chinese dialect, to qualify for promotion and his free home-leave passage after the initial five-year tour of duty. Failure would mean a one-way ticket home for his own account. He could effectively communicate with UP's employees in all three languages: the Tamil labor force at the less skilled levels and the administrative staff which was multiracial, mainly Chinese and Telegu Indian. The enlightened Danish management style went the extra mile to emphasize respect for all people at all levels, communicating with them in their own language and appreciating cultural mores and sensitivities. It was truly a merit-based management philosophy, which earned UP a reputation as the Malaysian industry's model employer.

UP's success in the plantation business was closely coupled with management's ability to motivate people—that is all sorts of people. This is true of almost any industrial and commercial undertaking, of course, but good communication had special significance when working with such a multi-ethnic, multilingual, multicultural and often uneducated human re-source. Hokkien and Cantonese, Tamil, Telegu and Punjabi, and Malay had to be navigated along with Muslim, Hindu, Sikh, Buddhist, Roman Catholic and non-conformist Christian faiths. One had to contend with the influences of class perception and income level among Chinese and Europeans, and divisions by caste structure among the Indians. All these elements guaranteed that few management issues were straight forward and simple.

The enthralling and uncommonly enchanting diversity of Malaya called for uncommon linguistic efforts and skills. On the estates, Hokkien was the commonly used Chinese tongue, reflecting the earlier migrant *coolie* population drawn from China in the first two decades of the 20th century, which then graduated to mercantile and administrative jobs such as clerks on the plantations, at timber companies, and in the trading firms. Hindi, Urdu and Punjabi were also spoken by the ubiquitous Indian tradespeople and money lenders, the turbaned Sikhs.

Native Malays constituted 60 percent of the total population, which meant that the Muslim faith predominated. This was before the start of extremist Islam's steady encroachment into the Malays' moderate, tolerant practice of Mohammedan faith. Many were devout, but very few were extremist. Islam arrived in Malaya with Arab traders in the 13th century and only gradually replaced Buddhism and Hinduism with an unorthodox Muslim faith. Its spread accelerated in the 15th century under the influence of the Sultan of Malacca, reaching up the Malay Peninsula and south into the Indonesian archipelago

United Plantation's cadets, trainees, or "first tour" planters were not allowed to marry on their maiden five-year tour of duty. Young planters lived modestly in bungalows located in the areas or *divisions* in their charge. The local Malay girls were almost universally alluring, often ready for a little infidel romance and the perks which went with it, especially in the most isolated plantation areas. Romance within their own Malay community was hard to come by, because good Muslim practice demanded female abstention until the wedding night, after marrying by arrangement. The taboos and prejudices of white colonial Malaya dictated that Eurasian matrimony would almost inevitably lead to difficult social and workplace complications, so the Danish company preempted the possibility of a cadet planter getting excessively involved with some lovely Malay or Chinese girl and deciding to marry her. The theory was that if it was the right relationship, it would survive the wait for the young man's second tour. Among the Brits it was an environment, where "fraternizing" across the ethnic divides, let alone overt romantic liaison, was verboten, and could be career-ending. Conservative as the colonial rules were, the Danish management's measured tolerance of the cadets' amorous escapades was almost as liberal as the permissive free-love practices in post-war Scandinavia. UP's management had a pragmatic don't ask, don't tell practice, akin to a Danish wink and a nod. Six decades later in Connecticut, reminiscing over a second *stengah*, *Far* would allude to these romantic adventures from his time as a rookie manager on the isolated Sungei Bernam estate, where his bungalow and the employee compound was surrounded by uninterrupted acres of oil and coconut palms. With a conspiratorial hint of a smile at the corners of his mouth and mischief in his eyes he would tell me "between-us-boys" stories.

> "Those were the days—long gone," PB would say almost wistfully, "Those were the good old days, I must say! I'd just love to turn the clock back fifty years—just for a few more of those young and carefree days, or—ha-ha—should

I say nights? Too bloody bad they're long gone. But then I'm past it now anyhow, my boy! Much too old for those tricks."

"Those good old days. What is it they call them, Flemming? Halcyon days?" he asked.

"S*kaal*, my boy!"

The financial crash of all time and following worldwide slump hit with a vengeance at the end of the 1920s. The Weimar Republic had come crashing down with rampant inflation. Germans were famously lighting cigars with 10,000,000 Deutschmark bills. In 1921, the Reichsmark was valued at 272 to one U.S. dollar, as post-World War I Germany had established its first democratically elected government in the central city of Weimar. Ironically, before Weimar became associated with the disastrous years of the republic to which it gave name, the city was known for centuries as a center of culture, art, and learning associated with names like Goethe, Schiller, or Frantz Liszt. Throughout the country deep depression, unemployment, labor strife, massive public protest, and hyperinflation were hallmarks of the time. The catastrophic inflation was fueled by reckless government spending on "passive worker resistance" and other national and social crises. This was facilitated by simply working the printing presses to create ludicrous, unlimited amounts of new Reichmarks. Soon, one single U.S. dollar bought 4.2-billion Reichsmarks. The utter chaos of Germany eventually led to the installation of Adolf Hitler as Chancellor. As leader of the Nazi party he had been in and out of prison several times in 1933. *Der Fuhrer* was on his triumphal way, but the world around him was stuck in the depths of the Great Depression.

The global depression took its punishing toll on every financial and industrial enterprise, and the commodity markets of the whole world. As palm oil, copra, and rubber prices just imploded, Malaya's plantation industry became a financial quagmire and a management nightmare. The tin mining industry and teak logging fared no better. In 1925, rubber was priced at five shillings a pound; by the end of 1929 it bottomed out at just over a single penny in Sterling currency, a 98 percent plunge. In the phraseology of millennium-age industry and commerce, the downsizing of every company was absolutely devastating. Planters were dismissed and sent home to the UK in droves; that was the fate of almost half the staff on most of British-owned estates. Some properties were simply shuttered; others were amalgamated with neighboring properties to cut costs to the bone as they struggled to survive. Hundreds of thousands in the labor force across the Malay Peninsula were rendered jobless. There were no colonial government bail-outs in the Great Depression of 1929 or during the 1930's. Nobody was too big to fail.

The desperate Danish general manager of the five United Plantations properties was overwhelmed and just could not cope with the pressure. He buckled mentally, panicked, and then sought to end it all. He electrocuted himself in dramatic fashion by walking barefoot into a flooded drainage trench holding live cables in each hand. PB, who had already won early promotion to estate manager of one of the smaller properties at a tender age, succeeded him instantly, appointed by telegram from the chairman of the UP Board in distant Copenhagen. *Far* was thus catapulted into the leadership of a large enterprise in crisis, the *tuan besar*—big Mr.—head man of a substantial business by Malayan or any other standards of the time. PB endured a baptism by fire at the height of the Great Depression, receiving ill-informed and unrealistic directives from a very nervous board of directors, as shareholders panicked in far-removed Copenhagen, where United Plantations Limited was listed on *Borsen*, the Danish stock exchange. As general manager on the spot, his focus had to be on simply keeping the wheels turning, propping up the morale of management and remaining staff, holding the surviving work force together, keeping all variable costs to the absolute minimum. He put a complete stop to all capital expenditure, had to cut corners on maintenance of equipment, and pared all fixed assets. Production had to be reduced to the minimum level dictated by cash flow requirements, leaving oil palm fruit and coconut crops rotting on the ground and rubber trees untapped. It was a unique challenge for a young 30-year-old rookie manager.

Things were no better in Europe. In the USA, Franklin D. Roosevelt was busy spending taxpayers' newly printed money to construct his New Deal which, despite the massive public spending, was to fail him and America until the economy, a full decade later, was eventually dragged out of its rut by the stimulus of World War II.

At Jendarata, *Far* worked 14-hour days, smoking a round tin of fifty English Gold Flake cigarettes each day. The world economy recovered at glacial pace as demand for industrial and agricultural staples was restored by tiny increments in the course of the 1930s. The frantic demands and pressures from the distant UP board of directors and shareholders back in relatively stable Copenhagen were enough to test any veteran manager, let alone a rookie. There was no Roosevelt-type New Deal, no 21st century Stimulus Package, TARP money, QE measures nor other attempts to assist Malaya's economy. Far had a very lonely job, hell-bent on protecting the interests of all stakeholders in a precarious balancing act. His impatient masters were far removed from the rough and tumble of the realities.

Only the jungle was immune to the tyranny of the Great Depression: it never ceased pressing in, attempting to creep in to regain territory lost to the agricultural initiative of the European planter. The jungle's appetite for revenge was irrepressible and simply had to be conquered. Banks, creditors, and suppliers also had to be beaten back. Meanwhile creditors had to be placated as cash flow was managed by delaying payments to the limits of the law while debtors were cudgeled for prompt response to billing. PB weathered the storm by leading from the front, working himself to the bone, commanding the respect of employees at every level and every race on the five estates along the Bernam River. UP finally pulled through and was returned to profitability. By the mid-30s, the price of rubber was slowly recovering from its lowest levels and some of Malaya's rubber plantations, which had been laid dormant, were cautiously brought back into production. Along with United Plantations, the strongest British companies like Harris & Crosfields, Sime Darby, Dunlop Estates and Guthries had survived. Long closed independent small holdings, owned mostly by Chinese, started to come back more slowly.

~~~~

After five years in Malaya, on his first three-month home leave, *Far* reconnected with *Mor* in Jutland and soon asked her to marry him. *Mor* was the younger daughter of a modest soft goods merchant on *Soendergade*, the main street of Horsens, a small market town in eastern Jutland, where they both had gone to school. *Far's* home farm, *Tammestrup*, was just eighteen kilometers north of Horsens on the highway to Aarhus, Denmark's second largest city. They had originally met during a summer when *Mor* was learning housekeeping as a kind of domestic summer intern on the farm, before she started training as a pediatric nurse in Copenhagen. The courtship was a whirlwind of visits to friends and relations before their wedding in the tiny Ousted village church nearby the family farm. It was a 16th century white-washed stone church, with walls a meter thick, a stubby square tower capped by a modest beaten copper steeple. Three generations of the family were baptized, married, and buried at that same small church. Today it still commands a singularly captivating view from the zenith of Denmark's highlands, across a broad patchwork of cereal, rape, mustard and beat crops, pastures and woodlands undulating down to Horsens Fjord to the south. The typical Danish countryside usually presents enchantingly intimate landscapes and views, but this particular vista has grand dimensions rare in this Lilliput land. Denmark's highest point, all of 178 meters or 550 feet, is but a stone's throw from Ousted church.

Mor's career as a pediatric nurse was promptly dropped, and the newlywed couple embarked for Malaya, where, in 1931, brother John came to this world in a primitive missionary hospital in Batu Gajah (*Batu Gajah* literally means stone of the elephant), a tiny outpost at the edge of the jungle of Cameron Highlands' foothills. *Mor* lost a baby girl a couple of years later, and I arrived in 1936, in the much more comfortable environs of a hospital in Penang. After giving birth to John in a bare-bones missionary hospital, *Mor* had chosen the relatively modern conveniences of a government hospital in the crown colony. I was born with a hair lip, which *Mor's* health care theories immediately attributed to tropical climate, preserved foods and poor vegetables deprived of the vitamins and minerals found in good Danish food—or maybe it was the human waste used by Chinese horticulturalists as fertilizer. *Mor* had these little medical fixations, often embellished by a touch of the hypochondriac's less than scientific speculation. Fortunately, my physical defect did not bring with it the oft-associated cleft palate, so the issue was shelved and later fixed when the family of four enjoyed a 1938 home leave in Denmark. My hair lip was mended in Copenhagen by an extraordinarily skillful plastic surgeon.

As always, the family's home leave in 1938 was spent catching up with relatives, getting acquainted with new arrivals to the clan, and mourning departures. It was the last time I as a two-year-old was to see my four grandparents and my aunt Ellen, the brilliant pianist. After seven years of World War II they were all gone, as was any childhood recollection of them.

Meanwhile, through the 1930s, the complacent western world simply ignored the increasingly ominous rumblings of Hitler and his viciously racist Nazi party, or made excuses to minimize its actions. Left-leaning commentators, many of whom were infatuated with the Bolshevik experiment, labeled any opposition to the coming rape of Europe as warmongering or arrogant imperialism. Others, like FDR and Chamberlain, waffled ad infinitum and looked the other way. At the end of the 30s, Europe, USA and the rest of the world were in deep denial. Only Britain's Secretary of the Admiralty, Winston Churchill, vociferously warned of the catastrophe that lay ahead if the Nazis were not checked. It cost him dearly—his left wing critics and revisionists still paint him as an imperialistic, warmongering blimp of the British aristocracy. Japan's bellicose moves were written off as Tojo's theatrical saber-rattling. Mussolini's fascist bullying and acquisitive African adventures were reported as harmless "Mediterranean posturing." The world's socialists and media, in an unholy alliance with philosophers, suffragettes, preachers and peaceniks, looked away and turned the other cheek. Their response to any serious threat was to advocate centralist socialism at home while encouraging cross-boundary labor alliances and appeasement. The empowered fraternity of labor, they declared, would never allow workers of the world to fight against their brothers in another country when the real enemy was the establishment and the ruling class at home. Doing nothing was so easy. In any event, they claimed, western democracy was under no substantive threat. Millions of tormented Jews lost their homes, their assets and livelihoods to Hitler's monstrous "redistribution," but that was not allowed to be an issue of note. Europe and America kept right on course, whistling past the graveyard. PB was never in doubt that his duty and job was the stewardship of the properties of UP headquartered on Jendarata Estate; but he grew anxious over what he saw and heard of Europe and was no less concerned over Japan's aggressive moves on China

Early in the fall of 1938, the family returned to Malaya on one of East Asiatic Company's vessels, Denmark's favorite passenger-cargo link to the Far East. A leisurely voyage back to the heat and routine of British colonial surroundings. John was again sent off to his convent up in the cool of Cameron Highlands. I was largely in *Amah's* doting care on Jendarata Estate in the throbbing heat, where I got both dysentery and malaria. This second time round, *Mor* fell into that Malayan routine more readily. Her first arrival years earlier had presented challenges of language, culture and the sometimes pretentious demands of life as a *memsahib*, wife of the boss. She had by now mastered two new languages and learned to handle the pseudo-genteel antics of English colonial women and to speak up for herself. She had, in fact, also learned to enjoy being spoiled by some aspects of a privileged colonial lifestyle.

~~~~

With the escalating aggression of Tojo's Japan to the north, *Far* had decided to take the Brits up on their offer of evacuation passages for women and children. While the government offered free evacuation passages, they did so in hesitant and inconspicuous ways. Singapore's *Straits Times* reported that supreme commander of British forces, General Arthur Percival, had warned that "overt European evacuation programs would have a negative psychological effect on the native Asian population of Malaya," so booking such a passage took proactive perseverance. This was how the families of less farsighted Brits later got trapped by the invasion.

PB booked us on the government-chartered Dutch vessel, *M/V Boissevain*, headed out of Singapore for Sydney under contract to the Brits. He equipped *Mor* with Thomas Cook travelers checks and an Australian bank account, to provide funds estimated to last up to six months. Everybody, even skeptical *Far*, was persuaded that the Japanese situation in Southeast Asia would be sorted out in a matter of months. This was the expectation despite what was going on in Europe as Mussolini sided with Hitler and every indication was that the Axis could take over that whole continent from Moscow to Madrid. *Far* had only scorn for Neville Chamberlain's wobbly appeasement of Hitler; he scoffed at the Prime Minister's pathetic promise of "peace in our time" upon returning from Munich, waving a piece of paper signed by the *der fuhrer*. He noted how the Vichy French viewed the situation through their own xenophobic lens of elitist complacency. He saw that the Americans were not even vaguely interested in getting involved in what they characterized as a confluence of European issues that did not concern America, even with Japanese aggression in China and the western Pacific region. *Far* wanted us out of Malaya, and yet did not foresee that there were five years of brutal World War II ahead.

He took a lot of flack from peer group planters at the Teluk Anson Club, almost all of whom were contented Brits under the spell of the government's propaganda and spin. Ironically, some of these colonial blimps—hard drinking, bloviating planters, accountants, and lower rank colonial service functionaries—were the first to take off when the situation later threatened them directly. They and their booze-induced bravado would vanish like the morning mist. Meanwhile, *Far* was quite determined to get his family out of harm's way while he would stay on to do his job. He was possessed by his responsibility for the interests of the company, shareholders, and its employees. He was driven by unswerving loyalty to more than two thousand people working on the five plantations.

PB had first made things clear to *Mor* before he spoke to the assembled family.

"Now please listen to me, dear ones," he said at the dinner table. "In my own mind it is just a matter of time before there is fighting in Malaya and Borneo, and serious bloodshed is inevitable. It is going to be no place for women and children. And there's no knowing how far it will spread … perhaps to Burma and India. I have thought a lot about it and, my dear boys, I have been talking with *Mor* about our situation. I am getting you all three out of here.

I am sending you to Australia, where you will be safe and sound until the British finally face the realities, come to grips with the Japs, and get things back on track and under control again throughout the Far East. Australia has to be the safest place to go, as Europe is obviously not an option, even if ships could get safely through the north Atlantic. Allied ships are being sunk by the dozens, and the Germans are on a march across Europe. Nor is India an alternative, because I don't think that country is safe from the Japs either."

Far paused for a moment as he could see that *Mor,* and therefore both of us boys, were struggling to stem the tears.

"You see, my dearest boys, there are times in life when you don't know enough, you can't predict for sure what is going to happen, so you simply can't be confident you're doing the right thing. Whatever the government says to reassure us all, there's no way in which I can tell what's going to happen here in Malaya, nor do I know exactly what *Mor* and you boys will find at the other end, or how she will manage in Australia. All I do know is that the three of you will be safe in Brisbane, Sydney, or Melbourne. I hear that the Australians are responding to this situation with kindness and generosity, and that refugees are being well treated. But I don't know more than that. Your safety is the priority, and I am convinced you are going to be in harm's way if I keep you here … so that's out of the question. You boys and *Mor* are off to Ozzie, sink or swim!"

Far's whole life was characterized by momentous decisions made on the basis of carefully assessed risk. He was bright, pragmatic and usually right; the family reaped benefit and progress as a result.

~~~~

The image which still leaps out at me, after all these years, is that of Far's gray silhouette waving his wide-brimmed straw hat at the edge of the dock in Singapore Harbor, as M/S Boissevain inched away from its berth. Cascades of water from a leaden monsoon sky engulfed all four of us.

Three of us in trepidation, waving from the ship's top deck, shedding torrents of tears as if to match the tropical downpour—Far, the only person in sight on the quay below, signaling his final farewell, hat held high. Although too young at the time to appreciate the dimensions or implications of what was happening, I still sense the reeling intensity of that moment's emotions and the appalling sense of helpless uncertainty. The memory to this day evokes a shiver and goes to the pit of the stomach. Ever courageous *Mor* simply could not stem the sobbing. None of us moved until minutes after the dark, dense curtains of water had completely engulfed the solitary gray figure on the dock. That moment changed life's direction as we plunged into the unknown on an uncharted odyssey.

I recall almost nothing of the journey into the Antipodes. The *Boissevain* made a stop in Batavia, where John first set eyes on eight-year-old Inge-Marie Nielsen, the girl he was to marry just a decade and a half later in Tokyo, of all places. *Mor* had arranged to look up Tage Nielsen, whom she and Far knew from their Danish school days in Horsens. Working for a molasses trading company, he lived in Batavia—today named Jakarta— with his Dutch wife and two children. The Dutch colonial government was no more alert or better prepared for the Japanese threat than were the Brits in Malaya, and life in Batavia was still complacently normal. Inge-Marie, her younger brother, and her mother were later put under house arrest by the Japs for the duration of the war, and father Tage spent the war in a Japanese prison camp.

The rest of the voyage is but a blur. Family legend has it that Japanese high speed torpedo boats were sighted by passengers as they patrolled the waters of Indonesia or the Dutch East Indies, as they were then known. I was later reported to have called them "speed potato boats."

Arrival in Sydney escapes me completely, but not the long train ride to Melbourne. It was an overnight affair involving a tiresome, sleepy transfer in the dead of night from the initial train from Sydney to another waiting across the border-station's single platform. The explanation for the mid-night inconvenience was a change in the gauge of the rail tracks at the boundary between the competing states of New South Wales and Victoria. The two Australian states could apparently agree on very little, and certainly not on railroad gauges. That was my early introduction to ludicrous practices of territorial hubris and protectionism in government, which I was to encounter later in linguistically divided Belgium, South Africa, and pathetically fractured Canada, with its ten parochial provinces—another country divested of national glue to unite it. That Australian idiocy prevailed, prolonging train transfers and billions of dollars of unnecessary waste for decades. To cap it all, the Sydney-to-Melbourne overnight "express" was pretentiously named "The Spirit of Progress." For the governments of New South Wales and Victoria, progress did not extend to standardization of railroad gauges, since that might mean more open markets and competition in interstate commerce.

Dread the thought!

A short spell in a cheap Melbourne hotel did not leave any lasting memory, except that the strange surroundings were never threatening. We were received with open arms. The Aussies were spontaneously and warmly generous without evident plan or coordination by government, extending a welcoming embrace to thousands of European refugees arriving from East Asia. Gregarious *Mor* quickly linked up with three or four other women, all British, who had left Shanghai, Hong Kong and Singapore with their children on various evacuation vessels, ending up for some reason in Melbourne. To this day, I do not know why we or they decided to head for the Victoria State capital.

Together they concocted a plan.

Things in Southeast Asia were getting more ominous by the day, as all-out war with the Japanese became a reality, and a full scale invasion of Malaya loomed. Geelong Grammar, an exceptionally progressive (truly progressive, as opposed to the American political sense of the word) boarding school, inappropriately tagged as the "Eton of Australia," threw its doors open to dozens of boys arriving with refugee families, including John Heilmann. He became the beneficiary of the finest education

Australia had to offer, absolutely pro bono for the duration of World War II. The governors of this private school, prompted by its visionary headmaster, James Darling, decided that the young refugees and their families should be guests not only of Australia, but also of Geelong Grammar until the planet's geopolitical convulsions were resolved. Meanwhile, the evacuee women, having hatched their plan, teamed up to rent an old Victorian house on a two-acre plot in the tiny seaside village of Barwon Heads at the mouth of Port Philip Bay, near Geelong and about 60 miles southwest of Melbourne. Here they formed a commune.

Barwon Heads was a peaceful, cozy seaside village, nestled under a beautiful large bluff sheltering it from the Tasman Sea. It was a fisherman's paradise with a tiny harbor and wonderful white beaches nearby, frequented by surfers and vacationing families. In this setting it was difficult to realize that history's most brutal world war was raging across much of the globe.

Mor and *Far* were able to keep erratic communications going via Red Cross letters and occasional cables during the early months of the separation. As the situation grew ever more threatening, they made a quite specific, preemptive deal to ensure that PB could contact us whenever he got the chance and would know where to find us in case we lost touch. The agreement was that while John went off to board at nearby Geelong Grammar School, *Mor* and I would stay in the Barwon Heads house, come hell or high water. This deal was only to be broken if or when *Mor* knew that *Far* was safely in the hands of the allies, was imprisoned by the Japs, was reported dead or if he actually arrived in Australia. Always pragmatic, PB took a very realistic approach and was able to send one more book of Thomas Cook checks, as he saw the hopes of an allied resolution of the conflict with the Japs dwindle.

The shared property in Barwon Heads did become a veritable commune in which the women distributed responsibilities for housekeeping and generating cash. All of them knew their cash resources were finite, and that they had to do something about it. Otherwise they would run out of funds before too long. A logical division of labor was developed.

The grounds of the property were transformed into a productive horticultural plot, where the women were individually responsible for different crops of fruits, vegetables, flowers and herbs. A garden shed served as a coop and a chicken run was fenced off. Hens and eggs became an important source of both food and income. Chicken prepared in every way became the staple diet: from *a-la-king* to *coq au vin, Bombay-curried, cacciatore*—stir-fried, boiled, sweet and sour, or just plain old roasted chicken. If it wasn't chicken, it was lamb or mutton. Australia was never short of sheep, so when the war impeded exports of lamb and mutton, the glut yielded an extremely inexpensive source of protein. Sheep's brains were a frequent main course, for which I never developed a fondness, despite attempts to disguise them in many presentations. That squishy, smooth texture in the middle, even when they were breaded and deep-fried to a crisp on the outside! Ugh! Tons of beautiful vegetables and fruits were grown for consumption and sale. Fish was a rare treat, although seafood was abundant and reasonably priced at the mouth of Port Philip Bay; it was still too expensive. *Mor* was a handy seamstress, so she was assigned specifically to the production of lambskin gloves, for both men and women, which fetched good prices at the local market and selected shops in the nearby city of Geelong. It was quite clear that Australian generosity and eagerness to give support boosted the income stream of the commune. The Aussies were not only extraordinary hosts, but also extraordinarily loyal and generous customers of the commune, who made sure that any hardship suffered by the refugees in Australia was minimized.

Being so young, living happily with other kids of my age, I was all but oblivious to *Mor's* chronic anxiety and the emotional hardships of the women in the group. I grew physically strong, enjoying a healthy diet of fresh food and the vigorous climate of coastal Victoria, no longer the somewhat sickly little fellow struggling with the heat, dysentery, malaria, or the other tropical disorders encountered back in Malaya. Mor's frantic scanning of all newspaper reports and obsessive attention to radio broadcasts covering developments in Southeast Asia escaped my attention. However, the news in fact deteriorated with every week.

~~~~

The Japanese fooled everybody, especially the complacent British, by landing on the northeastern coast of the Malay Peninsula to invade from the South China Sea. This happened only hours before the Japanese air force shocked the United States and allies by bombing the heart out of Pearl Harbor. The Japs made land among the fishermen's *kampongs* on the gorgeous palm-lined beaches of Kelantan, near Kota Baharu, and then used bicycles to move unchallenged southward in hordes towards Perak, then Kuala Lumpur, and eventually Singapore.

At 4:15 a.m. on December 7, 1941, the Japs struck Singapore with their first nocturnal air raid. The Royal Navy's base was ablaze with all its lights still on. *HMS Repulse* and the *Prince of Wales* supposedly guarding Fortress Singapore with several attendant escort ships were sent to the bottom of the China Sea or the Malay Straits by Japanese Zero dive bombers, or torpedoed by their submarines causing death and destruction deep into the Indian Ocean. The rest of the Royal Navy's East Asian fleet had fled in shame. Japan's disciplined and well equipped air force (those *papier mache* planes the Teluk Anson blimps had scorned) turned out to be state of the art. They meticulously bombed Singapore's strategic buildings, one by one, before annihilating squadrons of Royal Air Force planes— mostly Brewster Buffaloes—still parked on the tarmac aprons of their Singapore or Jahor airbases. The *Nips* methodically took out Britain's mighty tools of war, her fortifications and her strategic centers of communication and government.

Resistance from the overwhelmed Brits was notoriously pathetic. The official British surrender finally came on January 31, 1942. The Japanese renamed Singapore *Syonan-to*, City of Light, and within a month or two

their military police had killed up to 50,000 civilians in the *Sook Ching* purge
of ethnic Chinese from Penang to Singapore, claiming they were plotting a
revolt against the occupying forces. Thousands of Europeans, mainly
British civil servants and troops were locked up in Changi jail at the eastern
end of Singapore Island, where the nation state's proud airport now
thrives.

So much for Fortress Singapore!

Singapore, the fortified trading hub had been there as the eastern
cornerstone of the known world's trade for 800 years, a major port of call
on the ancient maritime silk route. Temasek, meaning Sea Town in
Javanese Malay, or Singapura (Sanskrit for Lion City) became part of the
Sultanate of Johor in the early 16th century. It was burned to the ground in
1613 by marauding Portuguese traders based in Malacca, the smaller rival
settlement on the southwestern Malay coast. The British did not really
make themselves seriously felt until early in the 19th century when Stamford
Raffles and William Farquhar established a trading post for the British East
India Company in 1819. At that time, they signed a treaty with the Sultan
of Johor to legitimize London's dominant role in the development of what
was to become today's flourishing, internationally influential city-state.
Singapore was later folded into the British *Straits Settlement* colony, which
was administered officially by the government of British India. Halfway
through the 19th century the wonderful natural harbor was deepened and
named Keppel Harbour; this eventually became the strategic East Asian
base for His Majesty's acclaimed Royal Navy.

With the fall of Singapore, communications between Malaya and the
Western World fell silent, including of course, those between *Mor* and *Far*.
Every line had gone dead, but sparse and spasmodic communication with
Europe was strangely still possible via Red Cross dispatches, which were
the source of some news snippets regarding the family back home in
Denmark.

In the spring of 1940, the Germans had turned their attention to
Scandinavia. Sweden had declared neutrality, but the Nazis announced that

Norway and Denmark had to be "protected from British attack" and proceeded to occupy Denmark on April 9, 1940, en route to taking Norway. The German fleet grouped in the Baltic and the North Sea while the little Danish navy was ordered by the government not to resist. German paratroopers started dropping into Denmark at 5:30 in the morning. The Danish army of less than 10,000 men was barely mobilized, and the only genuine fighting was limited to the region of northern Slesvig on the German border and skirmishes around Amalienborg, the royal residence when the Germans took Copenhagen. By 9:30 that same morning, the Danish government's surrender process was started. Varying reports of Danish lives lost point to numbers in the hundreds, including police and civil servants. Hitler had secured strategic locations for his airbases along the North Sea coastline of Jutland as well as the supply routes for German imports of essential Swedish steel. Seventy years later, Anders Fogh Rasmussen, former Danish Prime Minister and Secretary General of NATO, succinctly described the Danish government's position and reaction to the invasion as "morally unjustifiable."

Months went by while the evacuee families in Barwon Heads waited in limbo. The broadcasts and news stories became ever more distressing. Nerves were hardly calmed by Canberra's announcement of mandatory blackout disciplines and emergency coastal evacuation plans after reports of Japanese U-boat sightings off the shores of Queensland, Victoria and New South Wales. There was no news of PB or any of the other women's husbands. *Mor* knew that PB would stay on the job on Jendarata Estate to prepare for the worst until it was no longer safe to do so. That of course worried her all day, every day, and through every night. The news of Singapore's fall told of brutal roundups of Europeans conducted by the Japs throughout Malaya, the men being thrown into the infamous Changi Jail, or sent north as forced labor for the Japanese occupiers, many dying of sheer exhaustion or disease on construction sites of the renowned Siam Railway. Women who had remained in Malaya were interned with their children in special camps around the country, sometimes after weeks of marching from one location to another under the blazing tropical sun, deprived of shelter, food, and water. *Mor* and the other commune women, although spared the marches, were on the other hand tortured by nightmare images of their men on the run, or captured and starving in Changi— or dead.

The Red Cross's erratic overseas communication from Denmark brought distressing news. *Mor* received word from her sister that their mother, or my *mormor* as Danes call their maternal grandmothers, had died of a broken heart. She had lost her husband, my *morfar*, soon after the German occupation. *Mor's* sister with my half-Jewish cousin, Lone, had fled from the Copenhagen Gestapo to Sweden, helped by Danish fishermen who smuggled them (and about 8,000 thousand Jews) across the sound, *Oresund*, and the *Kattegat* to the Swedish coast. Aunt Harriet's Jewish husband, Uncle Aage Schoch, was a senior journalist and one of the founding leaders of the coordinated resistance movement in Denmark. The SS were looking for these families in order to prepare for the *Endlösung*, "the final solution." They caught *Onkel Aage* and locked him up on the attic floor of Gestapo Headquarters in Copenhagen's *Shell House*, which had been commandeered and taken over from the oil company. *Mormor* had thus been left totally isolated and alone in Nazi-occupied Denmark until she simply could take it no longer. After the war, an old friend and nursing colleague told my mother that *Mormor* had actually taken her own life.

At last, one of the Barwon Heads commune women got word that her husband had somehow landed safely in distant Brisbane. That reunited family, so favored by Lady Luck, immediately moved elsewhere. The remaining women could not suppress their jealousy over the good fortune of the couple. There was thinly disguised bitterness in the farewells as the lucky family departed Barwon Heads. Why couldn't they all be that fortunate? But reality had to be faced, and the remaining women buckled up and continued to work well together, so there was never any shortage of food, fuel, or clothing, thanks in part to generous Australian customers who, whenever they could, bought their produce, eggs, and chickens from the commune rather than the local shops. The Aussies stopped at nothing in their efforts to support the *pommies,* as the Australians characterized the Brits suddenly injected into their normally homogeneous Australian community. Other foreign women were also the beneficiaries of this rough and ready kindness.

> "Good on ya, sheila! Bonza greeens and stuff you're producing—they're reeelly dinkum freesh! Same for ya chick'ns 'n eeegs."

> "We're reeely happy to look aahfta ya here in Austrile-ya! Yo're a graaait bunch o' shielas, and we jus' love ya kids, bless'em."

> "Chin up, mite, you'll all be Ow Kai in good time! Thaooze little yella-bellied, slit-oyed baahrstards will be good'n fuck-ed before they knaoo what 'appened to'em! Bluddy Nips! Mark moy words!"

The British military performance throughout East Asia had been criminally inept and pathetic. Vainglorious Singapore of the 1930s, the British government, the British Colonial Service, the Royal Air Force and the Royal Navy were all totally discredited. Their inflated reputations, their frothy pomp and pride popped like soap bubbles along with their pretensions. The western world was stunned. Even the isolationist United States was shocked at the fall of Singapore, but not immediately enough to shake their own isolationist complacency in the face of Japanese aggression in their shared Pacific Ocean. Nor did they react to advances of the Hitler-Mussolini Axis in Europe and North Africa. In fact, prior to Pearl Harbor, Roosevelt had been persuaded by his political advisers to stay clear of a war, which "was a European problem in which America had no part."

With Siam, Malaya, and Burma conceded and India now threatened, the British were way back on their heels. Southeast Asia was in utter turmoil as the Empire of the Rising Sun raped the region, its brutal imperial forces crushing the territory like a steamroller.

Civilized Europe, East and West, was also being steamrollered by Hitler's Huns. Neville Chamberlain, that spineless, pontificating proponent of appeasement, had at last been succeeded by Winston Churchill as Prime Minister of the United Kingdom. The new leadership was the only good news around as the British Isles faced a seemingly inevitable German invasion. The Vichy government in Paris had cuddled up to their Nazi invaders while they, with equal cowardice, courted the Japanese in Indochina. For *Mor* and the family an excruciating wait lay ahead. Thousands of mothers and wives suffered this tortured apprehension and traumatic fear of the unknown in World War II, most of them with extraordinary courage and tenacity. It is a sad inequity that their particularly distinct, yet crucial, role in protecting our western civilization has never been adequately recognized. No decorations or medals for these moms and wives. *Mor* would have deserved a big one. She exhibited a stiff upper lip to match that of any Brit.

Chapter II

Island Hopping

"But if you only knew, deep down, what pains are fated to fill your cup
before you reach that shore, you'd stay right here ..."
Calypso to Odysseus : With apologies to Homer

AFTER SEEING US off on the *M/S Boissevain* from Singapore, PB
had hurried back to Jendarata and the estates to do his job and fulfill his
duty. Managing the business effectively had become impossible.
Communications, transport and essential supply chains broke down as all
resources were suddenly refocused on meeting the threat of Japanese
invasion. As the inevitable became obvious to the less educated, Tamil
laborers grew nervous and many left with their families to seek refuge back
in their homelands of southern India, the metropolis of Madras or the
northeastern region of Ceylon. Many Chinese clerical employees feared
that the Japanese invaders would perceive them as lackeys of the
Europeans because of their employment in European-owned companies,
so they disappeared from their jobs to melt into the huge ethnic Chinese
population. The Malays remained typically placid and complacent, sensing
no urgency, as there was no question of a *jihad* or Muslim call to action. All
the managerial staff of the five estates, mostly Danes, stayed on the job,
but knew that time was running out. Communications with United

Plantations' H.Q. in Copenhagen were interrupted and then eliminated. PB, as general manager, was flying solo with his loyal crew supporting him, including the chairman's two relatively young sons, who served under him.

Finally, when the first word of Japanese landings on Kelantan's beaches was transmitted from Kota Baharu, the Teluk Anson District Officer (local representative of the British Colonial Service) instructed PB and UP's European staff to evacuate. This meant heading towards Singapore via Kuala Lumpur, commonly known as KL, some 60-odd miles to the south. Far had anticipated this for some time and had taken the precaution of packing one large wooden crate with some of the family's most cherished possessions and had it dispatched; it was simply addressed to "Heilmann, Barwon Heads via Melbourne, Victoria, Australia." He had no other place to send it and precious little faith in the crate ever going anywhere at all. Nevertheless, he gave it a try. Nothing ventured, nothing gained.

PB's colleagues and staff were free to make individual decisions as to what to do and where to go. The married men had all followed his example in sending their families away. Most of the men headed south in search of escape routes, aiming mainly for Singapore. Some went for Penang, Malacca, or Port Dixon on the west coast, believing that the invaders would give their first attention to KL and the strategic priority of controlling Singapore. One or two decided to attempt riding out the occupation in the highland jungle of Malaya's mountainous spine near Cameron Highlands, or further south near Fraser's Hill, where they hoped to evade the Japanese. More specifically, they hoped that with the help of the indigenous jungle Sakhai population, they could survive and hide until things got sorted out. This strategy worked for some, who endured over three years in the jungle, while others got caught by the Japanese and were shot or interned. Yet others perished from malnutrition and tropical disease. Every one of them suffered all manner of horrors. Brother John's Danish godfather, Uncle Top, was caught by the Japanese after a few months in the jungle, interned, and repeatedly interrogated while they drove bamboo splinters up under his fingernails. He was thus compelled to talk, although he really had little of value to tell them. Those who stayed undetected in the jungle also went through hell in terms of uncontrollable fevers, physical disability, and mental health. Despite the helpful Sakhais, years isolated in the Malayan jungle is an eternity—an extreme test of mind, body, and spirit.

The Sakhai people are comprised of a number of different tribes. In today's politically correct nomenclature, they are known as *Orang Asli*, meaning original people in the Malay language. They had ranged throughout Malaya, mainly in the rainforest, until early Portuguese colonists and traders disrupted their lives and made them uncomfortable, driving them into the more remote highland jungle, where they have since lived mainly as hunters and gatherers. The Sakhais are famous for their knowledge of jungle flora and fauna, and for skilled use of blowpipes to shoot and secure their diet's protein requirements, such as monkeys or flying foxes which resemble giant bats. Their hunting technique involves propelling poisoned arrows, blowing them through rifled blowpipes. Sakhai tribes still populate the extensive wild mountain regions of Malaysia and southern Thailand, moving quite freely to and fro' across Kedah's and Kelantan's northern borders with Thailand. The Malaysian government has made concerted efforts to integrate this tiny segment of the population, but with little success.

PB first headed south to Kuala Lumpur, where he checked in with the military authorities because he was a member of the Royal Malay Volunteer Air Force. He quickly managed to head further south, as he was selected by the authorities to drive a top brass British Army officer to Singapore. Having delivered his big-shot passenger safely across the causeway from Johor, he sensed that time was of the essence. British defenses were visibly crumbling and control of the island was all but lost.

Singapore and the whole of Malaya were about to fall. The British media spoke of "courageous and determined stands" or "withdrawals to strategic fallback positions" as the Japanese forces marched or bicycled virtually unopposed down through the country, using the highways, rail routes, and plantation roadways, all clearly mapped in advance for them, from Kota Bharu to Singapore. The detailed cartography was the work of all those Japanese merchants, taxidermists, and engineers who had infiltrated Malaya in the years leading up to the outbreak of war.

By this time, escape was the only thought Far had in mind. But how? PB was always reluctant to talk about this chapter of his life. Most details of his escape and the uncharted equatorial odyssey remained a blur to the family, but images of selected episodes emerged over time, though a lot was never revealed. On one occasion, well after the war, I asked him to tell me more, but he did no more than simply hint:

> "There were too many times when events around us just happened because they had to, and exceptional things had to be done," he said, "some of them not very pleasant. We were running for our lives, Flemming, fleeing from imprisonment or death under conditions beyond imagination. So we did things that were inconceivable under normal circumstances— we were dealing with totally frenetic situations. I'm sorry, I just don't want to talk about them." Far looked away before he resumed. "Those terrible times are now long gone, and nobody can turn the clock back, thank goodness. From my point of view there's no need to dig up the past. Nothing can be changed, so there's no purpose served. We were very fortunate indeed. Bloody lucky! Let's leave it at that, please."

On his own, with Singapore literally collapsing around him, he instinctively gravitated towards the harbor without knowing exactly why, or what he would do there.

> "After all, Singapore is an island, and if you want to get off it, you go to the waterfront, you go for the sea! ... ha!," *Far*

chuckled during a later conversation, "even in a state of panic the logic was there. Options were hardly being offered, not much choice, so there was little call for strategy!!"

As luck would have it, he ran into five Englishmen near the docks, all of them RAF pilots who had fled from different abandoned airbases. They were members of different squadrons, but had suffered the same fate. The men were still in their gray-blue uniforms and slanted field caps, three of them with RAF trade mark moustaches, waxed and curled upward on either side. Far was still in his tropical whites, but now he wore long pants, and a Panama hat rather than a *topee* or pith helmet. Given his volunteer experience as a pilot he felt they were in some way kindred spirits, so he teamed up with them. The city was aflame as the bombing intensified and time was running out. The Englishmen had much the same spontaneous thoughts as Far had, and about as much to offer by way of strategy. All of them just knew they had better get off the island. Soon.

The Imperial Japanese Air Force continued their methodical destruction of utilities and administrative or command centers, and were now turning their attention to the harbor. The men knew that thousands were being killed or captured in Malaya and Singapore. No options presented themselves, so they "commandeered"—meaning they stole—a small vessel docked in a corner of the harbor. It was a flat-bottomed coal steamer designed for navigating only the shallows and estuaries of the Malay Straits, the east coast. The boat was sparsely equipped, little navigation kit except for a compass and a few coastal charts, but fortunately there was a lonely, panic-stricken Chinese stoker still on board. The six men simply walked aboard and took possession, including command of the Chinaman, who was only delighted to have someone make some decisions for him. With no radio or other means of communication, the escapees' knee-jerk objective was to immediately attempt a crossing of the Straits of Malacca to Sumatra by heading due west. Afterwards, they would head south, hugging the long coastline of the Java Sea wherever possible, around the island of Bangka, then all the way down to Batavia. Naïvely they thought they could hitch a ride to safety from there on a more seaworthy allied vessel. All five airmen destroyed their identification papers, because that is what the RAF had trained them to do. The Chinaman did not have any papers, but PB followed their example as he understood it was a security discipline, which anticipated the possibility of capture. The Brits also took all badges and rank insignia off their uniforms.

As soon as the stoker had fired up the boilers, the little steamer quietly slipped out of Singapore Harbor late that very night, one of the pilots at the helm. Japanese ground forces had advanced rapidly down the Malay Peninsula and were already putting their boots on the roads of Jahor, not far from the Singapore causeway. The escape was an exercise of shear bravado. Sink or swim!

> "If you are gutsy, determined and reckless enough, you sometimes get lucky, old boy," said the airman who had taken the helm, twirling one curly point of his moustache between thumb and index finger. "But if we just sit on our fat arses around here, we're fucked! I'd much rather surrender to old Father Neptune out there than some little yellow cunt of a Nip. Hell, we've just got to go for it now. It's our only chance. Not much you can usefully do around here, is there now?" He turned to Far with a grin. "So come on, my new Viking friend, the sea's got to be in your blood—you and your Viking longboats! You should be okay out there at sea, even if we know fuck all about where we're going! Nothing ventured, nothing gained! That's what I say, old cock!"

The voyage to Batavia was perilous beyond all expectations, despite calm weather and clear skies. Barely an hour after leaving the harbor on a westward course, all hell broke loose and the passage became a nightmare of terror, a prolonged and terrifying flirtation with death. Japanese Zero dive-bombers and submarines took not only Singapore in their sights, but all targets in the surrounding shipping lanes. Those waters were the Grand Central Terminal of Southeast Asian marine trade. Zeroes and U-boats were everywhere, death to be dodged as hundreds of vessels fled Singapore, desperately headed in all directions, but mostly west. Flames and acrid smoke from oil burning on the sea's surface. Stricken vessels sinking. Random life rafts adrift empty. Ominous luminescent trails of bubbles from torpedoes cutting through the water a foot or two below the surface, miraculously missing the slow-moving coal carrier although it was a sitting duck, unstable and cumbersome to maneuver. The Japanese probably thought they had bigger fish to fry than the pathetic little coaster limping westward.

The Royal Navy was of course nowhere in evidence. Its surviving, once proud, men o' war long gone in hasty retreat. The Royal Air Force was also a thing of the past in Southeast Asia. No heroics there—later commentators would be brutal in their assessment of the British political and military bungling.

If you ever believed in miracles, this one takes the biscuit! The tiny, vulnerable vessel remained navigable, and after what seemed to be an interminable voyage of many weeks made it to Batavia Bay, only for the escapees to find that all Dutch and allied vessels had long since departed for safety. Immediately upon learning of Singapore's fate, Dutch colonials and their meager military resources had fled as Indonesia braced for the arrival of the advancing Japanese. Neither Sumatra's nor Java's terra firma presented an option to the escapees, as the great Dutch colony was obviously about to suffer the same fate as British Malaya and Singapore.

Our family never really learned what the escapee group's plan was, beyond evading the care and attention of the Empire of the Rising Sun. Reaching safe haven in Australia was the only objective. For PB, of course, this goal ultimately meant Barwon Heads and the family. The vagueness of Far's account of this singular odyssey was perhaps the product of a healing process necessary to bury memories, or perhaps guilt over ghastly deeds never contemplated in a normal world. This reticence was not an unusual phenomenon among survivors of other such terror-ridden chapters of World War II history. This miraculous escape took place seventy years before the world understood the post-trauma syndromes of men and women who have lived through the terrors of war. Nobody in the family ever seriously tested Far's reluctance to talk, but snippets of his story escaped him over time, at his own pace.

We know that island hopping was the modus operandi, all the way down the southern coastlines of the Indonesian archipelago. They only steamed by night with the boat all blacked out, and then only if it were calm. Darkness provided shelter from the fighter-bombers, the periscopes of submarines and from roving torpedo boats. Even bright moonlight was a threat when cloud cover did not darken the bright lunar phase of the month. Calm water was a prerequisite for safety of a vessel built for estuaries and shallows rather than the open sea. A good tropical storm in open waters would likely send the vessel and its fugitives to the sandy bottom of the Indian Ocean. In daylight, they would make the vessel as unobtrusive as possible, anchoring in some cove, a sheltered nook or cranny of the Indonesian shoreline, or snuggling up to friendly Javanese fishing boats in order to be as much a part of the local scene as possible. Mangrove creeks and lagoons provided ideal shelter. What the men did for rations and fuel remained untold, but the vessels boilers must have been fired with wood, as there was absolutely no access to coal after the original load on board in Singapore was exhausted. The friendly native population en route was apparently very helpful. Far talked vaguely of "Javanese hospitality." He did tell us that his comprehensive grasp of the Bahasa Malay language—the *lingua franca* of the region from Thailand's border to the Timor Sea—was invaluable, as it allowed the locals to communicate and understand the plight of their unexpected white visitors. PB was thus the group's spokesman, which seems to have led to a kind of leadership role in making crucial choices, other than the technical navigation decisions.

After months of cautiously working their way down the coastlines of Java, way past Bali and the Lesser Sunda Islands, the fugitives reached the southern shore of Sumba in the southern arc of the Bandar Islands. Here they would bide their time, waiting for predictable, seasonal weather conditions. Then, when they sensed the weather gods would favor them, they made the daunting dash across open waters to Timor Island and proceeded to its southern extremity. This was where huge decisions had to be made, because from Timor they faced the even more terrifying ocean crossing, all the way to the northern coast of Western Australia. Japanese activity was still evident, albeit more sporadic, and the locals indicated that occasional torpedo boat patrols and aircraft reconnaissance flights could be expected. Sitting out the war on the island of Timor was not a choice, as the Japanese had long since declared that they intended to invade and occupy it, along with New Guinea to the southeast. Besides, all six white men and even the Chinaman were determined to reach the safety and comfort of Australia. A point well west of Darwin was the intended destination on the Aussie coastline, where the course would turn south-ward toward the ultimate goal, which for some unexplained reason was Freemantle, Perth's port, in Western Australia. Darwin would have been the shorter voyage as the crow, or the albatross, flies. The first leg required surviving almost three hundred miles of open Timor Sea, a corner of the mighty Indian Ocean, unprotected by the islands, bays, or inlets, which had given them cover and calm waters all the way down the archipelago. To avoid a watery grave, the situation called for some help from King Neptune and a good measure of luck.

They were beneficiaries of both.

At one point, in a rare moment of reminiscing, PB told of suffering endless days in calm, steamy tropical Timor waters under a brutal sun; but the heat and humidity was unreservedly welcomed if they maintained calm. The alternative of stormy rough seas could quickly have sent the vessel to that watery grave they feared. The frantically anticipated landfall was made some four hundred miles southwest of Darwin near desolate Cape

Bougainville on Western Australia's northern coast. Seventy years ago it was a wild, almost uninhabited shoreline all the way from Darwin to Perth. Today the halfway mark of that journey would have you off arid Port Hedland, the world's largest and most advanced iron ore terminal, handling Australia's colossal export of ore to China's steel mills and other global steel makers.

At least the refugees were in waters that were relatively safe from enemy planes and U-boats, although the Japanese did carry out a few raids on Darwin. The escapees still had no means of communication, so they may have chosen Perth because it was further away from possible enemy encounters. They apparently had some tiny land maps in somebody's diary to give them a rough idea of where they were, and of course the RAF pilots had navigation skills. The story does not relate what they ate or what the Chinese stoker used for fuel on the very sparsely populated coast. Perhaps they found driftwood and chopped trees ashore and caught fish.

Finally, arrival in Freemantle harbor was characterized by something near hysteria among the escapees and after causing astonished excitement on the busy docks, police arrived from the nearby city of Perth. PB immediately ran into problems specific to his nationality and name before anyone was allowed ashore. With a distinctly Kraut name like Heilmann, an accent weird to Australian ears, and no papers or ID, he quickly had the attention of both police and immigration officers. The name prompted poor jokes of "Heil Hitler" greetings and taunts of "Heilmann the Hun." They speculated that he might be a German spy and initially planned to turn him in to the poorly represented military authorities in Perth, isolated from the realities of the war in this remote western extremity of Australia. However, the British RAF men, who were immediately welcomed with open arms, vouched for him with passion and perseverance, recounting their joint escape from Singapore. They told of PB's invaluable role played en route and back in Malaya, including the chauffeuring of "the top brass British general" to aid his escape from the Japanese. They highlighted his command of the Malay language as he acted as spokesman and interpreter with the Javanese. My father's claim to Danish citizenship was for naught, since nobody in Freemantle knew what Denmark was, let alone where. The Brits and PB eventually got their way, and the confused officials issued Far a temporary immigration permit under threat of "deportation as an illegal alien" (without specifying a destination) if he did not report to the Melbourne police within twenty-one days to secure a more permanent status. The ecstatic men, along with their stoker, were allowed ashore. They were all predictably desperate to abandon the old coal boat, which by this time was probably quite happy to sink to its peaceful rest on the muddy bed of Freemantle's harbor. Once the officials were persuaded that the stoker was not Japanese, he quickly vanished into thin air, with nary a farewell despite the tight rapport that had developed between him and his white shipmates. He must have headed straight for Perth's little Chinatown district, having declined an offer to place him in the hands of the Red Cross.

Then the longed for and emotional contact was established. PB could not, for some reason, use the telephone to reach *Mor*, perhaps because of the outback quality of the service, or maybe he did not have a phone number or sufficient money, but he did manage to get a telegram off to *Mor* in Barwon Heads, nearly two thousand miles away on the far side of the massive Australian continent. To this very day I have in my mind's eye the vivid picture of *Mor* literally stumbling across the deep wooden porch of the old Victorian house, tears streaming down her cheeks, almost hysterical with arms outstretched, waving *Far's* telegram in her hand, screaming for me in the garden where I was playing with my mates.

> "*Far* is alive. He has landed. *Far* is in Australia—he's in Perth—and he's on his way. Oh, Flemming, he's alive and safe, *sanks Got! Sanks Got!* He'll be here in just a couple of days."

I didn't know what to do, how to share the moment with her. I just let her enfold me in her ample embrace and made my own contribution to the river of blissful tears. Suddenly speechless, she hugged me until I gasped, wet with our mingled tears as she stood there in the garden with heaving chest, silently stroking my cheek. She slowly recovered her composure, drew a huge breath and straightened her back.

"I have to go and telephone John," she whispered. "*Far* has landed in Australia, Flemming—he's safe."

Years later, PB's sparse account of their Freemantle landfall was to include his confession to an extended, very drunken celebration shared by the white shipmates, with many fond toasts *in absentia* to the Chinaman. A harbor-front bar owner had heard of their singular escape and remarkable voyage, so he declared that their drinks for the night were on the house. Without his generosity, the party would have been modest indeed, none of them had more than a few Straits Dollars to their name. Far speculated the stoker might have found friends with whom he could celebrate his good luck more comfortably. Eventually a Western Australia state law prohibiting the sale of alcohol after 6:00 pm prompted the men to think of saying goodbye and taking their next steps on life's path. After months of isolation as a group, intimately sharing fear, trauma, despair, hope and exhilaration, they bid each other an emotional but brief and unceremonious farewell, and then scattered. Far never had contact with any of them again.

Chapter III

Ozzie

"Once a jolly swagman camped by a billabong,
under the shade of a coolibah tree."
Waltzing Matilda

THE REUNITED FAMILY'S new base was immediately established in Melbourne, because that is where the action was in terms of *Far's* quest for a living. *Mor* was, of course, overjoyed, relieved and yet also sensitive to the feelings of the other women and children of the Barwon Heads commune, who had not yet had our luck. The farewells were emotional as everyone in the group was gripped by the team spirit and tight bonds that had been forged between them over more than half a year of sharing, months of mutual support and plain hard work. *Mor*, always the great communicator, remained in touch with several of the women for many years. It was almost equally difficult to leave our local Aussie friends in the Barwon Heads community, who had been constantly supportive and generous. These wonderful people openly rejoiced with the family in basic Aussie style, wishing us well in the big city.

"We towled you sao, mites! We seeed you'd be OW KAI!" they shouted, "congrats to you all, and fuck the bloody

Japs!—fuck ev'ry single one of theeem—baarsteds, all of
theeem! We're reelly chuffed for ya. Good luck in Melb'n,
mites! It's God's aown ciddy if you've reely gotta leave
Barw'n Heeds! Good on ya!"

The commune was joined soon by two new families and would in fact
continue to function very successfully throughout the war. Some of the
missing men never made it to Australia, either languishing in Japanese
prison camps until after the war or because they perished.

Melbourne, the capital of Victoria, was easily the biggest job market in
the state, so nearby Geelong was not considered an option as the family's
new home, despite its proximity to John's school. *Far* had arrived without
ID papers, but he must have had some limited access to financial resources,
as we soon moved into a tiny yellow-brick, single storied rental in the blue
collar suburb of North Balwyn. *Far* wasted not a moment before launching
his job search, as cash was very scarce. A strict routine was immediately put
in place. PB left home around six o'clock every morning, took the No. 47
tram to be in the city's center in time for the earliest opening of offices and
the pre-opening period of retail businesses, when staff would be stocking the
shelves, preparing for the day's commerce and hiring *ad hoc* help. He would
go from door to door on Melbourne's main commercial and retailing streets.
Up and down Bourke Street, Flinders and Russell Streets, in and out of
offices and the big stores such as Woolworths, Coles and Myer's. He pleaded
for work, any work, any menial job. His erratic sources of income were very
short term, from basic jobs in retail outlets.

He eventually got a residence permit of some sort from the authorities
in Melbourne, to whom he had been directed by the officials who allowed
him ashore in Freemantle. This may have been yet another instance of
Australian understanding and hospitality. The authorities in Victoria were
properly trained, well informed and much more competent than their
Western Australian counterparts, so they were sympathetic to PB's account

of his escape from the Japanese despite the total absence of identification documents. They actually welcomed him to Melbourne.

~~~~

The city's roots go to the 1830s spontaneous *de facto* settlement of Port Phillip Bay by restive migrants from New South Wales and Tasmania. A deal with Aboriginal inhabitants to buy 700,000 acres of their land validated further settlement, although this deal was later declared void by the Governor of New South Wales, who represented British rule along the eastern seaboard of Australia from the Gulf of Carpentaria and Torres Strait to Tasmania. Melbourne grew from the original settlement of the north bank of the Yarra River as its population exploded with the gold rush of the 1850s. The state of Victoria along with its capital, now independent of New South Wales, was recognized by London in 1851. When all the easy gold had been exploited and exhausted in the inland Bendigo and Ballarat areas, the rush subsided. The resulting unemployed poured back into Melbourne where industry and commerce were growing, or they sought a living in the burgeoning sheep raising and wool industry of rural Victoria. The city thrived and was named for William Lamb, Lord Melbourne, at one time British Prime Minister, who has been linked romantically with Queen Victoria early in her long reign.

The Victoria state capital in the 1940s was a warmly welcoming city, with a strong industrial and commercial base, a busy freight harbor and naval base. Outside the central urban grid of handsome tree-lined streets, parks and gardens offered attractive open areas, and the Yarra added its charm and sporting centers along its banks. Melbourne Cricket Ground, the botanical gardens, beaches on Port Phillip Bay, and the Flemington Race course were wonderful recreation choices, while sailing and surfing opportunities were never far away. Melbourne cannot quite rival Sydney in the scenic department, but its cultural and social life lacked nothing, given the era and the constraints of wartime. The two cities to this day compete on every front, as do the two states.

Australia was at the outbreak of war led by the moderately conservative Prime Minister, Robert Menzies, whose tenure after his election in 1939 was to be short despite his worldly understanding and vision, and despite his prescient geopolitical admonitions and leadership, all of which have withstood the test of history. In the early stages of the war, he lost an election to rival Labor Party leader, Arthur Fadder, because of a hung parliament, but not before he had strongly endorsed Britain's declaration of war on Germany and committed Australia's own troops in support of the *pommies*, as the Brits were known down under. Menzies directed the massive Australian contribution of forces to the Allied effort in Europe and, famously, in North Africa. He traveled to London to tell Churchill directly to strengthen the British position dramatically in Southeast Asia and he personally lobbied the hesitant FDR to join the Allied struggle against the Nazis and Italy. In his abbreviated term he persuaded the isolationist segments of the Dominion's population to take up arms, and he laid the foundation for Australia's gallant and steadfast role in Hitler's defeat five years later.

One of Churchill's bigger mistakes was not to heed Menzies' admonitions concerning southern Asia. This may have been a factor in the scandalous British failure in Singapore and Malaya. Robert Menzies, the son of immigrant Scottish crofters was born in remote western Victoria, continued to be very active in his country's politics, and made his come back in 1949 as the Liberal Party's leader and Prime Minister once more, this time for an extended tenure.

~~~~

PB's job search was frustrating and difficult. The strange accent and that German surname were not exactly helpful, even in those friendly surroundings. The country felt threatened with a Japanese invasion; people had been told by the federal government in Canberra that they should be vigilant and alert to the potential of spies working in preparation for a widely predicted invasion. Tens of thousands of Australians were already serving in the allied forces in the European and North African theaters. All Germans and Italians who were not naturalized Australians were rounded up and interned, except for their diplomats who were assembled under comfortable house arrest in Canberra.

Far had applied for a passport or similar ID document by contacting some form of Danish Government representation in Canberra, but it took many months before he had any positive response. However, he did get employment before too long: he took on the onerous and intellectually challenging responsibility of a "floor walker" in the downtown Coles Stores outlet on Burke Street. Coles was the Australian equivalent of today's Walmart in the US. His testing challenge was to patrol the aisles from nine o'clock in the morning to six in the evening, to apprehend shop-lifters and to ensure all shelves remained adequately stocked with mer-chandise. PB's intellect and management talents were not exactly tested. He became very frustrated, which resulted in irritability and a very short fuse at home, with *Mor* and me at the receiving end. John was safely out of range at Geelong Grammar School.

Mor continued to make lambskin gloves, as she had done in Barwon Heads, to supplement family income. She ran a micro chicken farm and tended a nano-scale vegetable garden with greens and berries in the miniscule backyard. The household budget was bare-bones frugal. Far had, without hesitation, swallowed his pride and simply found available work. It was a job, and it produced some cash for bread on the table. Over seventy years later, I wince at the arrogance of unemployed men and women out of high school, or even graduates and heads of families, who choose to be-come one-hundred percent dependent on the state or their own relations, rather than do something like flip hamburgers, unload trucks, or harvest potatoes until an appropriate job is found. In the challenging wartime of the 1940s, today's presumption of entitlement had not yet taken hold. The

21st century's obsessive sense of entitlement had not yet quelled appreciation of opportunity, the chance to earn a contribution to the family's financial needs. The emphasis was still on individual and personal responsibility, hard work and the need to grasp at every opportunity, or create it by learning new skills. PB learned how to catch shoplifters and keep shop shelves properly stocked!

As PB had realized in his late teens when he was bumped out of his childhood home to seek a living, he was poorly qualified in terms of formal academics and professional qualifications, which were readily marketable. Now the farmer's boy who had become an expert planter and accomplished operations manager faced a similar challenge in the wartime job market of Melbourne. The city's trees and plantings along the sidewalks, the exceptionally beautiful botanical gardens and manicured parks were all carefully tended and his expertise was irrelevant. There was little by way of agricultural activity in that part of Victoria, except for the inevitable sheep stations just beyond the sprawling suburbs, so his experience and moxie in plantation management or farming did not impress too many people. Then one day he read an article in Melbourne's *Argus* about the work of the Victoria State Forest Commission, which claimed to be committed to "the improvement of forestry practices, lumber yields, the marketing of timber and prevention against bush fires." Here was an organization where he could add value if he did a bit of research, some self-education in order to adapt his skills. He plunged into the study of all aspects of the Australian bush, its species and forestry management, all from literature he researched in Melbourne's municipal library. The Victoria Commission's head office on Collins Street opened at eight in the morning. PB decided to risk arriving late for his eight-thirty clock-in at Coles after calling on the nearby forest commissioner's office every single workday morning. At first he was unsuccessful in seeking audience, but would then sit for a while in the commissioner's reception room, making himself felt every morning and then leaving a written reminder that he wanted to work for them. As one of his RAF mates had told him that fateful night in Singapore harbor, he thought that if he were sufficiently persistent and audacious, he just might get lucky. Nothing ventured, nothing gained! After being ignored or dismissed daily for over a month, his tenacity paid off and the commissioner caved. PB was invited into the agitated commissioner's office, where he must somehow have been quite persuasive.

The Victoria State Forest Commission offered Far a job as a kind of field inspector in the area around Bendigo, the old gold mining town almost exactly one hundred miles north of Melbourne, surrounded by endless indigenous bush and the occasional sheep-farming station. While it lasted, the 19th century Bendigo gold rush was the richest gold strike in the world, spawning ornate hotels and concert halls in the style of that era, and typically pretentious residential excesses of wealth accumulated too fast. At the beginning of World War II, Bendigo was a sleepy bushland backwater with empty buildings and little commercial activity.

Mor packed our very modest possessions, and we moved to another tiny rented house in Bendigo, this time red brick. Far would set out each day "at sparrow's fart," as he said, in a rattletrap pickup truck, powered by a wood-burning gas generator to do his "inspecting" deep in the Victorian bush. Endless blue gum and every other eucalyptus variety, wattle and thick, bone dry brush: a tinder box. Bush fires are a chronic Australian curse. Millions of man-hours and fortunes in other resources are spent every summer of every Australian year on wild fires, which the Aussies fought as a matter of dreaded routine. It seemed to matter not whether the Commission's fire prevention disciplines were observed, but breach of the regulations was rightly subject to severe and extensive punishment. The summer's predictable scorching north wind blew in from the outback, from the burning center of this desiccated continent, and it dried everything to a frazzle. That febrile air stream from the interior was a seasonal feature: it blew frequently and in strong bursts for days on end, every single summer. Any spark, cigarette butt, or shard of glass magnifying the sun's rays could, in an instant, cause this tinderbox to explode in flames. The resulting inferno would race, driven by the wind, through hundreds of square miles of bush in a matter of an hour or two, leaving a charred landscape looking like the aftermath of the Battle of the Somme.

John was still at Geelong Grammar and I had reached the age when I too was ready for real school. During the following twelve itinerant school years, I was to attend ten very diverse institutions in two hemispheres and in three different countries before I ended up spending four continuous years at English boarding school from the age of fourteen. The very first of these institutions was Gravel Hill State School, a small public day school in Bendigo, where I relished every moment of the experience. The headmistress, Miss Skinner, who was also my classroom teacher, introduced me to Longfellow's Hiawatha, thus kindling a deep childhood fascination with the people we called Red Indians. At Gravel Hill I learned a lot about the slaughter of Red Indians, the American Indian wars, and stories drawn from *The Winning of the West*. We studied Captain James Cooke's many exploits and the 1788 settlement of British prisoners in the penal colony at Botany Bay which became Sydney. However, absolutely nothing was said about the Australian aboriginal peoples, who had been on that continent for 45,000 years before the English arrived. Nobody addressed their plight in the outback. There was no talk of discrimination in urban areas or their generally depleted land rights. They were referred to as *Abos* in the first grade history book, and we were curtly told that theirs was a simple life!

"They live happily in the Outback with their didgeridoos
and kangaroos, where of course those people belong."

Such were the parameters of ethnic sensitivity and tolerance in the Australia of those days, where the fear of a Japanese invasion was reflected in terms such as "the lurking Asian menace to the north," or "the yellow peril." Anyone with an Asian complexion or dark almond shaped eyes was a prima facie threat, so the occasional Polynesian, Chinese, or Filipino would have no easier passage of entry than PB with his German surname and strange accent. However, that never got in the way of the warm Aussie generosity and hospitality enjoyed by thousands of Caucasian refugees.

During school vacations when John came home, weekends were often spent in the bush with new local friends, either camping or in Spartan bush cabins. The bigger boys would shoot dozens of wood pigeons and rabbits, which were skinned and cooked into a crude and sticky pot stew with a few potatoes, tomatoes, turnips and carrots, laced with Vegemite or Marmite (salty extract of vegetables and beef respectively, which were also popularly spread on hot toast). That was supper by the camp fire, washed down with lemon-and-barley-water prepared at home by somebody's loving mum. It was all very innocent, uncomfortable, and boring; but it was a required vacation ritual in up-country Victoria. The bush was generally uninviting, prickly-hot in summer and powder-dry. Every discomfort of Bendigo and its surrounding bush territory was magnified ten times when the dreaded north wind blew. Billions of green-gray gum trees and weary wattle were waiting to explode into flames, given half a chance. No exotic kangaroos, wallabies, or duck-billed platypuses in Bendigo to provide a schoolboy thrill. The greatest excitement was a glimpse of the occasional dingo, another indigenous creature, more like a dog than a wolf, which was a menace to sheep and even human infants. A more cheerful member of the bush community was the laughing kookaburra, named for the sound of its call. The bird looks like a kingfisher, but as a carnivore it is not dependent on rivers and waterways for food. Snakes were also quite common and a constant fear of mine, playing on my personal phobia. My relief from boredom on these dreary escapades was provided by swims and little-boys' water games in the opaque, orange-brown *billabongs* of a bushland creek, in which the tepid water gave cool respite from the searing wind.

No priceless memories linger from our dreary sojourn in parochial Bendigo, other than the thrill of finally being allowed to go to school, enjoying new chums, the caring attention of Miss Skinner and her Hiawatha stories. However, *Far* had a job and there was bread on the table. We were together, we were safe and surrounded by friendly, welcoming

Aussies, who treated us as welcome curiosities out there in bushland. Nobody in the family had any complaints.

PB must have done his "inspecting" very competently, because in less than a year he was promoted to a bigger job, which took us back to the Victoria Forest Commission's Melbourne headquarters and the little yellow-brick house in North Balwyn. I went to my second school, East Kew State School, a two-stop tram ride away, where a couple of the nastier kids called me "The Nazi," poked fun at my hair lip and ridiculed the boots I wore—they were handed down from *Mor* and worn with two pairs of thick socks to fill them out. I soon figured out how to smuggle my Sunday shoes out of the house, change into them halfway up the street, hiding the boots in a rabbit hole on an empty lot while I was at school. On the way home I would make the reverse change, to avoid *Mor's* attention. That way, the boot problem was solved, but little could be done about the surname or the hair lip, so East Kew was not one of my happiest social experiences. The kids were tough, but probably not more so than kids of that age around the world. After all, I was an outlier, very different and an obvious target; yet I don't remember being that devastated. I just sucked it up. There was no alternative.

As things improved on the economic front, thanks to PB's promotion, I moved to a private day school called Carey Baptist Grammar School, which charged especially low tuition fees for children who were "victims of the cruel war." This philanthropy was effective, but labeling people as victims is a bad idea, because this label tends to cause people to abandon their sense of individual responsibility and blame others for their plight. There was nothing particularly Baptist about the place except support from the church of that denomination; it simply had the standard protestant morning prayers and a hymn, followed by typically banal school announcements. Mor's religious leanings led her to appreciate the "Baptist" component of the school's name, so she was happy. In fact, I enjoyed my days there. I was introduced to the thrills of competitive athletics, track and field. Australians have always been extraordinarily competitive and engaged in their sports. I loved my class mistress, Miss Wilson, a pretty young lady who taught me arithmetic and periodically came to tea with us on Sundays at the little yellow-brick house. PB would be especially attentive and clearly also thought she was attractive, which went unobserved by *Mor*, who simply proclaimed that she was a good and very kind Baptist! My mathematical education got off to a good start, which was tragically reversed in later years at boarding school in England.

When old enough, towards the end of the war, I gleefully joined John as a boarder in Geelong Grammar School's junior section, nine months before we left Australia. I basked in the aura of big brother John's success and accomplishments in the years ahead of my arrival. He had his name engraved on a prominently displayed trophy called "The Lempriere Cup," awarded to the "Best student-athlete of the year." I auditioned and failed selection for the junior choir. Games and sports were important components of every day, much of which spent outdoors. *British Bulldogs* was a favorite game played by groups of boys every evening just before dark on the lush green quad of the junior school. Years later, the renowned school drew the world's attention as Prince Charles spent half an academic year there in 1966. He has proudly told of his experiences there, including being labeled "a little pommie bastard." The institution had much in common with Gordonstoun in Scotland, where the prince spent most of his schoolboy years. Both institutions emphasized life in the rugged outdoors, fending for yourself, and learning to become self-sufficient. Geelong Grammar was also quite tough—Australians have this singular ability to be tough while also being fair and generally kind. The fine reputation of the school was owed largely to the visionary headmaster of 30 years, J.R. Darling, who in retirement became chairman of the Australian Broadcasting Corporation as Sir James Darling. There were no "victims" at Geelong Grammar, because nobody was allowed to abdicate from individual responsibility.

John was on one occasion called "a bloody Nazi" (again thanks to our surname) by a particularly edgy kid named Zach Ashkenazy, to which John reacted with a sharp and well directed jab to the prominent nose of his tormentor, shouting, "Shut up there, you Hebrew monkey!" as the kid dropped to the floor. Political correctness was perhaps not Geelong Grammar's strongest suit in the 1940's, perhaps because the notion had not yet been conjured up, certainly not in Australia. The whole notion of such behavioral standards, according to one theory, originated from a telegraphic exchange between President Harry S. Truman and his two representatives, MacArthur and Nimitz, in Tokyo at the time of the Japanese surrender. The president was urging caution in the US military's use of language in dealing with the vanquished foe and was advocating "political correctness," which he was then prompted to define. One citation indicated that the president's proffered telegraphic definition was as follows:

> "Political correctness is a doctrine fostered by a delusional minority and promoted by the media, offering the proposition that it is possible to pick up a piece of shit by the clean end."

John's close contemporary and housemate at Geelong Grammar, Rupert Murdoch, was surprisingly not a stand-out in the school community, nor did he make any particular waves while he was there. The total experience enjoyed in academic, social and developmental terms at the school was nothing short of marvelous. The institution seemed to be a distillation of all that is good in Australia. The greatest enduring benefit was derived from being part of a particularly open community, divested of pretense, blind to social rank and bestowed with a sense of uncomplicated decency and fairness—qualities reflected in the country's role in our global society today.

~~~~

Midway through our Australian adventure another little miracle broke our way. After making tentative, but frequent enquiries about the possible arrival of the wooden crate he had dispatched from Jendarata in Malaya, PB was contacted by the Australian Customs & Immigration office in Melbourne. His first fear was that his official resident's status was being challenged. That, however, was not the matter on the customs officer's mind. A junior staff member had reported that there was a large unclaimed wooden box set aside in a dockside warehouse in Melbourne's freight harbor, with some discernible clues of the intended addressee and destination painted on it; but words and letters had been partially obliterated. The crate had indications that it was part of a cargo from Penang, off-loaded by a Norwegian tramp freighter calling on Melbourne. A customs officer had decided to pry the crate open to inspect the contents, and on the very top layer had found a silver-framed photo of PB's identical twin brother, Johan Ernst. The photographic portrait rang a bell with the officer. It prompted his recollection of PB's repeated enquiries and visits to the office, so he was persuaded it was a photo of the persistent enquirer. He had therefore made the call. It turned out that the crate had, in the hasty panic caused by the Japanese invasion, been loaded onto an old Norwegian tramp steamer leaving Penang at the eleventh hour. The vessel had been bound westward for Europe during the last days before the enemy forces took over the port. She got as far as Madras (today's Chenai) when the Nordic skipper decided, like so many other merchant mariners, that the voyage through the submarine-infested North Atlantic was not for him and that he should try his luck plying the Australian coast until things got better in Atlantic waters. By then, Norway was occupied by the Germans anyway. That was the serendipitous chain of events that led to the wooden crate reaching us in Melbourne. Several of the recovered artifacts and family heirlooms from the crate are treasured by family members in the USA to this day.

PB's reputation for efficient plantation management in the Malayan rubber, palm oil, and coconut industries had apparently spread far and wide among the allies' government and administrative organizations dealing with Southeast Asian territories. Poul Bent Heilmann, the Danish head of respected United Plantations Ltd. in Malaya, was methodically tracked down by an organization called UNRRA, acronym for United Nations Relief & Rehabilitation Agency. It was launched in 1943 (well before today's U.N. was even contemplated) in anticipation of victory over the Japanese, to plan for the restoration and rehabilitation of the infrastructure and strategic industries in occupied countries. In Southeast Asia, UNRRA was largely focused on agriculture, tin mining, hardwood logging, tea, rubber, palm oil and copra, along with infrastructure, power generation and trading. The agency was established under the auspices of the allies and the wobbly old League of Nations organization. More importantly, the Southeast Asian effort was led and directed by experienced British, Dutch, and American government appointees, who had dealt with the realities of finance, commerce, and industry in the region before the war. Its effectiveness in Malaya and Indonesia was secured by top British colonial administrators and senior international businessmen taking the initiative and by the Americans funding it most generously. The Dutch government did little more than assign some civil servants—as always, Hollanders were quick to recognize a good deal when one was offered. The League of Nations, per se, was actually not involved nor more effective than its successor, the pathetic UN bureaucracy. UNRRA's refugee and food-aid programs were assigned to the League and were the victim of the same incompetence, corruption, and waste that characterize today's United Nations.

PB was recruited as the senior expert in operating oil palm, coconut palm and rubber plantations, and refining the products they yield. He was fitted with a sharply tailored American-style uniform generously adorned with gold stripes, a lot of badges, name tags and flags, all of which made a great impression on me. I thought *Far* looked incredibly important and smart. He was then shipped off to a comfortably equipped military in-stallation in Brisbane, where rigorous briefing, planning and training of the recruited experts were administered. Detailed strategic and operating plans for immediate postwar action were defined and coordinated. Similarly trained groups were established at other locations around the war-torn world, to address the differing needs of ravaged territories.

While *Mor* did not welcome *Far's* renewed absence, his significantly enhanced income was enjoyed by all. The quality of life in wartime Australia quickly improved for the whole Heilmann family, as UNRRA remunerated its recruits significantly better than the Victoria State Forest Commission. *Mor* was simply delighted to know with such certainty that her husband was safe and well looked after, mainly owing to generous American financing and oversight in Brisbane, where the Australian government had promptly provided accommodation and all needed facilities. She never once complained over the recurring separation forced upon her. *Mor* was a good soldier.

The UNRRA initiative was launched against the background of long delayed but escalating American incursion into the war's Pacific theater. Early in 1943, the US Army's XIV corps came into play and the Russell Islands were taken back from the Japanese. In the Philippines, however, they continued to wreak unchecked havoc and commit atrocities duplicating their exploits in Malaya and Burma. In 1942, they had killed up to 10,000 American and Filipino POWs in the Bataan Death march, when almost 80,000 men were force-marched 60 miles under vicious tropical conditions. Thousands were beaten and bayoneted, and others beheaded as Japanese officers on horseback practiced using their Samurai swords. Meanwhile, the Soviets had turned the tide on the Huns in launching assaults on Stalingrad, Leningrad, and into the Caucasus. The Jews of Warsaw had mounted their renowned ghetto uprising. The Casablanca Conference saw Churchill and Roosevelt agreeing on plans for the invasion of Europe as their coordinated air forces bombed the heart out of Germany. There is still speculation as to whether Stalin joined the two leaders in Morocco. Eisenhower was later made Supreme Commander of Allied armies in Europe. The *Chindits*, a specialist British long-range-penetration group, was launched in Burma, where they eventually succeeded in cutting the rail link that supplied the Japanese occupation of Burma as far as Mandalay and beyond.

Nearer home, the Australian hospital ship *AHS Centaur* was torpedoed and 268 people perished off Queensland's Stradbroke Island and *HMAS*

Australia suffered, but survived, the war's first Kamikaze bombing attack at the cost of 20 lives and a lot more wounded. The first Aboriginal Australian was commissioned in the army, and the governing United Australia party was replaced by a new Liberal Party, which was to be led by the great Robert Menzies after the war ended.

Although the European campaign ended with German surrender in May 1945, it was of course months before the Japanese actually came to heel and capitulated. Three months before the Japanese surrender, PB, with the family in tow, was ordered to embark on a 29,000-ton troop ship called the *M/S Dominion Monarch*, destined for England with just under five thousand people jam-packed aboard. The fact that the Pacific Ocean was still teeming with Kamikaze aircraft and U-boats on suicide missions was lost on nobody, but the complete UNRRA team for Malaya had to be assembled in London for final briefing and preparations for imminent action. The ship, which in peacetime was a Shaw Saville luxury liner, was said to be the largest diesel vessel afloat at the time. John and I wondered at her size and beauty from afar. We were all billeted in a cheap hotel just across a corner of Melbourne's Hobsons Bay, waiting for orders to board, and the *Dominion Monarch* was clearly visible from the window of our shared room. In June 1945, she made her exit from Port Philip Bay, easing her way past Queenscliff at its mouth, only a couple of miles from Barwon Heads, packed with humanity and bound for distant Liverpool.

Denmark had been liberated on May 4th as the British forces under Montgomery and the Americans finally drove the crumbling German forces out of Italy and the occupied territories of Western Europe. In Australia, we had received news via Red Cross signals from family and friends, whom we had not seen nor heard of in seven years. All four grandparents were gone, as was the twins' pianist sister, Ellen, but my mother's only sister had returned home with my cousin Lone from their refuge in Sweden to be re-united with Onkel Aage. *Far's* twin and his family on the old homestead in rural Jutland had survived the Nazi occupation with nary an incident and minimum discomfort but for the general wartime deprivations suffered by the whole country. That part of the family, tucked away on Tammestrup's lovely land had been little disturbed by the Germans.

Leaving Australia was gut-wrenching despite the prospect of returning home for a long-anticipated reunion with loved ones in Denmark. The family had found not only safe haven in Melbourne, but all four of us had struck up deep and treasured friendships with Australians of all stripes—young and old, rich and poor. All four of us had, in different ways, done some significant growing up and maturing under testing circumstances, but always with the attentive help and generosity of the Aussies. Their kindness and caring never left us. John had thrived at Geelong Grammar, excelling as an all-round pupil, doing particularly well in sports, absorbing a particularly Australian sense of fair play. I had received a good academic grounding in my earliest school years, learned to take some knocks as an outlier, and had gained robust health. Out of the torment of war, positive experiences had emerged and invaluable lessons had been learned. At age nine and fourteen, John and I had matured well beyond our years. Australia had opened her welcoming arms to us and thousands of other refugees in times of desperation and frantic need. My gratitude for the unreserved warmth of those people through nearly five wartime years remains indelibly imprinted in my heart and mind.

Europeans and Americans tend to shortchange Australia as a nation, not always heeding the sacrifice of her people, their gallantry and persistent efforts in defense of civilization during two world wars. How many Americans and Europeans remember their 1915 sacrifice at Gallipoli, tens of thousands killed at the hands of the Ottomans? Again, their role on the European continent and in North Africa in the Second World War? The same can be said of the Australian position in countless more recent international issues and geo-political conflicts. Australians tend to speak out and act, predictably on the right side of any issue. They live by their word, and have the guts to defend their own values, casting political correctness to the winds in defense of their nation's integrity, sovereignty and proven values. As a nation of immigrants, Australians like to keep Australia Australian, doing so with pragmatic integration measures for those who enter their country legally. Other countries might gain from embracing such common sense.

Chapter IV

Danish Homecoming

"A tale is but half told when only one man tells it."
From the Viking Sagas

A MOTLEY CREW it was indeed on board the *Dominion Monarch*: British troops from all three services being repatriated; Italian POWs and a few Germans from Australian camps due for release; civilian families of enlisted people like PB, who were urgently needed back in Europe for specific postwar priorities and to jumpstart rehabilitation and remediation of the planet. There were Jewish families who had fled from Nazi persecution, ending up in Australia and now allowed an accelerated return to their home countries. Tension was added to excitement by the fact that the Japanese war in the Pacific and to the north and east of us was still raging. The ship's passage, crossing that vast ocean, was fraught with danger and real risk of disaster. Transporting the hordes of people on board was an exercise of continuing warfare. Japanese suicide U-boats, torpedo boats and dive-bombers were still terrorizing the allies on Kamikaze missions, which were commenced as Japan's equipment losses started to outpace the country's ability to replace materiel. Suicidal missions were undertaken mostly by volunteers seeking to defend the honor of the Imperial Empire of the Rising Sun: to sacrifice life in defense of Nippon was much more honorable than staying alive for the increasingly inevitable defeat by the Allies. These planes, attack boats, and submarines were virtually manned explosive missiles aimed at killing the maximum number of Allied military personnel and civilians by crashing into any vessel at sea—even hospital ships. They would take off from Japanese bases or leave home waters, never to return, determined to hit a last allied target before they ran out of fuel to perish in Pacific depths.

The Kamikaze campaign dictated that the *Dominion Monarch*, painted camouflage gray and armed only with a couple of heavy machine guns mounted in the bows, endure an evasive zig-zag navigation protocol across the vast Pacific. She varied speed constantly and changed her course by 15 to 90 degrees at random but frequent intervals. Total blackout at night was observed. Every open deck was stacked with lifeboats and primitive inflatable rafts. Everyone, including children, understood that if a person were to go overboard, there would be no search and rescue procedure. The value of one person's life with five thousand at stake was not debatable. A necessary but disruptive schedule of emergency exercises was instituted while the ship was still in the calms of Port Philip Bay. Extraordinary turmoil was precipitated whenever fire or lifeboat drills were called without notice. The pandemonium caused almost as much angst and egocentric tantrum as a real enemy attack would have done. The drills somehow shortened everybody's fuse, encouraged hyper-anxiety and brought out the worst in some people, who were normally responsible and civil.

The level of discomfort in sleeping quarters varied, depending on your individual station in life aboard the troopship. Men and women generally slept in hammocks hanging in single-sex dormitories, packed like sardines in a tin, head to toe. Mothers with very young children or infants could be lucky enough to share smaller dorms, and the ultimate luxury was a min-uscule cabin with two-tier bunks affording just a few spare inches for access. *Mor* and I had inexplicably been allocated one of these preferred slots, while John and *Far* slept in separate dormitories of a hundred people or more. How the Italian and German POWs slept in the extreme bow and stern quarters of the ship was left to the imagination. The British—many of them military people—were dominant on board, *pommies* at their very best, doing everything possible to turn discomfort and boredom into a voyage of camaraderie and as much convivial fun as possible for adults and children alike. They made sure that attitudes remained positive and considerate of others' needs. During the crossing of the Pacific, there was absolutely no food or drink beyond Spartan rations to cheer people up; but games were organized, debates were staged, plays produced, sing-along concerts and talent competitions were devised. Years later, as a young man in the Cockney neighborhoods of London's East End, I was again to benefit from the wonderful capacity of the Brits to handle adversity with humor, fortitude and sensitive concern for others. This characteristic trait is somehow linked to an admirable British respect for other people's demonstrated leadership.

Within a week of embarkation, John had his first real teenage crush on a very pretty English girl named Annette Lansbert. The romance was as hot and heavy as inexperience and the cramped quarters allowed. In my nine-year-old's assessment, I could understand why John was so smitten. She was a very pretty, nubile teenager whose father was a senior officer in some Scottish highland regiment, who proudly donned his kilt, given the slightest occasion, like a concert or a debate evening.

The strictly segregated sleeping quarters, which ruled out any hope of privacy, may have played a part in providing me with an accelerated sex education based on observation and sightings on deck. Lack of space and privacy inspired some sex-starved youngsters and their elders to engage in feats of gymnastic copulation in lifeboats and inflatable safety rafts. One impressively athletic performance—in a hammock suspended between two lifeboats—was particularly riveting, with illustrative sound effects to make up for the darkness of blackout conditions. For this nine-year-old, the bit about the birds and the bees instantly became obsolete and superfluous.

While the *Dominion Monarch* made her deliberately erratic way across the Pacific, the war was racing into its climactic, closing stages. The world's military and political order had again been turned upside down as the allies finally succeeded in reversing the early dominance of the Nazi and Japanese war machines and their colossal territorial gains. The US forces had invaded Iwo Jima and finally took it after a ghastly, bloody battle. American men o' war had bombarded Tokyo and Yokohama. Manila was captured by the US VI Army and the Australians had taken Brunei. The Soviets were busy trying to secure their stranglehold as imminent occupiers of all Eastern Europe and Berlin itself. The UN charter was signed and the first of its endless broken promises and empty pronouncements were broadcast to a naïvely expectant and credulous world. The first nuclear weapon had been successfully tested in New Mexico. The Labour Party was in the process of taking over Britain, causing Churchill to be shamefully dumped by the Brits and replaced by socialist Clement Attlee. The allies were already preparing to sign the Potsdam Declaration defining the terms and conditions of Japanese surrender. Our troop ship survived its perilous Pacific crossing just as the final blow to Japan on August 6th was being planned and prepared by America. Only weeks later, the Boeing B-29 *Enola Gay* dropped the calamitous bomb nicknamed "Little Boy" on Hiroshima.

When the vessel was within a few miles of Central American shores, after weeks of pitch black nights and edgy nerves, the blackout was lifted and there was an instant explosion of light, emotional relief and excitement. That night, every deck of the great ship's gray superstructure, the enormous single funnel, and the masts were brightly illuminated by spotlights remaining from the passenger liner's glory days in the 1930's. The spirit of every soul aboard was lifted, as if the menace lurking in the dark Pacific nights had been vanquished. There was cause for celebration. The vessel was finally out of Kamikaze range. *M/S Dominion Monarch* headed into the haven of Bahia de Panama, as adults celebrated with a drink or two, or more—many quickly getting a little tipsy. Despite stern discipline, strict security, and the suffocating lack of space on board, an astounding abundance of booze miraculously appeared from nowhere. The heavy predominance of rum-and-orange libations suggested that the British Merchant Marine, with excellent foresight, had honored nautical tradition in stocking the ship properly with the most essential element for celebrations afloat. It was a party of singular dimensions.

While anchored off Bilbao harbor, a daytrip ashore was a fairytale for schoolboys. Scores of launches, barges and lighters ferried civilian passengers ashore. There was chewing gum to be bought, there were friendly American GIs giving rides in open Jeeps, there were smiling faces of swarthy Central American Indians and gesticulating Latinos vocally peddling their wares as they welcomed us. It all created a relaxed holiday atmosphere in happy contrast to the four weeks of discomfort and anxiety. The passage through the Panama Canal was an education for adult and child alike. All were enthralled as the giant ship was gently, deliberately nudged and coaxed, first through multiple locks, each of which seemed too narrow and tiny, and then into the canal itself, all of which happened in an almost eerie silence. Passage through the lake midway offered breathing room for the ship and glimpses of the tropical rainforest along its shoreline. Over the ship's Tannoy system, the *Dominion Monarch*'s skipper carefully explained that while the Atlantic Ocean was off to our east, the canal route actually took us on a counterintuitive northwesterly course toward the Atlantic because of the snaking geography of the famous Isthmus of Panama. That was an interesting geography lesson for a nine-year-old.

Once into the Caribbean, the skipper took a southerly course to pause off Trinidad before heading on our final northeastward leg, making a beeline across the Atlantic for Liverpool. No explanations were offered for the diversion. One theory was that British colonial Trinidad, with its refineries and fuel storage capacity, was the designated port for refueling UK ships while other British West Indian possessions were perhaps not adequately equipped.

The approach to Trinidad left a single vivid memory: a little boy's observation of a mesmerizing maritime pattern in the sea as the tropical Atlantic abruptly changed from gorgeous peacock blue to an opaque *café au lait*—the exact color of the Bernam River meandering by Jendarata in distant Malaya. As we left the open sea and engaged the muddy river waters billowing out of the huge Orinoco River estuary, hundreds of miles from the giant river's mouth, a spiraling design swirled in the waters below us. At the very edge where the murky river waters encountered the clean blue Atlantic there were huge twirling spiral patterns of *café au lait* and peacock blue, just like the swirling pattern of colors trapped in glass marbles. A little boy's magic, an aquatic marble design, a fascinating image, which in my mind's eye has survived age and the passing of time.

We lay at off-shore anchor, dead still for two excruciating days of 105 degree temperatures and no hint of a breeze or cloud in the sky. Five thousand people gasping for air, no escape ashore, no air conditioning, no relief—much sweat, foul smells of human bodies, while a slow stream of small fuel lighters finally quenched our ship's thirst for diesel. The Atlantic was crossed on a direct course for the Irish Channel and then Liverpool at full tilt, with waves of happy news of liberated Europe reaching us by the hour. It was all fun despite the unchanged, cramped quarters, some heavy weather and queasy discomfort induced by forty foot ocean swells. The moment we steamed into a calm Irish Sea, booze was once more miraculously sprung loose from every nook and cranny. High seas one day, and high spirits the next, as we cruised up the Irish Channel, turning east around the Isle of Anglesey for the final run in to the Mersey River mouth. The berthing in Liverpool's Merseyside docks was poignant. Thousands of Liverpudlians and Lancastrians crowded dockside, British passengers hanging over the ship's railings, waving, yelling, and weeping with joy on that early August morning of 1945. A spontaneous unison choral outburst from each of the ship's decks sent the moving strains of *Land of Hope and Glory* rolling through the docks. The dockside crowd responded with tumultuous cheers, waving Union Jacks. The moment was one of tear-jerking emotion, whether you had endured the trials and agonies of wartime abroad, or had been at the gruesome receiving end of Germany's vicious *blitzkrieg* on Britain's cities blasted by incendiary bombs, V-1 rockets and V-2s.

Liverpool was one of the worst hit.

Vast mountains of rubble in the bombed-out segments of Liverpool, stretching from the docks way back into the heart of the gutted city provided the backdrop. The old Great Western Line steam locomotive heaved and strained to pull the crowded train out of the Mersey Side docks, bound for London. After barely fifteen minutes, the gasping loco-motive groaned to an asthmatic stop, somehow stuck in the middle of the pitch black Mersey River Tunnel. The half hour incarceration and blackout swept us all back into the choking below-deck claustrophobia of the troop-ship nights. When the train finally resumed its slow and arduous trek to-wards London, we emerged into stunning stretches of lush English countryside, which gave exquisite relief from the urban devastation and chaos of blackened Midland cities, smashed to smithereens by German bombers. In the countryside, we could still marvel at "England's green and pleasant land."

Great Western's aged locomotive eventually managed to drag the long train through London's grimy northern suburbs and trundle into King's Cross station, heavily smothered in soot and filth. It took hours before we could check in at Devere Gardens Hotel where UNRRA had the family billeted. The very next day PB was whisked off by the RAF and flown to Copenhagen. He had been granted three weeks leave, to allow a little time with family at home and meetings with UP's board of directors, after the seven years of separation. PB was immediately elected a member of that board. He was then to report for duty again in London for departure to Malaya with the team recruited for the British colony's rehabilitation.

The rest of the family spent ten tumultuous days at the Devere Gardens, which consisted of a string of four-story Victorian townhouses on a Kensington side street for which it was named. Here we were to await news of arrangements for the final leg of our journey home to Denmark. Passage on the Danish passenger-freight ship M/S Erria, again an East Asiatic Company vessel, was provided, departing a week later from the begrimed coal-exporting port of Middlesborough in the industrialized northeast corner of England.

During our London sojourn, just over three months after the allied victory over Germany was celebrated in Europe, the Japanese Emperor announced his country's reluctant surrender on August 15, 1945. The actual signing of capitulation documents was on board the *USS Missouri* in Tokyo Bay, and only to take place on September 2nd because they were crafted according to the Potsdam Declaration. But the ultimate allied victory and VJ Day had arrived. War-ravaged London instantly burst not into flames this time, but into massive, careless, street-filling, gleeful celebration and abandon. One million people clogged the streets of London's West End from Piccadilly and Trafalgar Square to Buckingham Palace, Whitehall and Westminster. The throngs were screaming, yelling, dancing, and singing—and drinking. Along with the celebrating hordes, King George VI and Queen Elizabeth braved downpours of rain in an open carriage as they made their way along the narrowest of passages through the crowds, cleared by London bobbies, from the Palace down the Mall to Westminster. It was like Moses' parting of the Red Sea.

All of London was drinking and dancing in the streets, hugging and kissing in one glorious, ecstatic whirl of humanity. Here and there bonfires briefly blocked traffic until the police, with benign humor, took firm control. Fireworks filled the air and every official building was suddenly illuminated as if to say a final goodbye and good riddance to wartime's sombre blackouts. Cars and buses in the West End were unable to move for a full day. Piccadilly Circus was jammed solid, with Eros newly reinstated atop his perch in the epicenter of the chaotic celebration. The one-and-a-half mile "walk" back from Piccadilly to Devere Gardens was an exhausting four-hour exercise in patience and tenacity, bumping into and squeezing around thousands of people. Londoners knew that Asia and the Pacific were finally at peace, that sanity and civilization could now be restored on the planet. They knew that the celebration of VE day three months before had marked the end of their European misery and torment, but sensed that their comrades in arms and allies fighting the Japs were not yet done. In fact, at that very time in mid-August 1945, tens of thousands of American and allied POWs were still enduring torture, starvation and gruesome disease in prison camps across Japan, unaware of the official Japanese surrender. It took many days and sometimes weeks before the news reached them, let alone relief supplies, which were eventually parachuted in from B-39 bombers of the US Air Force. The physical release of POWs held in domestic Japan took much longer than it did in Japanese camps located in liberated Southeast Asia, where the Allies immediately took over.

The slaughter, atrocities, and human sacrifices from Hiroshima to Hamburg and from Singapore to Stalingrad had devastated the world and should never be forgotten. With passing generations, however, recollection and understanding of these horrors are fading, along with westerners' ability to endure and address real adversity. Yet, for those few magical days of euphoric elation, the terror was put aside as confidence in the future of the civilized world had been restored. The barbaric onslaughts of Japan, Italy, and Germany were at last vanquished. It was a climactic day in history. *Mor*, John, and I were swept up by the occasion, memories of which never faded. At age nine, I knew it was huge. This time, unlike the 1940 departure from Singapore Harbor, I grasped some of the dimensions and dynamics of the events unfurling around us. With the family having escaped capture, I had spent five childhood years at the very edge of World War II action, experiencing the peripheral effects of warfare, some of which had lasting impact. People raised in the uninterrupted freedom and security of the United States and Canada, or those who have never known enemy occupation, rarely have an understanding of that impact. Our family's exposure to World War II was *de minimus* compared with that of so many others; but on the other hand, some of those events and circumstances were more traumatic than anything experienced by people in the distantly insulated Americas or the antipodes. Such adversity can encourage a broadness of mind and an appreciation of divergent views, that the more fortunate have to work harder at before enjoying those benefits.

The anxiety of evacuation and leaving *Far* behind in Malaya, being driven from home by an invader, fear of the opaquely unknown, apprehension over the Spartan communal life with total strangers, living at subsistence level, a troopship crossing of the Kamikaze-infested Pacific in deadly peril—they were all occurrences of the type that can sharpen appreciation of freedom, a sense of personal responsibility, recognition of leadership and acknowledgement of other people's better informed views, sensitivity to the needs of others—all required for liberty and democracy to be sustained. These were all lessons that demonstrated that the paramount freedoms of choice and movement in any society can only be secured by the sacrifice of lesser freedoms and personal preferences. Too many glib activists, politicians, and professed advocates of freedom—freedom of choice, of speech, movement or religion—have not learned those lessons. Their circumstances have not always imposed that intellectual discipline of putting the needs of a sustainable community ahead of themselves and their personal preferences and dogma. A free society absolutely requires sacrifices of personal choice for the sustainable benefit of the whole, of all its members. The 21st century's obsessions with entitlement—often unconditional—and instant gratification get in the way of understanding these dynamics, these building blocks associated with enduring liberty in any given society.

During our wait in London, there were days of boyhood boredom at the Devere Gardens Hotel. Walks in Hyde Park, rowing boats and feeding ducks on the Serpentine could not fill our time. So John and I had to find ways around the ennui, devising new games. Our room was on the fourth floor, with big sash windows overlooking the sidewalk of quiet little residential Devere Gardens, where the locals would amble by, commuting to work or going about their domestic shopping. With practice we developed and honed our skills in harassment with water bombs, utilizing thick brown grocery bags filled with cold water. By the end of a day's target practice, we could almost guarantee a perfect drop for the water bombs, which would explode on the heads or shoulders of innocent passersby, causing shock, fury, and drenching. The stunned victim's reaction of incredulous exasperation gave us a hilarious thrill before we drew in our heads from the window frame to avoid detection. We howled and wept with mirth until we almost choked. How we escaped censure and punishment from the hotel management or even the police remains a mystery. Our victims were perhaps simply grateful that, after those years of *blitzkrieg*, they were no longer contending with V2 rockets falling out of the sky. Patiently, we would cease fire for several minutes to allow the street to clear before we leaned out again to select our next unsuspecting victim. Whole mornings were spent on this mischievous sport.

At last the awaited call came from the Danish Embassy to give us embarkation instructions.

~~~~

After another arduous train journey through blitzed urban areas and gorgeous English countryside, this time on *LNER* (London & North Eastern Railways), the passage to Copenhagen from Middlesborough was short and very sweet. The East Asiatic Company's *M/V Erria* was powered by diesel, again with no funnel, but with four strange masts that served no apparent purpose. This peculiar design was the hallmark of the East Asiatic Line's passenger-freighters. She was the very first ship of that once proud shipping line to return home to Denmark after five years of wartime exile in the service of the allies. This arrangement was parallel to the action initiated by the Danish A.P. Moller-Maersk shipping line, which formally put all of its free vessels in the hands of the US government when America joined the war. Sometime before, Mærsk Mc-Kinney Møller himself arrived in New York from Copenhagen to safeguard the interests of the company's dispersed assets through the war.

From the open North Sea, *Erria* rounded Skagerak into Danish waters and cruised southward through an unusually tranquil Kattegat. The late summer sky was almost cloudless, with only the odd puff of pearlescent grey or white drifting in from the west, the coastline bathed in soft afternoon sunlight as we pulled into the northern reaches of Oeresund, the narrow strait that separates Denmark from Sweden at Helsingor. We gazed in awe at the spectacular 17th century renaissance Kronborg Castle, Shakespeare's home to his mythical Prince Hamlet. King Frederik II was responsible for the elegant castle, set atop the star-shaped earthen ramparts and parapets of the original fortress built by King Erik VII of Pomerania in the 1420s. Barely two miles across the narrowest part of the Sound to the immediate east lay Helsingborg on the Swedish coast, smug and at peace after a comfortably neutral World War II. To Danes, Kronborg is first and foremost the guardian fortress of Oeresund from medieval times. Nordic saga tells of the heroic Viking *Holger Danske* slumbering at a heavy wooden table deep in the ancient catacombs, his long white beard growing into the oaken tabletop, yet always ready to spring into action in defense of the homeland at first hint of enemy threat. Sadly, old Holger Danske overslept and did no more for Copenhagen when the Germans invaded in 1940 than the British guardians did for Fortress Singapore when the Japanese attacked Malaya.

Right on cue, a salute of cannon fire blasted across the Sound from Kronborg's ramparts as *Erria's* diesels were throttled back and she came to a near stop; clouds of billowing blue smoke chased the thunderous welcome-home signals across the calm waters. The ship drifted slowly in the current as dozens of journalists from surrounding launches and motor yachts boarded and mobbed the decks to photograph and interview the fifty-odd passengers aboard. With the reporters arrived young girls selling *hoestblomster* or harvest flowers made of paper, sold in support of the prevention, control and cure of TB, which had not yet been totally eradicated. The tradition, which raised millions of kroner, originated early in the 20th century and had become an integral component of late Danish summer and harvest time. The sight brought tears to *Mor's* eyes as she explained it all to John and me. With tuberculosis vanquished today, the tradition has disappeared.

The vessel then eased her way smoothly down the last twenty miles of Oeresund into Copenhagen's newly liberated free port, again with thousands of celebrating Danes lining the docks and perched on the window ledges and rooftops of the great old 17th century red-brick warehouses of the harbor. Cheering crowds, happily waving small paper *Dannebrog* flags, the national flag with its gleaming white cross on a field of bright red. Others threw red and white streamers towards the ship as it nudged the dock. An ecstatic, tumultuous welcome home. A dancing sea of red and white on the quay. A huge brass band was playing patriotic songs, marches, and cheerful umpa-umpa music. Scores of men were still wearing the distinctive green, red and white armbands of freedom fighters in celebration. As the ship was secured, hundreds of packs of cigarettes, chocolate bars, oranges, and bananas were heaved over the railings into the pulsating crowd below. Such treasures had not been seen in Denmark for five years. *Mor* managed to spot *Far*, who had come to town from the family farm in Jutland to meet us, standing with *Mor's* sister, Harriet Schoch, and my cousin, Lone, themselves just repatriated from their wartime refuge in Gothenburg. Ingeborg, *Mor's* still unmarried roommate from her nursing days was also there. Half the country, it seemed, was assembled to welcome us and the good ship *Erria* home. A moment of excitement, cheers, and some joyful tears.

~~~~

After five years of German occupation there was cause for celebration. Across Europe, there had been slaughter, deprivation, loss of freedom, agony, and heartbreak, but Denmark escaped the massive destruction and gruesome loss of life suffered by near neighbors, particularly the industrial cities of Germany and England, which had been bombed to rubble and dust. The diabolic mountains of scree and debris in Hamburg or Dusseldorf, in Liverpool or London, were not replicated in any Danish city. In fact, the German invasion in 1940 had triggered little by way of immediate or effective Danish military action. A feeble effort during the hours and days following the actual invasion did cost some lives; but the Social Democratic government of Prime Minister Stauning caved without heroics and with little delay. However, somewhat disorganized resistance was very soon evident in most parts of the country; but it was only in 1943 that the Danish resistance movement really came together effectively and established a coordinated leadership in the form of the Freedom Council. Before that, resistance was growing via small underground cells operating independently and with limited impact on the occupying German administration. The successful evacuation of most of Denmark's 8,000 or so Jews was extraordinary. It had been achieved by coordinated cells of the resistance movement, for the first time working closely with each other and with the nation's fishing fleet. This cooperation was the catalyst underlying the establishment of coordinated resistance to Nazi rule. It achieved ever better results, causing significant damage and obstruction of Nazi objectives through the war's end in May 1945. Danes had eventually realized that their subjugation to Nazi tyranny would not be alleviated by random initiatives, printing illegal pamphlets, ad hoc sabotage, protest marches, or singing patriotic national songs.

The initial Freedom Council was an assembly of six men. They were all leaders of underground cells such as *Ringen* (The Ring), and "*Free Denmark*," which was the core of the Danish Communist Party, joined by influential businessmen, journalists, and newspaper editors like my Jewish uncle, Aage Schoch. He represented one of these key resistance cells and had initiated direct contact with British parachute units, which dropped UK-trained freedom fighters around the country to assist the cohesive organization of the underground movement. Aage Schoch had refused to take the escape route to Sweden, but did not manage to escape the reach of the Gestapo or the SS. In 1944, he and another council member, Mogens Fog, were arrested and incarcerated with other active patriots in the attic of Shell House in the middle of the city, where the Gestapo had commandeered the building to establish it as their headquarters. The Danish prisoners were locked up in improvised cells right under the roof to provide a human shield against British bombers. However, the RAF later pulled off one of the extraordinary technical accomplishments of the war, when their Mosquito fighter-bombers, skimming the treetops of the adjacent boulevard, managed to lob small incendiary bombs into the lower floors of the building, affording an opportunity for the prisoners to escape in the subsequent pandemonium, if they could get through the flames or survive a perilous leap to ground level. Aage Schoch was one of several to survive, virtually unscathed, and disappeared into hiding again to hook up once more with the Freedom Council. Some less fortunate Danes perished, while German casualties were much heavier. This remarkable feat, however, was linked to tragedy: in an earlier air raid, the RAF had mistakenly bombed a convent school, killing dozens of children and nuns.

After a few days of emotional reunion parties in Copenhagen, lubricated by many a celebratory *skaal*, we took the overnight Aarhus ferry to spend time at Tammestrup in Jutland. The family farm in the hills overlooked the undulating highland topography of the gorgeous Skanderborg and Silkeborg lake region. PB's twin, his wife, and my cousin Peter, were falling over themselves to welcome us home. Tammestrup was the family's center of gravity after more than seven years of separation. It continued to play that role for many years after the war since we had no home of our own in Denmark at the time. The twins had lost both parents and their incredibly talented pianist sister since our last home-leave from Malaya in 1938; but nothing could dim the elation and sparkle of this reunion.

Years later, as an adult, I learned that our homecoming had caused some nervous tension. *Tante* Ditte, married to PB's twin, Johan Ernst, the designated heir to the property, apparently had concerns that PB would challenge the status quo of ownership. She apparently feared that he might demand his pound of flesh and insist on getting his share of the property's value now that his life's savings and financial assets had been totally wiped out by the war. The family politics and dynamics of the situation totally escaped me at the time, but her angst explains why *Tante* Ditte was always a highly territorial and somewhat prickly matriarch of the Tammestrup homestead. In fact, PB, as his personal finances recovered over the years, twice bailed out his twin in order to protect the brother's continued ownership of Tammestrup. Johan Ernst was a dear and charming fellow, a great shot with a 12-bore shot gun or deer-hunting rifle, but less accomplished as a businessman or manager of his farm's simple finances. He had little ambition and limited appetite for modern farming technique, nor did he anticipate the cycles of agricultural markets, so he was not the best steward of his inherited real estate assets. Meanwhile PB and his twin were close as only twins can be, and would have died for each other or for the family homestead. Maybe *Tante* Ditte never knew of this, but her tensions never really diminished, even after PB's retirement to his own little forest property in Zealand many years later.

Beautiful Tammestrup was approached from a local country road via a long avenue of elms, oaks, and horse chestnuts running along the crest of a big round hill from which the view stretched northward and down to distant Skanderborg Lake, over a glorious patchwork of mixed farming and forest landscape. It was an iconic Danish farm with its four-winged structure and layout, white-washed walls and red-tiled roofs, surrounding a large cobbled courtyard: the long, low homestead in the northern wing, the stables, cowshed and barn on the other three sides. Only the stables were constructed of black and white timberwork with straw-thatched roof giving home to patches of bright green moss. A huge circular river stone and mortar drinking trough for the horses marked the courtyard's center. From the homestead's north terrace and garden, one looked down over a quilt of wheat, rye, oat, and barley crops, bright yellow mustard or gray-green beet fields. Rolling meadows, dotted with black-and-white Frisians grazing and mixed deciduous and evergreen woodlands could be seen in the distance, tumbling down to the twinkling lake. The garden was dominated by a large lawn circumscribed by a gravel walkway, two giant trees—one a linden, the other a horse chestnut—and a great tall flagpole from which the red and white *Dannebrog* would billow on any day calling for celebration. Such celebrations were frequent: a birthday, the arrival of welcome guests or a national holiday. It was all so deeply Danish, never more beautiful than when set under a blue summer sky adorned with chubby silver-white clouds scurrying before a brisk western breeze. Every time I was reunited with Tammestrup as I grew up, after any period away, this scene was cause for pause, for swallowing hard and taking a very deep breath. Imagine returning to this beloved homestead after seven years of separation, anxiety and virtually no communication. PB's very evident emotion was something I later shared over many years as I sank my deep Danish roots. The powerful aura and tradition of this beautiful place still underpin a lifelong love affair with and loyalty to Denmark, her culture and her best values.

~~~~

Tammestrup's origins are not well documented, but it was certainly the agricultural holding of a very early Catholic order resident in nearby *Oem Kloster*—a 13th century monastery—and was known at the time as *Thomistrop*.

Danish village names often end in variations of the ancient word *torp*, which means hamlet or village—for example, trop, trup or thorp. A landowner's identity would be reflected in the first half of the name. The common English equivalents would be the many towns and villages throughout England's Danelaw territory of the Viking occupation, ending with the suffix "thorpe," as in Scunthorpe on the Lincolnshire coast or Saxthorpe in Norfolk. Tammestrup's name, then, originated as "Thomas's Village."

The Reformation, as it did in most of Europe, transferred Catholic property to the Danish Crown. By the 19th century, Tammestrup belonged to the widow of Royal Counselor Gerhard de Lichtenberg, and then passed through the ownership of several commoners until my grandfather Christian Adolf Heilmann bought it, in about 1890. The property's history is not without romance. Legend has it that in 1212 AD, the powerful Nordic King

Valdemar Sejr, riding to the deathbed of his Queen Dagmar in West Jutland's historic town of Ribe, passed through the forest of Thomistrop causing a roving pack of wolves to halt their prowl, tilt their heads skyward and howl in sympathy with His Majesty in his hour of distress. Almost 700 years later, the bucolic scene of a farmer tilling his land with a horse drawn plough was depicted on the back of the Danish 500 kroner bill. It was painted by my grandfather's first cousin, Gerhard Heilmann on Tammestrup's land. The homestead and farm buildings were built during the time of the Napoleonic Wars, most of the structures completed by around 1812. When my own first cousin, Peter Heilmann, inherited Tammestrup in the 1970s, there were nearly 500 acres of mixed arable, grazing and forest lands—also a substantial dairy operation.

Colorful characters were associated with the property. Gerhard Heilmann, known as *Onkel* Gerhard, was not only an impressive artist, he was Denmark's foremost illustrator of ornithological textbooks and famous for his eclectic work in oils, including landscapes and village scenes. Gerhard was a vocal atheist and publicly scornful of the world's addiction to what he called "religion's emotional crutches of blind faith." He was an equally vocal pacifist, so he was assigned to eighteen months of peeling potatoes instead of serving military time under Denmark's conscription laws. Gerhard produced a deeply researched, beautifully illustrated family history, in which he traced the Heilmanns' roots to Krefeld in western Germany, whence they migrated to settle in Denmark in the 16th century. Finally, he extended his ornithological knowledge to the study of dinosaur species from which birds evolved. He has such a creature named for him in the literature.

Another noteworthy cousin of my grandfather was another Johan Ernst Heilmann, a pastor in the State Lutheran Church of Denmark in the early 20th century. He was in charge of a rural parish in Eastern Jutland between nearby Skanderborg and Aarhus when trouble arose because he increasingly neglected his parishioners and other duties. He was particularly delinquent in catering to the congregation's spiritual welfare. Sunday services were truncated as he distilled prayers and readings, while sermons were cut to a matter of minutes. He would occasionally skip a service altogether. Johan Ernst's flock saw less and less of him as he pursued his all-consuming passions for early amateur flying and fox hunting. He would try out every new bi-plane as it was developed and would, for hours, put them through his favorite aerobatic maneuvers. His second predilection was hunting, particularly shooting foxes and buck. These secular interests incrementally took priority over his congregational obligations, so eventually his delinquency was pointed out to the Bishop of Aarhus, his boss in that Lutheran hierarchy. The Bishop chastised Pastor Heilmann, warning him that his tenure would be in jeopardy unless he mended his ways. The warning fell on deaf ears: Foxes and roebuck continued to perish in numbers at the hands of the pastor as his air-manship and aerobatic talents were honed. After further ineffectual ad-monition, Johan Ernst was de-frocked. In the equivalent of an ecclesiastical plea bargain, the pastor-no-longer was assigned to missionary work in Greenland, where under the Lutheran Church's direction he was to spend some years spreading faith and goodwill in the Arctic, and thus mitigate the ethnic prejudice of colonialist Danes living among indigenous Eskimos. Up-on receiving his assignment, unburdened by contrition, he wrote to the Bishop, placing on record that he drew much consolation from the fact that, while piloting his airplane, he had spent a lot of time nearer God than the bishop would ever be granted.

The role of missionaries in Greenland encompassed certain duties akin to that of a colonial administrator in the course of traveling the hinterland and interior regions. Johan Ernst Heilmann made good use of Eskimo lore, which hospitably offered the warmth and general comforts of shared fam-ily beds to travelers, who braved the hardships of the Arctic to serve the populous. This resulted in a growing number of Greenlander Heilmanns, who still thrive there today. Two Danish parliamentary delegations to the UN's annual General Assembly in the early 2000s included Greenland delegates of that name, representatives of their arctic colony in the Danish parliament.

~~~~

Far's home leave was largely spent at Tammestrup, but he was quickly gone, flying back to Jendarata via a slow and torturous RAF itinerary with stops in North Africa, the Middle East and India to reach Malaya's UNRRA headquarters in Kuala Lumpur. He was back at work on his old stomping grounds, Jendarata, by the end of September 1945.

UP's plantations were in total shambles, undergrowth and weeds choking the rubber trees and palms, drainage systems clogged, impassable estate roads, communication and power lines cut, water supplies polluted, buildings falling apart and the bungalow plundered—a filthy mess after years of abuse by Japanese occupiers. The residential quarters for the labor force were in disarray if not burned down, the administrative offices converted to dormitories. The estate clinic and school were literally destroyed by tropical decay. The latex and palm oil processing plants were rusted solid. PB's challenge was the rebuilding not only of United Plantations' estates and processing plants, but also to coordinate the rehabilitation of the crucial rubber, palm oil and copra industries of Perak and Selangor.

John flew to England to start boarding school at Gresham's School in Norfolk. He was over fourteen and considered too old to make any sensible switch to Danish school. The consensus was that his future would be in an Anglophone environment. *Mor* and I stayed some weeks at Tammestrup, where I learned to use the Danish language at the local village school. John and I had always understood Danish as our parents inevitably used that language between themselves and with us, but we never spoke it ourselves. We would respond in Malay or English, depending on who was addressing us. John somehow mastered the language over time, spending his vacations in the old country without ever going to school there.

A few weeks later, *Mor* was asked to house sit the grand country mansion of a former colleague of PB's from pre-war Malaya days. Sofren Ingemann, after he made a perfunctory attempt to train and qualify as a planter with United Plantations, had married Irene, a wealthy heiress of a

Scottish newspaper publisher in Dundee, who financed Ingemann's acquisition of a major Danish agricultural estate, *Egebjerggaard*. The residence was large and handsome, almost Georgian in style. They lived the life of landed gentry, ensconced in North Funen's fertile flatlands, where wife Irene could be kept in the manner to which she had always been accustomed. With the constraints and immobility of the war years behind them, the Ingemanns were anxious to spend time with her Scottish clan and then decided to take a joyride through Africa, so they asked *Mor* to help them out as the acting lady of the manor house.

We were transported to *Egebjerggaard* in the Ingemanns' ancient 1929 LaSalle sedan, powered by a wood-burning generator, and moved into the well-staffed 12-bedroom edifice on several thousands of fertile acres, some of which were managed by tenant farmers. The idea was that after three months, the Ingemanns would return, by which time *Mor* would know her next move. It was a carefree life of unfamiliar luxury and pampering. I went to the village school to hone my language skills and welcomed the attention of a well built, long-legged 19-year-old nanny called Mudde, who was hired to look after the Ingemanns' two little adopted daughters. Wealthy friends of the Ingemanns, some with impressive titles, invited us to visit them in romantic castles dotted around Funen. Two of them actually had moats and drawbridges in true fairytale style. Unaccustomed as we were to this life, we had a right royal time!

As *Mor* prepared to join Far again on Jendarata, I was sent to boarding school at an insanely evangelical, very un-Danish institution fifty miles south of Copenhagen in a sterile little market town called Haslev, which was Denmark's evangelical headquarters. Most of the boarders were boys from broken marriages with domestic problems of some sort, or part-time orphans like me, with parents posted abroad. The place was populated by earnest bible-thumping teachers, all of whom, except the soccer coach, were dour, dull, or disapproving. This gelded missionary town's only spark was that generated by fire-and-brimstone sermons. The atmosphere was totally alien to me; I had a hard time coping. The boarding pupils around me were not kindred spirits and I was clearly an outsider. My better friends were day pupils from more normal families in the surrounding area. One of them regularly brought me delectable lunch packages, as his mother understood that the school cuisine of the pious was less than exciting.

The oppressive evangelism of the institution backfired. The boarding school functioned on obedience to rigid Calvinistic rules. Excessive time was assigned to compulsory bible studies or pious pontification. Civility and manners were given strangely short shrift in the mentoring of the boarders. The demeanor of the zealots in charge provoked resistance and protest, in turn inducing antisocial behavior, and my own behavior was no exception as it steadily deteriorated. My academic progress was halting, to say the least. The only subject in which I got a decent grade was English (my English being a lot better than my teacher's—the Australian accent went undetected and thus un-penalized). I far too readily participated in the antisocial activities of a nasty group of young boys, who often reflected a mean streak. This behavior could verge on vandalism as my conduct sank to the level of the lowest common denominator. This could not be excused by the fact that boys of this age will almost invariably do everything they can to conform to their peer group. After all, I clearly knew better, so the environment fostered an inner conflict. I was very unhappy.

The nasty little gang of preteens was constantly looking for mischief. On occasion we would roam around the dreary little town looking for buildings with door locks accessible from the street. We would insert the biggest firecracker that could fit into the given keyhole, light the fuse, and flee into the shadows on the other side of the street to watch the whole door lock explode and shatter, sometimes causing the door to fly open. Guffaws of laughter! On one occasion, this vandalism very nearly got us into real trouble with the authorities. As our target we had chosen the big sturdy garage door to the local firehouse. The explosion of a fire cracker only slightly smaller than an M-80 demolished the lock and caused the heavy door to spring wide open, which triggered a deafening alarm system so that all hell broke loose in the whole neighborhood. Firemen and police scrambled from all corners as our gang fled in terror, scattering in all directions. *Haslev Gymnasium*'s headmaster was called by the police as part of an official town inquiry, prompting him to spew extra fire and brimstone at assembly next morning. *Rektor* Peter Kaestel called insistently for confessions, but nobody owned up. The whole student body stood as silent as statues before the podium as Kaestel's face grew purple, eyes popping. The situation demanded that one hundred boarding school boys were to suffer, so the regular 90 minutes of bible study the following Sunday was extended by a full hour.

Another less wicked trick was played on the unsuspecting people out strolling on weekend afternoons along trails giving public access to woods outside the town. (All woodlands in Denmark are open to the public on foot, irrespective of their ownership, provided people stay on the footpaths. It is a Danish civil right.) We would tie a wallet, stuffed tight with paper, to the end of a solid long string and then place it visibly in the middle of the path. The string running into the bushes at the side of the path would then be covered by dirt. We would then hide behind the bushes, the string kept taut, until weekend strollers ambled by to discover the stuffed wallet lying on the path. As some poor soul bent over to pick up the wallet, we would tug mightily at the string, yanking it away, causing the victim to levitate in a state of shock. Guffaws of laughter were followed by scattered escapes through the woods.

Most serious was the bullying—real bullying, which would keep today's talking heads and pediatric therapists busy for days. The targeting of particularly homesick boys, or the more timid, for victimization was deliberate and nasty; but it went unchecked by our bible-thumping mentors. My own experience of this counterculture was just short of torture, administered by a patrol of young *KFUM* (Danish equivalent of YMCA) scouts in green uniforms—Christian scouting was part of the Haslev paradigm. They cornered me, forced me to the ground, opened my pants, peeled back my shirt, and pounded my bared stomach with a floor brush of stiff nylon bristles until little droplets of blood oozed from the pinholes pierced into my skin. That was how their Christian scouting mission for that particular Sunday afternoon was accomplished.

Haslev was so un-Danish in almost every way—revoltingly so. Away from Haslev, I enjoyed a treasure trove of wonderful experiences and created indelible memories during vacations. They far outweighed this wretched school. The grounding I received from family and friends in the best of Danish culture and traditions has stayed with me to this day. The introduction to Danish and Nordic music—Grieg, Nielsen, Gade and Sibelius, for example. Appreciation of clean design. The folklore, the deep pride in house and home, the seasonal celebrations, the food, the national sense of fairness and sensitivity to the needs of the less fortunate. All of this came from my extended family, friends and my surroundings, rather than my schooling. One lasting benefit bestowed by the evangelical school was an appreciation of Denmark's beautiful national songs and lyrics woven into the institution's weird daily life. The time at *Haslev Gymnasium* was not optimal, but those years brought many positive developmental aspects and understanding of Danish values despite the school's religious perversions. In hindsight, I often wonder why the Haslev experience did not cause me to complain, and why I did not question my mother's religious positions earlier in life. However, both my parents eventually realized that a bad choice had been made for me and that I would do better with a major change. Adjustments were called for.

Regularly during these post-war years, there were times when one or both our parents were home to share vacations with us in Denmark; but John was always home for his school and university vacations. When neither parent was in Denmark, we would stay with aunts, uncles and numerous distant cousins, all of whom were warmly welcoming with their generous hospitality. Tammestrup was particularly cherished as the constant, welcoming substitute for our own home. The vacation pattern would have us in Copenhagen with one of several families for half the time, the other half always spent in Jutland on beautiful Tammestrup. We had only two first cousins: Peter at Tammestrup and Lone, our maternal cousin in

Copenhagen, but we enjoyed the hospitality and traditions of several other wonderful family homes.

~~~~

Everyday life under-pinned Danish values and traditions. The Danes have a concept of *hygge,* for which there is no known word in any other language. (Foreign writers and linguists have always failed to capture its spirit and true meaning in translation, perhaps because it is in large part a Danish state of mind). In 2016 there was an international, highly commercialized fad which made *hygge* a buzzword, without ever capturing the true meaning of the concept or notion. Lifestyle consultants, writers, shrinks, "behavioral" researchers, coaches and shallow magazine columnists wrote pages of worthless rubbish, books and articles about their ill-informed, concocted understanding of *hygge.* The exclusively Danish word describes the notion of a relaxed and peaceful ambience, which generates warm human sensations, emotions and relationships. It melds human feelings like coziness, security, comfort, relaxation and intimate conviviality. It is usually associated with gatherings of friends enjoying each other's company, perhaps relishing something delectable to eat and drink as they appreciate attractive surroundings. *Hygge* is almost inevitably associated with soft light and candles to enhance the ambient atmosphere. No nation on earth uses more candles. *Hygge* cannot manifest itself in cold, ugly or untidy surroundings; it is absolutely incompatible with any hint of enmity, hubris or confrontation. The noun has an adjective, *hyggelig,* as its partner, used for example to describe a cozy restaurant, a picturesque old timberwork farmhouse in the countryside or a gathering around the dinner table to celebrate a birthday. Danes cannot get enough of it.

The eternal quest for *hygge* influences almost all aspects of Danish behavior, the Danes' values, traditions and lifestyle. It places uncommon emphasis on architecture, interior design and decoration, enjoyment of food and drink, the use of space and light in the home itself, even shared enjoyment of the arts and the way people interact. This was the Danish culture into which I sank very deep roots.

I learned how important food is to Danes. It is a cornerstone of Danish culture and tradition. The quality of food is as high as one can find anywhere in the world, and not just at gourmet level. Everyday food is consistently excellent, meticulously prepared, not at all fat-free but balanced, wholesome and nutritious.

Danish cuisine is varied, but does emphasize *smorrebrod*, iconic open sandwiches beautifully decorated and presented or simply prepared for a lunch break at work. Fabulous seafood of every variety harvested fresh out of the frigid Baltic, Kattegat or North Sea. Delicious dairy, beef and pork products. Traditional dishes for specific holidays such as Christmas, New Year and Easter. Danes pay equally serious attention to what is imbibed, whether it be an imported Bordeaux, Carlsberg or Tuborg beer or varieties of Akvivit or *snaps*. Their concern for culinary excellence is neither obsessive nor pretentious, but it is surely serious. When one Dane tells another about a recent dinner party he attended, the immediate issue is not where it was or who was there, but what was served?

Family life, the home and its design, along with that of the furniture, artwork and lighting are all crucial elements of the *hygge*-level sought by Danes. I found it logical that the people around me should be as focused as they were on architecture and furniture design. This focus took hold after World War I and endured from the 1920s through the 20th century. Danish furniture design became the paradigm for modern interiors throughout the world. Designers such as Kaare Klint, Arne Jacobsen, and Hans Wegner led the way for later luminaries like Boerge Mogensen, Poul Henningsen (literally a luminary by way of his ground-breaking design of lighting products and systems), Verner Panton and Poul Kjaerholm. They all created beautifully clean lines and sound ergonomics, which were enhanced by texture and color, using leather, textiles, hardwoods like teak, beech, ash and cherry. Arne Jacobsen's avant garde buildings still cause excitement in urban landscapes. Joern Utzon's Sidney Harbor opera house, when its mechanical and acoustic functions were finally fixed by his offspring, is an international icon—as is Henning Larsen's more recent harbor-front opera house in Copenhagen. The best of silver, porcelain, ceramics and stoneware reflected singularly Danish qualities of shape, texture and subtle color. Sheerness and purity of style.

I also learned that Danes are imperfect. A significant segment of the population had fallen prey to an alarmingly perverse syndrome in the form of *Janteloven,* or the Law of Jante, which scorns and punishes individualism while promoting a collectivist sense of entitlement readily accepted by socialists— all of it embracing an egalitarian approach to civic structure and society.

In the mid-1930s, a Danish-Norwegian author, Axel Sandemose, wrote *A Fugitive Crosses His Tracks,* a novel about the community living in the small town of Jante. The story describes the town's rejection and condemnation of individuality, creative self-expression and personal accomplishment. Its collectivist philosophy sought to punish individual achievers, who behaved outside the boundaries of mediocrity or performed at levels beyond the average in any way. Jante's Law encompassed ten commandments, all of which made it verboten to think you were any different from everybody else, let alone better, or that you could impart knowledge or experience of value to another person, or even be of help. Janteloven said you should forever be comfortable in the belief that others don't know, and should not know, about your weaknesses or shortcomings. Underlying this dogma was the innuendo that individual achievement could only be accomplished by exploiting others—the collective. One has to wonder if Ayn Rand had become acquainted with *Janteloven* before writing her short satirical novel *Anthem* about the futility, tyranny and counter-productivity of collectivism and the banishment of individualism. The attitudes dictated by *Janteloven* characterized much of Danish left wing politics for almost sixty years under the Social Democratic party and its coalition governments. Their credo, policies and practices had a huge detrimental effect on the country's financial sustainability, and it contributed to the near collapse of Denmark's post-war welfare state.

Successive Social Democratic governments after World War II led Denmark into an era of economic stagnation caused by escalating deficit spending and crippling taxes siphoned off private sector employers in order to create government jobs. Entrepreneurial achievement and growth were thus plundered to fund massive subsidy ("compensation") of the unemployed, while discouraging investment and thus reducing the tax base. Public sector employment soared while unemployed people fell off the safety net. Inflation and a mounting national debt combined to create a downward economic spiral until the system imploded. The basic obligations of government, such as the provision of good education, law, order and security, protection of property rights, effective health care and support for the most vulnerable were rendered beyond reach. Denmark's once proud and effective public education and health care systems went into decline. Unemployment became endemic; living off inflated unemployment benefits became a chosen way of life because the "compensation" made it comfortable for many to do so. "Compensation" financed vacations in Mallorca for the unemployed, while sour discontent festered in the population at large. One symptom was the vindictive keying (scratching with car keys) of nice looking automobiles in the cities. Another was graffiti displaying the words "Capitalist Pigs!" on buildings. Much of this was precipitated by widely held preconceptions justified by *Janteloven*.

Only late in the last decade of the 20th century did a right-of-center coalition government, led initially by Anders Fogh-Rasmussen, turn things around. Labor and capital was allowed to move more freely, incentives for performance and hard work were restored with less confiscatory income and capital gains taxes. The new order in the 90's transformed the economy with investor-friendly reforms resulting in prosperity driven by the private sector. Interestingly, the Danes were soon defined by international media polls as the "happiest" nation on the planet.

In 2004, Prime Minister Fogh-Rasmussen spoke thus to Danish voters:

"We must become better at recognizing, appreciating and rewarding those who dare, can and will. Success should not breed envy, but recognition—there are too many examples of success or achievement by entrepreneurs creating envy, along with the innuendo that cheating was their way to success. That is the mentality we have had to contend with."

And contend with it they did. Most Danes eventually recognized the indisputable truth in Fogh-Rasmusen's pronouncement, even if they did not implement all his reforms

This was the history and my cultural back yard as I grew into pubescence and during the teenage years which followed at school in England. In these formative years I became very Danish in a way that can only happen when you are truly immersed in a culture during your formative years.

~~~~

In 1945, our family began another protracted period of physical separation. The physical distances, however, were always bridged by my very communicative mother. *Mor* would write to John and to me at least twice a week, following every event and development she could learn of our lives at school or university and during the parentless vacations. It was tougher for her than it was for the rest of us. She lived for the family. It was the all-consuming focus of her life, her driving force. She in turn was helped by her strong religious faith, which *Far* did not share. She found similarly devout believers among friends outside the family. She derived great comfort from them and various churchgoing communities, where her sweet personality was always embraced. PB was totally agnostic, perhaps atheist, ever dedicated to and absorbed by his pioneering work, which he tackled with a strong intellect, great energy and pragmatic realism. His decision-making, even in the face of the wildly unpredictable, was always deliberate and sound. This was as true of his managerial decisions as his determinations for the family.

Peacetime had returned, but we remained an itinerant family, which was close in terms of the tightest possible emotional bonds, but separated by whole continents between us. After five postwar years of regrouping, the family had changed gears and sensed it was time for change in young Flemming's life.

Chapter V

Selamat Datang!
—Welcome Home!

"The first condition of understanding a country is to smell it."
Rudyard Kipling

EARLY IN 1949, *Mor* and *Far* concluded that it made little sense to have me unhappily attending a school that isolated me from them as well as John; but they were unsure of where to send me. The alternatives were to have me join John at Gresham's in England at the very end of John's time there, or have me return to Geelong Grammar School in Australia, with its easier access to Malaya for vacations. School in Malaya was not considered an option for teenage European students. Catholic convents in the cooler hill areas were adequate for younger children, but there was very little by way of high-schooling at European standards. Despite some brilliant Jesuit institutions, strong academics were not a feature of life in postwar Malaya. I never quite understood their reasoning, but they decided to have me travel out to Malaya with *Mor* to spend time with them during the European spring and summer of 1949 while they deliberated over my future. In any event, I was thrilled to escape from *Haslev Gymnasium* and to enjoy the adventure of a voyage to Malaya to revisit the scene of my earliest childhood. It was an opportunity to acquire a deep attachment to the country and its people at an age when I could absorb and retain it all. I accumulated endless new and indelible memories of that wondrous, colorful, and vibrant land, but not without a couple of hair-raising experiences thrown in.

Mor and I traveled by train from Copenhagen to Antwerp to embark on the East Asiatic Company's flagship at the time, the *M/V Jutlandia;* again that strange, hybrid four-masted passenger-freighter design carrying no more than 50 passengers. The month-long voyage parachuted its passengers back into Somerset Maugham's world of the 1920s, maybe with a touch of Noel Coward added. In fact, Maugham himself had been aboard a similar East Asiatic vessel when PB was on his first eastward passage to Malaya as a UP cadet. Evenings aboard *Jutlandia* brought terribly jolly cocktail parties and fierce competition between the socially ambitious for invitations to the Captain's Table for dinner. Late morning games of mahjong, rummy, or bridge for the intellectually qualified, lubricated by Pimm's or *ginantonics*. Long evenings of cheek-to-cheek dancing on deck to very slow foxtrots and pre-war crooning favorites, awkward Charlestons performed by younger women dressed inappropriately in *New Look* frocks of 1949's mid-calf length

Balmy ocean nights. On-board romances, some attempting to be clandestine, others enjoyed more openly with brevity and timely disengagement clearly in mind. Undetected romance aboard a small ship is very difficult to accomplish. Women trading gossip in stage whispers over mid-morning tea on deck. Competitive fancy dress dances. Equally competitive deck tennis tournaments.

After passing through the Straits of Gibraltar, there were excursions ashore in Marseilles, Genoa, Port Said, Bombay, and Colombo. The short bunkering call in British Yemen's capital, Aden, allowed no time to visit that desolate, desiccated protrusion of grey rock, which was home to the strategic British naval base ensuring British control of Red Sea access and exit, the seas around the Horn of Africa, and the western reaches of the

Indian Ocean. For one lone preteen passenger the voyage generally meant days of boredom.

The approach of journey's end brought excitement as we entered the Andaman Sea. Penang Island broke the aquamarine horizon to the south and, just to its east, Kedah Peak's dove-blue silhouette rose graciously to extend mainland Malaya's welcome. The narrow strait between the island and Butterworth on the mainland was teeming with ships at anchor in deeper waters and lighters, tenders, sampans and fishing boats scurrying to and fro. *Jutlandia* was small enough for a couple of tugboats to nudge her into a quayside docking slot right on the Weld in the heart of Penang's bustling harbor-front, where hordes of hustling laborers and merchants were overlooked by the city's iconic white clock tower. Customs and immigration officers instantly swarmed aboard to expedite the landing formalities in the comfort of the passengers' smoking lounge, where the captain and second officer in gleaming whites stood ready to bid us all a smiling farewell.

Waiting on the dock, *Far* and our beloved *syce*, Abdul Rahman, were ready to whisk us off in the customary shiny black Buick parked just yards from the gangplank. There were excited embraces, including a huge hug for me from a tearful Abdul.

> "Flemming! Pemuda Flemming!" he cried. "Selamat datang!
> Sudah besar! Sekarang tuan besar, selamat datang!"

He welcomed young Flemming home, joking that I had grown up to become a big boss. My Malay was still good enough to express my joy in response.

The Buick's course was immediately set southward to the Butterworth ferry for the crossing into Perak, then on to Teluk Anson, and Jendarata Estate for the reunion with my very first plantation home of the 1930s.

~~~~

Malaya's recovery from the destruction of Japanese occupation, plundering and looting had been immediately and efficiently launched in 1945 by the British government, UNRRA and organizations akin to it, despite the UK itself being under acute duress. Malaya's agriculture, mining, and food production had collapsed hopelessly under the Japanese, so serious wartime food shortages and famine continued into the postwar years before Chinese smallholdings, Malay peasant farming and industrial agriculture were restored to normal. Rehabilitation was aided by huge rice and other grain imports from the USA and the British dominions of Canada and Australia. Progress, however, was impeded by an embryonic but growing organization of Chinese communist insurgents: militant groups working in Malaya with direct and ample support from Chinese Maoists and the Soviets. These groups were eventually organized as the MNLA—the Malayan National Liberation Army, the military arm of the Communist Party, which set out to obstruct infrastructure repair, damage the country's strategic resources even further, and generally hinder the administration. Their aim was to take over from the British at the expense of native Malays and Malayan Chinese. The Malay independence leaders were hardly activists, but they did feel that their plans and dreams of Malay rule were threatened by the communists.

Ethnic Malays, constituting 60 percent of the population, are the product of a millennium of migration and trade, descended from sub-groups from all over Maritime Southeast Asia and the Australasian islands, drawing also from Polynesian, Indian, and Chinese precursors. Today they range from parts of southern Burma and Thailand through the Malay peninsular, Borneo, Java, and Sumatra down as far as Timor. The identification of Malays as an ethnic cluster dates from the 14th century with the rise in power and regional dominance of the *Melaka* Sultanate, which brought political and religious—Muslim—structure to the territories north and south of modern Malacca.

~~~~

Soon after we had settled into a daily family routine in the general manager's bungalow on Jendarata, all hell broke loose on UP's estates and in the surrounding lowland plantation districts of Perak and Selangor. The communist Chinese uprising, which had been gathering momentum throughout the Federated States of Malaya, finally erupted just as Britain addressed escalating Malay pressure for independence. Britain's accelerated postwar withdrawal from Burma, granting full independence, had whetted all the activists' appetites for control and had boosted the revolutionary aspirations of communist insurgents across Southeast Asia. Insurgent activity was, from the start, focused on strategic non-urban areas, which were home to the plantation and tin mining industries. The situation was dubbed *The Emergency* by the Colonial Office and media, who also referred to the insurgents as *bandits*. The nomenclature was strange, but there was a reason for its use. Lloyds of London had declared that the relevant insurance contracts and policies covering damage arising from insurgent action would not cover losses defined as "results of war," but in a bizarre twist of logic and reason Lloyds allowed compensation for results of "one or more emergencies" in the country. The government was quick to name the whole situation and all its local and national aspects *The Emergency*. The insurgents were *organized bandits*, not guerrilla warriors.

The insurrection was clearly well financed. The insurgents were well armed, organized and trained in guerrilla warfare with the objective of causing maximum disruption to the infrastructure of the country, its productive assets, and its commerce. The sultanate of Perak, particularly the Teluk Anson and Ipoh areas, provided lots of opportunity to do just that, and the nearby jungle of the foothills inland of UP's Jenderata and Ulu Bernam properties provided ideal cover into which the guerrillas could disappear between attacks. A communist Chinese takeover of what today is independent Malaysia was their overall objective. Their strategy was first to cause administrative and economic breakdown of the colony, gain control of all essential resources, and thus disrupt any orderly handover to an independent, democratically elected government.

In the end, the British prevailed, but it was a long, bloody and expensive struggle. The Brits eventually did a brilliant job of countering the guerrilla tactics: they grasped that there was no point in seeking to neutralize the mercurial Chinese communist leadership or its chain of command because the leaders were never assembled in one location long enough to be pinned down. Conventional military supremacy of personnel and conventional equipment like cannons and tanks were useless and irrelevant.

The British High Commissioner of Malaya, Sir Henry Gurney, was ambushed and shot dead in his car on his way to a hill station retreat at Fraser's Hill in 1951. He was succeeded as head of the government by a little-known military man, General Sir Gerald Templer, who purportedly was given more powers to do his job than any British soldier since Oliver Cromwell. He ended up in total command of the Malayan situation on both the political and military fronts. He insisted that the colony's finite resources be deployed widely (and therefore very thinly) and then focused entirely on alert preparation and readiness. The next step was to cut off the Communists' supply lines—stepping on their wind pipes—and beating the guerrillas at their own game in thousands of small but vicious skirmishes. Templer turned Malaya's conventional policies and bureaucracy on their heads. He swore like the trooper he was, cursed like a cockney, and declared,

> "I am going to put fucking ginger up those Chinese commie arses!"

Sir Gerald also had more subtle ideas. He pursued a strategy of "winning the hearts and minds" of the non-Malay population, particularly the Chinese. For one-million-plus of them he secured Malayan citizenship. His policies entrenched "political and social equality for all Malayans," irrespective of race.

Anxious Malay nationalist leaders were terrified of a potential communist victory and consequent political intervention, which would upend the developing plans for their *bumiputera melayu* program—an ethnic Malay takeover from the British upon gaining independence, which they called *Merdeka*. The *bumiputera* program's name is derived from the Sanskrit words meaning "sons of the earth." It was, and still is, a nationwide affirmative action program to secure overall control of the country by ethnic Malays and ensure participation in business and government by means of ethnic quotas. The legislation ensures 30 percent Malay ownership of any enterprise employing more than 50 people throughout commerce and industry, which protects Malay interests from the competitive pressures of large Chinese and Indian minorities. Chinese businessmen, especially, have always been a driving force in the country's industry and commerce, thus stimulating its economic growth.

It was Sir Gerald Templer's dynamic personality and leadership that persuaded the Malays as well as the Brits that they were going to win. He was described by colonial officers as a human dynamo, driving himself and everybody around him tirelessly. Desperately fatigued, he would sometimes lose concentration as his subordinates dutifully reported to him; but a single word could then catch his attention, causing him to bolt upright like a jack-in-the-box to shout, "that's absolutely right, Old Cock!" and immediately order vigorous follow-up action in support of the given recommendation. The field marshal applied tactics based on a program known as the "Briggs Plan," which set out to isolate the guerrillas from their sources of food, intelligence, and arms—namely the Chinese squatters living at the edge of the jungle, who were instrumental in providing support to the *bandits*. He resettled the squatters in deliberately attractive "new villages ," introduced identity cards or passes, established food rationing and the formation of home guard units, a bit like the Brits did during World War II in the UK. His special branch agents infiltrated the Chinese in the new villages, cunningly creating false defects in the system set up to deprive the guerillas of food, and then set up a terrorist rendezvous, which in turn would facilitate a pre-arranged ambush. This very effective technique was known as "creating honey pots."

Another Templer innovation was the creation of "white areas." The territory of Malacca, which had been a relatively minor field of guerilla operations, was the first to be combed and cleared of "bandit infestation." This allowed Sir Gerald to lift all emergency restrictions including food rationing, curfews and other unpopular controls, and then broadcast the move throughout the country as a victory, and declaring Malacca a "white area." He saw this as "a carrot we can hold out, so everybody will want to work with us against the Communists."

And it worked.

As a component of the British Army the famous Gurkha Regiment was key to British success. Gurkha skills, fanatic commitment, and their ferocious agility set them apart. It would have been impossible to overcome the insurgents by relying on conventional warfare and conventional force of numbers and armament. Templer showed the world that tanks and heavy artillery were no good at chasing squads of highly mobile Chinese guerillas, who would scatter in the jungle or melt into the crowds of a market place. The Gurkhas, on the other hand, were masters of face to face combat, the arts of ambush and aggressive pursuit. They were lethal and blood-curdling in action.

Sometime before Templer took over, a dozen planters and several more staff families were murdered in the course of one dreadful night of raids on their homes in the plantation districts surrounding Teluk Anson and Ipoh. Soon after that, Jendarata and its sister estates got the attention of the guerilla leaders. United Plantations' model estates were perfect targets as their disruption would be seen as great accomplishments, adding ammunition to the insurgents' propaganda campaign aimed at the Chinese component of the population. PB saw to it that steps were taken to see that Jendarata and the other UP estates were particularly well guarded by military and police units, including a Gurkha platoon assigned by the British Army to Jendarata Estate.

A raid on the bungalow of UP's general manager at three o'clock in the morning was launched a month or so after my arrival. The attack was immediately detected by alert military guards the moment the *bandits* broke cover of total darkness provided by the adjacent rubber plantation, the very edge of which was behind the bamboo hedge at the back of the garden. Pandemonium broke loose in a matter of seconds, as the raiders sprinted across the great lawn and vegetable garden, automatic guns crackling and bloodcurdling screams replacing the animal cacophony of the Malayan night. Tracer bullets cut through the darkness in every direction as the army and police units sprang to action.

For months the British authorities in Teluk Anson, following Sir Gerald Templer's instructions, had been preparing meticulously for exactly this sort of incident. Police intelligence had allowed them to be preemptive, so guards had been posted, road blocks set up, sandbag walls built inside and around residential and office buildings. Searchlights were installed along the upstairs balconies of the bungalow and at both entrances to the long U-shaped driveway. In the middle of the house, on the landing at the top of the stairwell serving the bedroom area, there were more sandbags to provide shelter inside a kind of mini-bunker.

Within moments of the attack, lights went on everywhere except inside the house. Sweeping searchlight beams immediately picked up the attackers storming in from the jungle and plantation's edge. The police, mostly Sikhs, were quick, cool and efficient in their response with fire-power; but the pivotal element of the defense was the savage retaliation of the Gurkha platoon. They were the world's toughest and most brutal hand-to-hand fighters. The Gurkhas are an elite regiment of the British cum Indian armies, hand-picked from the *Rajput* clan of Nepal, intensively train-ed to kill in close combat, and then kill again. They must have invented the concept of fighting to "take no prisoners." The typical Gurkha is sturdy, but relatively small in stature with round, smiling hazel faces, high cheek-bones, and slightly Mongolian features. However, they were ice-cold, vicious combatants, totally committed to their combat mission, physically agile and completely ruthless in using their bodies and any available wea-pon, from their own razor sharp, dagger-like *kukris* or Malay *parangs* to automatic firearms and hand guns. They used their favored *kukris* with breathtaking skill and precision. When standing down, at ease in hours of relaxation, they would spend hours sharpening their weapons, and whenever asked, would eagerly show off their prowess. With one lightning stroke they could slice a mango or a papaya in half, one part ready to eat, while leaving the other half still hanging by a stalk on its branch or stem. Being at the receiving end of the Gurkhas' martial arts was no sport. The Chinese *bandits* learned this at enormous cost.

Not a single *bandit* got closer than twenty feet from the bungalow before falling to the barrage of bullets, or to the cold steel of a Gurkha's stab or slash to the throat. I experienced the raid from a very secure place inside the sandbag bunker with *Mor*, well protected from the action. The setting of the hand-to-hand combat was the lawn between the edge of the plantation or the jungle and the house, or in the shadows of the servants' quarters at the back of the bungalow. With lethal athleticism the Gurkhas' confronted and terrified the insurgents, many of whom turning tail and attempting desperately to return to the protective dark of the rubber trees, which most of them never reached. They fled the merciless, daemonic defense they had triggered. Although *Mor* and I were tucked away safely in our bunker, we heard and sensed much from our interior vantage point. Blinding white stripes of light darted to and fro' on the plaster ceiling, as the searchlight beams swept back and forth across the outside walls of the bungalow and penetrated the hedges and bushes around the garden. The *bandits'* random bullets punctured outside walls and penetrated the ceilings high above us, inside the house, while staccato gunfire from the Sikh police and British soldiers strafed every corner of the property and pierced the corridors between the trunks of rubber trees. Orders screeched by platoon leaders at frantic decibel readings. Bloodcurdling groans as Cantonese *bandits* encountered the sharp end of a Ghurkha's *kukri* or bayonet and slumped to earth with a macabre thud. Ominous muted thumps of occasional bullets slamming into a nearby sandbag. But, in a matter of five minutes it was all over.

Despite the protection of the sandbags and knowing *Far*, armed with an automatic, was downstairs ready to protect us with his life, I trembled and shook with fright. However, after these minutes of frenzied tumult, earsplitting noise and desperate combat, total silence suddenly fell as the last surviving bandit scrambled back into the black of night. The eerie silence lasted but a minute or two before Malaya's nocturnal sound-blast resumed, uncontrolled like a full symphony orchestra blaring its final discordant tune-up. The cicadas, crickets, all sorts of owls, night jars—all of Malaya's tropical nocturnal fauna recovered from the rude interruption and again took over the darkness and the airwaves. Methodically, the police and troops regrouped to clear the battle field and take score. Eleven dead Chinese insurgents to one wounded Sikh sergeant, who took a bullet to his shoulder, his pristine powder-blue turban spattered dark red. The British officer in charge praised the performance. The Ghurkhas, expressionless and totally unmoved, again took their appointed positions around the property as if they had only been on a tea break.

Far, apparently cool and calm, eventually came up the stairs to the sandbag bunker and assured us quietly that everything was all right, all was under control. The sun would be up in a couple of hours. However, his hand was trembling as he reached around *Mor's* shoulders and kissed her on the forehead. He gave me an unusually tight hug as he bid me goodnight for the second time.

"Well, it's time to turn in, my dears. Go back to bed and get some decent sleep. Everything's just fine now," he said. "The police and troops did their job well, and the Gurkhas were just incredible. They certainly looked after this particular group of commie bastards for the time being. We're probably okay now for another few days. We've been a lot luckier than some of our friends in the Teluk Anson and Ipoh areas. Our fellows did very well and we're all in

one piece and the Sikh's shoulder will be fine." Turning to
Mor he said, "We are in good hands, Hedde."

Mor's rather Teutonic name was Hedvig, but she was universally
known as Hedde, pronounced *Hedda* in English. She was reassured by PB's
words and his anchored composure. She was a good soldier, too, admired
by the other staff wives for the way she handled her concern for others on
the estate and the raid itself.

That was our first and last attack on Jendarata while I was in Malaya,
but Ulu Bernam, the UP's oil palm estate way up the Bernam River—hard
by the jungle refuge of the *bandits* in the foothills—had to beat off several
later attacks, unfortunately with some loss of life.

PB's leadership and management skills were once again put to the test
by the emergency, just as they had been during his first years as general
manager in the great depression and again in the testing months leading up
to the Japanese invasion. Now, as on previous occasions, he had one or
two nervous and erratic managers on the team, but his senior staff was
strong and resolute. He was a cool customer to observe under pressure and
seemed very much in control, but beneath the façade he was tense. He was
always an example to others, particularly to those who were more prone to
panic and rash decisions. PB's leadership style never allowed him to take
full credit for what he accomplished; he was always quick to acknowledge
the contribution of his subordinates. Just every now and then, however, his
short fuse could let him down, especially if some avoidable stupidity or
negligence was the cause of a problem. He was up tight during these
challenging times, so his tin of fifty Gold Flake cigarettes would barely last
the working day. The tin, with its bright yellow label, would travel with him
everywhere. This soldered tin was the only form of cigarette package used
in the humid Malayan environment. PB's leadership example was not
limited to dramatic situations such as the terrorist attack. He was also a
frugal administrator when it came to stewardship of UP's assets and funds.
He would not permit shareholders' funds to pay for anything non-essential

to the business; he would use his own money if he deemed his own needs to be irrelevant to the needs of the business. Because he led from the front, he was hardly self-effacing; yet his style was certainly not that of a cheerleader. Even at my tender age, I sensed the respect PB commanded at every level of the population, within and well beyond the United Plantations community.

The insurgent attack in the middle of my Malayan visit unsurprisingly accelerated the parental debate and decision-making regarding my future schooling. In early September 1949 I was to sail back alone to England. A passage was booked on East Asiatic Company's *M/V Selandia*, again bound for Liverpool to join John in his last year at Gresham's School in Norfolk. However, that was still many weeks away, and I had time to savor and drink in the wondrous aspects of stunning Malaya, all the colors, smells, sounds, people, fauna, flora, beliefs and traditions that constitute the uniquely diverse and captivating land.

In the colonial setting of the time, the chasm between races, particularly between Europeans and the rest of the population in this multi-ethnic country, was yet to be bridged. This was a weakness of most colonial regimes, but in colonialism's late stages this was perhaps more prevalent in the case of the British than the Europeans who had fewer and lesser taboos in matters ethnic. The Mediterranean colonists were somehow more relaxed in their attitudes to color, reflected in the proliferation of mixed-race populations in their colonial territories throughout Latin America, Africa, and Asia. So, in post-war Malaya, I was not actively encouraged to seek friends among the children of non-European staff employed by United Plantations.

My early childhood relationship with Abdul bin Rahman, flourished anew. It had quickly redeveloped on the dock as *Mor* and I disembarked in Penang and when he welcomed me "home." Squatting, relaxed and at ease on his haunches as all Southeast Asians so readily are, he again introduced me to Malay manners and food, corrected my baby Malay language, taught me Muslim lore and explained the five pillars of Islam, the rules and rituals that shaped his life. The language, long buried in childhood's sub-conscious, came gushing back to me. Abdul's high golden brow and enormous ebony eyes were those of a gentle and devout man. He saved enough over many years to make the pilgrimage to Mecca sought by every devout Muslim in the world, so he now wore the prestigious white cap, the badge of a *Hajh,* instead of the common Malay *songkok.* Abdul was no great sage, but a considerate and simple man; yet he was my beloved teacher, mentor, and companion. I only caught a fleeting glimpse of my erstwhile playmate, his beautiful daughter Fatimah. This was because of our age at that time. She was obviously nubile, quite lovely, and physically more mature than I was, so Muslim sensitivities would not encourage a relation-ship that could conceivably develop beyond the platonic. The innocent childhood bond between us at age four had never presented any concern. Fatimah, in fact, was married in splendid Malay style a barely a year later.

I had lots of exciting meals with Abdul, prepared by his wife who was ever busy in the kitchen right after sundown at six o'clock, in their little staff house close to the general manager's bungalow. Appetizing wafts of Malay food announced the imminent serving of supper. Although there were ingredients common to Malay, Indian and Chinese food, their many scents and aromas were quite different—they each added to the rich array of distinctive smells of Malaya. We sat on woven reed mats or *tikar* thrown on the hardwood floor, eating with the left hand, while chatting endlessly. My parents encouraged my relationship with Abdul; we all three loved this gentle, loyal, communicative man, whose constant smile hinted at self-confident artlessness.

Abdul's coaching in the ways and beliefs of Malay Muslims presented Islam with a smiling face, which accounts for the majority of the planet's Muslims—then and indeed today. Independence was to mark the later start of nationalist politicians' escalating embrace of "Political Islam" to further their goals. At the time, Malay girls and women usually did not wear the *hijab* to cover their heads. Outside the very limited community of extreme Islamists, the Mohammedan religion was practiced with relaxed moderation, tolerance, and benign understanding of "infidels." There was nary a sign of resentment of the widespread Buddhist and Hindu traditions and practices. Only rarely would a *fatwa* be pronounced, causing Malay men to carry a *kris*—a dagger, which was often a ceremonial accessory—as a demonstration over some relatively minor political or religious issue. The Malays simply went quietly about their daily business, sanguine and content as they were, even in Kelantan's tranquil paddy fields and idyllic fishing *kampongs* along the pristine China Sea shoreline, where more radical Islam first took hold in Malaysia. The roots of stricter, orthodox Islamic practice grew in the northeast Kelantan sultanate, where today the most extreme PAS party rules. The broader Malaysian political arena was and is dominated by the nationalist Malay party, UMNO—it has thus been since independence or *Merdeka*. Only in Kelantan did PAS recently succeed in banning the sale of pork in open markets and passing laws to have young couples caned for holding hands on the street. However, modern Malaysia's religious and racial fault lines in the new millennium are sadly deepening. My days with Abdul, in 1949, left me with a perhaps infatuated, yet deep and lasting respect for moderate Muslim beliefs and traditions, which stand in such stark contrast to the extremist abuse of Islam in the 21st century.

Beyond the housing provided for Jendarata's clerical staff (Chinese, Sikh or Telegu) were the *coolie lines* where the Tamil labor force was housed. Political correctness was not much of a consideration in the language of post-war Malaya. *Coolie* was the term originally used for imported, unskilled Chinese labor in the early 20th century and was still used by everybody including the Indian and Chinese clerks. Thus, in the common nomenclature, *coolie lines* were simple but functional wooden row houses for the estate's many Tamil families. Beyond them were the Hindu temple, the estate's elementary school, a general store and the well-staffed and equipped medical clinic. This is where UP's resident M.D. tended to the medical needs of all employees. Jendarata's self-contained Tamil community thrived there in the compound, where the air was loaded with thin, blue spicy smoke from cooking stoves, scents of frangipani, aromas of curry and ripe fruit occasionally invaded by whiffs of less appealing durian fruit, cow dung, or rancid oil. Behind this housing compound the latex curing plant and warehouses stood. The palm oil extraction operation was located away from the community in another division of Jendarata.

Almost fifty years earlier, just after the turn of the century, Malaya's labor force had consisted predominantly of Chinese migrants, but by the 1930s, these workers had mostly been replaced by Tamil Indians. That's why PB had been required to learn both Tamil and the Hokkien dialect in his early days as a *cadet* or trainee. The Chinese generally were more ambitious, industrious and therefore upwardly mobile, so they tended to move up the social scale to trading, commercial, and administrative jobs if they didn't go home to China. The housing provided by the company consisted of spartan but solidly built wooden structures, with good sanitation, potable water and electricity. The unsophisticated Tamils from northern Ceylon and the Madras region of southern India enjoyed strong sexual instincts and multiplied at a high rate. They were extraordinarily enthusiastic and uninhibited in pursuing their sex lives, quite happy to copulate with gusto in full public view on the hardwood benches on their front porches. Their children, dogs and cats simply continued to play and scurry to and fro', oblivious of the ecstatic grunts and groans of their impassioned seniors. It was an eye-popper for a pubescent Danish schoolboy fresh out of Haslev's pious strictures ... an ear-opener too! My racing mind took me back five years to the nocturnal sport I had witnessed in that hammock on the deck of the blacked-out Dominion Monarch, halfway across the Pacific.

The *emergency* did mean that everyday life was affected by security precautions and constraints on movement, but the community played down the hardships and went about life as normally as possible. There were no other white children around, so I tended to engage in somewhat adult pastimes. I became an accomplished driver of a surplus US Army jeep, of which there were dozens on the plantations, bought from Chinese dealers who had swept up unwanted equipment and supplies as the Allied forces withdrew from the Southeast Asian theater after VJ Day. Unfortunately, arms and ammunition were also acquired, later to be sold into the hands of people who had dark plans for the future of liberated Malaya. With *Far's* permission to roam any of the company's private roads, the adjacent rubber, coconut and oil palm estates were explored, as well. I befriended Malay families in the *kampongs* all along the Bernam River. Here they made their living from fishing in the muddy waters and growing bananas, coconuts, vegetables, other local fruit and of course a bit of rice in crude and poorly tended paddy fields.

Observing the basic processes of harvesting and producing crude palm oil and copra, as well as the production of raw latex sheets was an educational bonus. All these semi-processed products of the plantations were sold to large wholesale traders and representatives of multinational rubber companies or soap, food and animal-feed producers around the world. Before World War II, the Japanese had also been big customers, but it took years for commercial relations to be restored as Japan's industrial economy was rebuilt and as deep animosity dissipated. The company had not yet invested in downstream refining of palm oil for its many different uses, but that was to become important in UP's future operations. Nor had it embarked upon its sophisticated research and breeding of hybrid oil palms using West African and South American strains to improve yield and nutritional qualities. Years later, I was to realize how these products touch us all in our daily lives, whether we are vegetarian, omnivores, or organic food devotees. They were all strategic materials at some level. I also learned that Malaya was a global player, almost on the scale of Bolivia and Peru in the mining and refining of tin. Pahang Consolidated Tin's mine in Sungei Lumbing claimed to be the largest single tin mine in the world, employing 8,000 people at a single location. There were different smells attached to each of the raw material refining processes. The pressing, extraction and refining of palm oil belched steam into the air and gave off a heavy sweet smell—almost a sticky smell—while the drying of coconut meat stripped from inside the nut's shell loaded the air with an appetizing aroma reminiscent of Asian food markets, kitchens or cake bakeries. The latex factory, on the other hand, smelt like some sort of animal waste depository, rotten and sour, again with billowing clouds of fume-laden steam as water was sprayed on solid sheets of rubber to set and cool them for curing.

It was brought home to me that the United Plantations group was a component of a truly strategic group of global industries. The rubber, coconut, and oil palm estates were starting points of vast supply chains that eventually spanned the planet to reach consumers of soap, cooking and other edible oils, margarine, baked goods, animal feed, condoms, gumboots and automobile tires via huge corporations as disparate as Unilever, Durex, Slazenger, Johnson & Johnson, Proctor & Gamble, General Foods, Nestle, Sarah Lee, Dunlop, Goodyear and Firestone—giants of industry and commerce by the score. The dominant producer companies operating in Malaya included Dunlop Estates, Fraser & Neave, Harrison Crosfields, Guthries, Sime Darby, Berjuntai Tin, Tronoh Mines and Kuala Sidim, along with the smaller rubber and oil palm growers. The financing of it all was handled by banking giants like Hong Kong & Shanghai Banking Corporation or HSBC, OCBC, and the traditional British banks.

Much later in life, tinplate became an important part of my own career, and it was in Malaya that I learned that palm oil was a crucial element in the old-fashioned conversion of cold-rolled steel sheet into hot-dipped tinplate for making cans and other "tinware" goods. In Malaya I discovered that semi-dry coconut meat was chewy and delicious before it became copra. I even got to sample a little *samsu*, fomented juice of coconut palm shoots, which was the prerequisite of any Tamil wedding party, wake, or other celebration—the essential path to a night of Tamil or Telegu oblivion. *Samsu* also caused sleep problems for those who overindulged, as it would lead to nightmares and intoxicated panics about *hantu's*, as ghosts and evil spirits were called in Malay.

~~~~

Far insisted that I should not be idle for weeks on end, so *Mor* arranged that I had an hour of German language coaching three times a week with a nice, homely Arian *hausfrau* of Teutonic dimensions, married to an English planter on a neighboring Guthries estate. The lessons were very chatty but ineffective. My contemporaries in Danish schools would have had German added to English in their curricula at about this time. Over weekends, *Far* would insist on coaching me through multi-digit multiplication, division, square root tables, some geometry and chemistry formulae.

However, there were also trips to the colorful towns of Perak and the neighboring sultanate of Selangor. The nearest of them, apart from Teluk Anson, was Ipoh, a bustling market town and tin-mining hub two or more hours away, depending on how fast the honking, lumbering trucks (*lorries*, as they were called by the Brits) would allow Abdul to pilot the big black Buick. Progress was frequently halted by road blocks manned by huge, dignified Sikh policemen, or by Gurkhas of half their stature hiding their iron purpose behind big smiles and friendly salutes. They were checking out every two or three covered *lorries* for concealed weapons, supplies and contraband destined for guerrilla groups, or even bandits themselves hidden under dry grocery goods or produce piled up in the back. The drive was a treat for me, as the road wound through exquisite and exotic landscapes of tall limestone columns, turrets, mounds and bluffs jumping out of the lowland flats, mostly covered by jungle growth, clad in rich tropical flora, vines, brightly colored lilies and wild fruits. The exceptionally lush scenery belied the insurgents' sinister use of its hidden limestone caves and crannies for refuge and storage. In between, sleepy Malay *kampongs* gave off their appealing smoky-blue scent of fire and spice-laden cooking. Buffalo-drawn ploughs struggled through the mud of inundated rice paddies, driven by lean sinewy Chinese farmers, shirtless under their broad conical hats, goading on the beasts with whips, shrill cries and dire threats. Colorful young Malay girls in brilliant sarongs sauntered gracefully along the roadside at a relaxed pace with feminine Malay allure, chattering through captivating, carefree smiles, not one of them in a *hijab*, let alone a *burka* in those days of benign Islam.

Ipoh's market, like any Malay market, was a palette of vivid color and a clamorous confluence of commerce. Chinese and Indian merchants plying their trades with an intensity suggesting that every sale or purchase was key to their lasting prosperity. There was a phenomenal range of produce and goods on offer. Conical mounds of rich red, orange, maroon, ochre, and brown spices—all the curry ingredients, each with its distinctive aroma. An infinite variety fresh fruit, vegetables and exotic blooms. Chickens dead and alive; fresh fish displayed on costly blocks of ice or dried and displayed in huge woven baskets, other seafood delicacies. Brilliantly colored and patterned textiles from finest wool and silk, linen and cheap cotton, woven materials and batiks. Ebony and ivory carvings; earthenware and fine ceramic pots; bronze Buddhas and incense urns. Toothpaste, brushes and shaving kits. Shoes, sandals and sneakers—also known as "plimsols." Foreign currency, semi-precious stones, rubies, emeralds and opals. Small ingots of gold, silver and tin. Cheap jewelry. Hats for every taste and purpose from solar *topees* for the *sahib* to wide-brimmed floral silk creations for the *memsahib's* afternoon at the races, wide woven straw cones for the rice paddy people. Nary a gun for sale, but endless genres of knife, *parangs*, daggers, and *krises*.

Throngs of querulous, vocal customers of every ethnic origin driving the hardest possible bargains at the highest possible pitch. Vibrant hawker commerce in the market place, ultimately driven by Chinese merchants, Punjabi money lenders and Telegu pawn brokers operating from offices on the side streets. Ipoh's narrow streets of multi-story shop-houses, home to merchants and retailers of every ilk, metal traders and mining company offices, all teeming with people hustling and bustling in energetic commerce. Chinese clan houses and storage spaces. But the main outdoor market with its hundreds of stalls was the fulcrum about which it all turned. In all of Malaya, only distant Kota Bahru in Kelantan could offer a bigger, more brilliantly colorful market. More of Jendarata's industrial and commercial supplies came from Ipoh rather than from nearby Teluk Anson because the variety was greater and the competition was so keen.

Kuala Lumpur, affectionately known as K.L., was farther away in Selangor to the south. As the crow flies, the distance was not great, but the Bernam River forced a circuitous route to reach the nearest bridge. K.L. was an exciting metropolis with its government buildings, hundreds of mosques, temples and churches of every denomination, grand hotels, cheap dosshouses and department stores scattered between thousands of shop-houses and multistory residential row houses. In 1949, it was not only the seat of Malaya's colonial government and the country's military headquarters, but it was also the bustling corporate and financial hub of the Malay peninsula, second only to Singapore with the latter's huge port and international trade. The architecture reflected the fusion of disparate ethnic groups into a remarkable cultural conglomerate. Gorgeous wide boulevards provided the main thoroughfares, shaded by flowering trees, dazzling crimson *Flame of the Forest* and almost violet jacaranda, frangipani shedding their delicate bridal white and gold blooms, versatile bougainvillea in rich hues of purple, red, orange and pink. Gardens and parks sharing their treasure of bright pink sakuras, golden chains, tecomas, giant hibiscus, and Thai myrtle with the frantic foot and motor traffic. Sharp copper steeples of Anglican churches competed with shiny onion domes and needle minarets of mosques to pierce the skyline while busily sculpted Hindu temples throughout the city exhaled wafts of incense and wisps of blue-grey joss stick smoke. Gaudy Chinese temples, divested of all inhibition, brandished every Buddhist theme in gold, bright red and black,. Malay and Indian women in flowing attire of luminescent to soft pastel colors melded with multicolored Sikh turbans, while the trees and flowers enhanced Kuala Lumpur's stunning urban palette. Although unrevealing, the Malay women's Muslim dress withheld nothing in their use of gorgeous color. Young Malay girls, observing prescribed modesty of dress, moved elegantly along the sidewalks, somehow managing to offer less modest hints of feminine figure through their flowing gowns of light chiffon or soft cotton batiks. The occasional *hijab*, head-covering scarf, was used only by older women.

Kuala Lumpur's British colonial culture projected its well-ordered bureaucracy and stodginess through unimaginative red brick or white-washed government buildings with windows curiously smaller than called for by the heavy architecture. Departmental edifices were ranged along the four sides of the vast central *padang*, which would have been called a green in England, complete with cricket pitch in the middle and a fine club house, right across from K.L.'s pseudo-Mesopotamian onion-domed railway station. Thousands of civil servants in standard uniform of starched white open-neck shirts with sleeves to the elbow, long cotton pants and immaculately burnished black shoes. Towering turbaned Punjabi Sikh policeman nudged the traffic along with confident dignity, instructive arm movements, nightstick in white-gloved hand. Cars, rickshaws, motorbikes, bicycles, tricycles, buses, and *lorries* yielded dutifully to the gentle discipline applied by the police. Chinese and Indian businessmen aspiring to the style of their European peers in tropical suits of crisp white, ivory and beige linen or soft sharkskin cotton. Senior British officers in gleaming white or khaki, wearing polished silver insignia and peaked officers hats banded with black-and-white checkered ribbon and gold foliage decorating the black visors.

The city was Mor's beloved shopping destination. Meandering tours of department stores were interrupted only for substantial morning and afternoon teas, complete with English accoutrements: warm scones with clotted cream and strawberry jam, thinly sliced cucumber sandwiches or anchovy toast, even hot crumpets toasted to a golden hue and then buttered heavily. Endless specialized boutiques and tiny stalls offered male and female tailoring services. There were also infinite varieties of textiles, embroidered linen ware; carpets and rugs from Persia, Afghanistan and China; ethnic or religious artifacts and artwork from Qum to Karachi, Batavia, Hong Kong and Peking all the way to Yakutsk.

Once more, KL's teeming markets tempted with seductive scents, sounds, and vibrant color. Enticing displays of flowers, textiles, fruits, vegetables and any food of the Orient you could desire—peddled to noisy negotiating customers and traders of the capital and its visitors from Selangor's market towns and *kampongs*.

A trip to Penang was the best excursion of all. It was a long car ride in the black Buick, north through Ipoh and Taiping to Butterworth, whence in those days Penang Island could only be reached by a shuttle ferry. Just off the northwestern coast of mainland Malaya, this was a British Crown Colony of captivating scenery and urban bustle. Its easily addressed isolation lent a singular romance to the island-city's ambiance and to the setting of the old Georgetown settlement at the foot of towering Penang Hill. It's a nice place to have been born.

~ ~ ~ ~

A Crown Colony, by strict definition, is a British possession which has been acquired by military means, such as Hong Kong or Trinidad, as opposed to a territory garnered into the Empire by peaceful settlement, such as Australia, New Zealand or Canada. Historians, however, have referred to the current American state of Virginia as the very first British Crown Colony, so one has to wonder whether the Brits claim their erstwhile American possession as an historic military acquisition. The Brits, in fact, abolished the nomenclature in the 1980s, perhaps because they were running out of possessions that complied with the definition.

Only a short distance from hectic Georgetown and its ever busy harbor, palm-lined white icing sugar beaches beckoned at the luminous brink of the turquoise Andaman Sea. The iconic coconut palms arching gracefully over a powdery beach were to become my lasting personal symbol of all I find so enthralling about the coastlines of the equatorial tropics. The breeze just beyond the skirts of the steaming city was always soft and soothing, even when the temperature in town was unbearable. The lush equatorial flora of the island was beguiling in its variety of shape, perfumed scents and vivid color. Perhaps most stunning were the ubiquitous Flame of the Forest trees, which would periodically defoliate to show off brilliant clusters of crimson blooms before re-growing dense green canopies to give deep shade from the burning sun. Georgetown itself was a very busy merchant port and important trading post. Its commercial center of gravity was the Esplanade, where the elaborate clock tower, which rang out hourly chimes, provided the marker from which all distances on Penang Island were measured. All roads led to the clock tower. The route to every hilltop temple and *kampong* of Penang Island started at the clock tower. The Chinese population of the colony gave the edifice to the British when Queen Victoria celebrated her Diamond jubilee.

For ages, the island had been ethnically very Chinese, so the dialects of the island, besides Cantonese, included Hokkien, Hakka, and also Teochew from the eastern Guangdong region of China. Chinese commerce had driven the vibrant economy and business development for two hundred years. The growing Chinese political and commercial influence throughout Malaysia in the 21st century has its roots in Penang, which is today home base for the Democratic Action Party or DAP, Malaysia's second largest political party. A majority of its members are ethnic Chinese; but it is also well supported by Indian Malaysians engaged in commerce and industry, as well as some liberal, well educated Malays. In the 21st century, DAP has been creeping up on the long dominant nationalist Malay UMNO party, which has been in uninterrupted power since *Merdeka*, independence from the British.

This Chinese predominance was very evident in the culture and traditions of Penang. Chinese New Year and a stream of other festivities produce eruptions of dazzling, highly athletic dragon and lion dances in the streets, fantastic fireworks as only the Chinese can manage, great exotic feasts meticulously prepared: abalone, dried oysters and mushrooms, black seaweed, waxed duck and Canton sausage. The early 18th and 19th century immigrants from China were known as *Babas*, or Straits Chinese, many of whom had originally settled much further south in Malacca, a centerpiece of Asian spice trade in the 16th century. The Malacca Chinese, who were also known as *Nyonyas*, are still famous for their exquisite cuisine enjoyed through the centuries by locals, passing travelers, and also by the Portuguese colonists of the 16th and 17th centuries. Malacca, to this day, is a destination for gourmets and tourists, who also appreciate the old town's Portuguese architecture of townhouses and ancient villas, Chinese mansions and Buddhist temples. Penang had no similar European history before the arrival of the British.

Many of the Penang *Babas* belonged to *kongeis*, associations that were basically benevolent societies established by early immigrants wishing to preserve their heritage and the welfare of their families and cohorts. *Kongeis* also served as places of ancestor worship where they could ceremoniously pay homage. A number of important *kongei* houses are still links to the past and to Chinese tradition in today's Georgetown. At the top of the social ladder, well-to-do Chinese were called *towkays,* which categorized them as successful merchants and business people. Way down the social scale were the "sea people," who lived beyond Weld Quay, in houses built on stilts as part of the jetties over the water itself. Here were shops and merchants supplying fishing gear and other daily necessities for life on and over the water. The sea people would only occasionally visit terra firma, possibly for funerals or rare visits to a hospital or clinic. They are descended from very early Chinese settlers who lived off fishing, or as laborers in the lighter traffic, working on *toukangs* plying between shore and the freighters anchored in the outer waters of the harbor. The quayside swarmed with toiling shoreline laborers in blue cotton shorts and white singlets, permanently drenched with sweat. The Weld and harbor together comprised one big human beehive of industry and commerce supported by industrious, tireless coolies. The Penang longshoremen outperformed investments in mechanization because of their very low cost, and they strangely had no interest in unionization for several decades. They trusted their own physical strength more than the communist union activists.

Georgetown's Chinese culture was tempered only by distinct Malay, Indian, Burmese and Siamese communities, each with varying impact on the cosmopolitan life of the beautiful old town, today a World Heritage Site being restored and preserved under the auspices of UNESCO. These distinct ethnic enclaves are in some spots separated by a single street or narrow lane. They are centered round the Indians' Chowrasta Market, the Malays' Kling Mosque, and the Chinese community around Chulia Lane and Kimberley Road. On Lorong Burma, a Burmese temple stands cheek by jowl with the Siamese Wat Chayamangkalaram, both more strictly traditional Buddhist than their Chinese counterparts. With only one or two unfortunate exceptions, all new construction in Georgetown has been limited in elevation to help preserve its old magic.

Weld Quay Street was a frantic waterfront thoroughfare, choked with every type of wheeled vehicle and pedestrian, where the Butterworth ferry would dock to disgorge its crowds of passengers and all types of vehicles from the mainland. Launches from the ocean-going vessels of the ever present P&O line would drop off passengers. The P&O enterprise, an icon of Asian colonial travel, originated as a small London shipping contractor serving the Iberian Peninsula, Gibraltar, and Malta in the mid-19th century. However, after the opening of the Suez Canal, it became the leading means of passenger transport between the UK and the Far East, boasting grand white flagships such as the *Canton* and later the *Chusan,* calling on British ports such as Colombo, Penang, Singapore, Hong Kong and Shanghai. These vessels were elegant settings for some of the wonderful Somerset Maugham and Noel Coward stories and lyrics. Every kind of merchant plied his high voltage trade along the Weld, buying and selling absolutely anything, but more often than not, rooted in the traffic of tin, rubber, palm oil, copra and some tea from Malaya's highlands. Warehouses lining the quay were known as *go-downs* because the storage rooms were generally below ground level, under their office facilities at street level or above.

A large number of Penang's relatively small Malay population lived in a more rural district outside Georgetown called *Pulau Tikus*, meaning

Mouse Island; mice and rats in this part of the world were not perceived as undesirable rodents in quite the way westerners view them. Malay life here, as always, was conducted at a slower pace and centered on fishing, horticulture and raising poultry to serve the town markets. Malays are not hustlers.

Penang offered an array of elegant hotels, but none to match the grandeur and romance of The E & O, Eastern & Oriental, with breeze-cooled bedrooms and verandahs enhanced by the sound of lapping water at the very edge of the Andaman Sea. In the vast bathrooms both the tub and the WC were placed on elevated teak platforms like two thrones—one reclining and one upright—two steps above the cool marble floor. Spectacular views across the strait to the smoky blue silhouette of distant Kedah Peak on the mainland to the east, a palm-lined coastline almost all the way to Batu Ferringhi Beach on the western horizon. The hotel's circular entrance driveway was matched by a grand circular lobby leading to public rooms, havens of polished hardwood paneling and furniture, maroon leather armchairs, benches and sofas, gleaming marble floors and exquisitely carved teak screens shielding guests from the glare and pulsing midday heat right outside. In the lounge and bar natural ventilation was bolstered by an Indian *punkha wallah*, a man who would use a pulley system to swing a large expanse of heavy linen curtaining back and forth, generating a draft—a relic from pre-electricity days, before the powered ceiling fan. When overcome by fatigue, the old *wallah* would sometimes cause the *punkha* to sway to and fro' by tying the pulley cord to his big toe, so he could look after his duties while half asleep, reclining on a comfortable chair. Sundowners, a cold beer, a pink gin, or a *stengah* on the waterfront terrace watching a golden sunset or even a distant thunderstorm gathering over the horizon celebrated the end of every scorching day to perfection.

Georgetown's shops and street stalls tempted at every street corner and in every narrow alleyway. There were luxurious silks and cottons, every imaginable fruit or flower, more conical piles of spices, all russet and

yellow shades. Chinese alternative medicines, some of them products of
nature, others of pure superstition. Whitewashed clubhouses with black
ceramic roof tiles for the white elite offered sparkling swimming pools,
English and other European members sipping Pimm's or perhaps a pink
gin in *ratan* chairs and chaise lounges. A few exceptionally opulent tea-
sipping Chinese *towkays* accompanied by short, plump wives flaunting their
gaudy jewelry. To enjoy these clubs, one's face and personal provenance
certainly had to fit, and only rarely was it not white. Your wallet also had to
fit if you weren't white because it took money for the Chinese to buy the
required social status that opened doors. Some old school *towkays* were
never interested despite enormous wealth. They were usually descendants
of very early *Nonya* or *Baba* settlers, whose pedigree was quite enough to
satisfy their vanity.

In dramatic contrast to the hustle of the Weld, the old town, and
harbor front, there was the *Ayer Hitam* black water temple, or Buddhist *Kek
Lok Si* high above Georgetown up Penang Hill, an eerie mystical island
icon, where thousands of joss sticks and hundreds of incense bowls
perfumed the air and dozens of scary but allegedly harmless snakes
slithered across polished floors. The temple beckoned peaceful funicular
excursions up the great hill, which presented tranquil breezy views of the
low-rise city below, the romantic island coast along the northern shore,
Butterworth and the mainland to the southeast across the strait. The cool
rainforest's extremities drooped over the funicular track, perhaps heavy
from an early morning shower, raindrops clinging to the tips of leaves,
catching the sunlight like sparkling crystals. Buddhist monks who were not
meant to work or engage in commerce urged visitors to take tea or try their
dumplings in a lowly cafe with the grandest of views.

Secluded residential enclaves of Penang nestled contentedly in a quiet
atmosphere of elegance and evident privilege, totally undisturbed by the
city's hustle, let alone any sense of insurgent threat from the mainland.
There were no guards, nor were the heavy wrought iron front gates closed
to bar entry or block views of immaculate English gardens, velvety lawns,

or enormous shade trees and reflecting pools inside. Even glowing pink and pale yellow English roses seemed to thrive in this incongruous tropical island paradise. It was here the Chinese *hongs* (of elite merchant or trader pedigree) and British heads of large trading companies lived, or aspired to do so, in gleaming white mansions behind large shuttered windows under gleaming black or navy blue tiled roofs. The whole of Penang Island seemed isolated from the tensions, threats, savage attacks and brutality of the communist emergency.

What gave Penang that apparent immunity? It may have been the wealth of the Chinese community. The island's riches were largely generated by the intensity of trade and commerce driven by ambitious, extremely competent and industrious Chinese capitalists. The *towkays* and *hongs* were the very first to organize obstacles for the ambitions of communist insurgents, determined to protect their business empires built by their families' hard work over multiple generations. They would unite and spring to action at any hint of threat to their way of life. Penang was relatively free of the unemployment, extreme squalor, shanty towns and slum areas so common in other cities; the island had largely avoided conditions which bred discontent and encouraged crime. The geography also made it difficult to infiltrate unnoticed or make a quick exit. Thus the island was spared Malaya's many tensions, violence and disruptions caused by the emergency and the counter-measures taken. Penang's magic, prosperity, and the wellbeing of its people seemed to outweigh the forces of evil on the mainland. Very few wanted change. It remained the perfect pearl of the tropical Andaman Sea. Those postwar, pre-*Merdeka* years were perhaps the peak of Penang's Halcyon days.

~~~~

Life of almost any European in colonial Malaya was dominated by "the club," as it had been for a century or so. It mattered not whether you were a civil servant in the great colonial bureaucracy or a planter, miner, banker, merchant, or professional—club life ruled in the cities, smaller towns, and on the plantations and in the mines. Every tiny community of five or six white families had a club of sorts. A place to meet for drinks in the evening and at midday on the weekend, for tea, mahjong, gin rummy, or bridge; a setting for children's birthday parties away from Spartan staff bungalows or civil servants' quarters. Many of the clubs had tennis courts, swimming pools and cricket pitches, especially in the urban areas. They were mostly white clubs, where even light-skinned Eurasians would very rarely set foot. Each was the social nucleus of a given community, large or small. They provided some comforts and facilities in a still relatively undeveloped land, in European terms. Malaya's clubs, however, were not exactly sources of political, cultural or intellectual inspiration. They did little to promote social progress despite well lubricated and often ill-informed debates in their bars throughout the country. The clubs were watering holes where alcohol or hubris could inadvertently stimulate racial and class prejudice; clubs in the cities and suburbs served as social ladders up which snobs could climb, and as incubators in which gossip was spawned.

United Plantations Ltd. was a distinctly Danish enterprise, clearly progressive in a management context compared with its British competitors, and socially in the context of its colonial environment. The company was, in its values and modus operandi, removed from the racial prejudice of almost all organizations and civic structures of the colony. In fact, one of the company's founders, Lennart Grut, had married a gorgeous Franco-Japanese Eurasian woman just before World War I and fathered five beautiful children, two of whom worked for the company. One later became its CEO some time after when PB left Malaya. However, against the background of British Malaya, not even my parents or their Danish colleagues were entirely immune to the prejudice, bias, and taboos of that age and culture. It was often in the matter of club membership that especially Eurasians were at the receiving end of racial prejudice; so many were desperate to penetrate that pure white world despite its wicked bias and taboos. Occasionally pale Eurasians were willing to suffer dreadful humiliation and affront, just to become members—technically—of certain clubs, even if it was painful to appear in them. The color bar was alive and well in various forms and practices. It was a stubborn and pervasive cancer of society in those years leading up to independence. It was the unacceptable face of colonial Malaya.

"Oh, but he does have a touch of the tar brush, you know. It's such a shame! Otherwise a damn good chap, I'd say, with real potential!" said the D.O. (District Officer) sipping his *ginantonic* on the club's porch.

"She really IS dishy, as so many of them are … and SUCH fun, darling! What a frightful pity she can't join us here at the club and really be part of it all," said the estate doctor's wife between hands of bridge at Guthries Planters Club.

"It's the Bengali temperament he inherited from his grandma. It tends to cause him to panic under pressure and get things arse-about-face. He's just not predictable, old chap—not when he's tested in any way. It's a Eurasian trait, you know! He'll never make a leader!" concluded the head of Sime Darby's personnel department. "And he's completely plastered after just two Tiger beers and then gets really narked over nothing. So I wouldn't promote him if I were you—he's a *chee-chee!*" said the Sime Darby personnel officer, using a colonial pejorative to describe a person of mixed Anglo-Indian heritage, "and that's all there is to it."

"Despite his deeply local background, they did give him a shot at a shift manager's slot in one of their mines—because he is actually quite capable, you know! I'm sooo glad he is being given a chance—but I do wonder if he'll make it. You know, my dear chap, most *chee-chees* just *DON'T* seem to."

"Mr Patel will do well supervising the Indian tellers. Just you wait and see! He's a good choice, he'll keep 'em straight! There'll be no bloody filching of small change by the tellers in my bank from now on," chuckled the local Lloyds Bank branch manager over his pink gin. "You know, most of our tellers at the counters are Indians and he knows his own crowd. It TAKES one to CATCH one, doesn't it, old boy?! Ha, ha, ha!!"

These colonial blimps and their social-climbing wives were to be heard everywhere, many of them remittance men of limited talent and education, who could never have dreamed of a comparable lifestyle back home in "Old Smokey," as Brits often called their homeland. Many developed affectations of speech and manners in efforts to climb the social ladder. Yet, by way of curious contradiction, most of the same people—nearly all Brits—would have given their right arm in defense of the very people of color whom they disparaged with such condescension and contempt. During the emergency, the Brits were generally very protective of their Eurasian employees because the Chinese communists despised them so, and the bandits sought them out as targets, labeling them as lackeys of the white man.

For some, the club was more than the social center and gathering point. To many, it was home in their time off. Not everyone had a bungalow like those provided by UP to its planters and division or estate managers. The staff of smaller estates belonging to other companies often led more primitive lives, with few modern conveniences, and were usually isolated with very little company in the vicinity. The club was a social refuge and source of comfort in their spare time. The clubs were serious watering holes, where *stengahs* and *ginantonics* were consumed at a pace: the former to get flying speed and the latter only for the quinine content, of course, to ward off malaria.

> "The quinine in tonic, you know, puts the mozzies off! True as God, old chap! Five *ginantonics* a day keeps the malaria away! Ha ha ha!" proclaimed the Teluk Anson D.O. as he shouted for number three, "BOY!!! Another *ginantonic*! PDQ, please boy!"

The globally preferred *Schweppes* brand of tonic water had been around for a very long time, but Johann Jacob Schweppe, who founded his carbonated water company in Switzerland in the 18th century, must surely have applauded from his grave. It was more than 150 years later in Malaya that Schweppes Tonic Water was first marketed as THE way to combat malaria—a perfect prophylactic protection from mosquitoes when enhanced with a good shot of Gordon's or Gilbey's best. It made perfect marketing sense to emblazon their formula's nano-dose of quinine on bottle labels. This marketing message was duplicated around the world, wherever any species of mosquito took to the air. Fight malaria; drink plenty of gin with Schweppes Tonic!

At clubs one played tennis, or bridge, poker, rummy, liar's dice or mahjong. The daylight hours of Saturday and Sunday were spent drinking anything from lemonade, or barley water, or tea, to Tiger Beer, one of Pimm's five numbered offerings or Singapore Slings, the latter favored by Danes perhaps because of its Cherry Heering component (a Danish-made cherry brandy). As shadows lengthened and Mother Nature then precipitously lowered night's velvet curtain, the fountain of *stengahs* or *ginantonics* would gush. The club was the clearing house for gossip, the parochial debating forum or venue for erudite analysis of last week's cricket test between England and Australia. Who would win, lose, or keep *The Ashes* in the never-ending contest between the two countries? Other British

Commonwealth countries such as India, South Africa, Ceylon and the British West Indies were part of this globe-spanning competition.

A regular male member's prolonged absence from the club would trigger the nomination of a search party, because he must obviously have had an accident or fallen seriously ill if he were not already dead. Or maybe he had just gone native with some irresistible Malay girl, causing a reallocation of his time off, in which case the search could be discretely called off. But the club gossip, recharged, would rage on for a week or more, loaded with creative speculation and titillating detail. If it turned out there were two community members of the opposite sex AWOL simultaneously, it quickly triggered an escalation.

Neither Godfrey nor the somewhat younger Penelope had been seen at the club for a couple of days, and yet their spouses had both been spotted shopping at the market.

"My darlings, they're probably having a lovely little toot! Isn't that too exciting—just to think of it! Where on earth would the love nest be, I wonder? Hotel Victoria in Ipoh is so far away, darlings! My golly, more than an hour's drive, just for a quicky? But they've been gone for four days! It could, of course, be worth it, couldn't it?" asked Phillipa, "I've never seen Penelope starkers, Godfrey must have fallen for her arse-over-tit! But at least they're both white, so they'll have no problem checking in at the Victoria, will they! Ha ha ha!" Then a pause. "Tut, tut!—aren't I *NAUGHTY*? But by golly what a story! I do hope they're having fun!"

Sensing the mischief, others would immediately join in the fun, right there and then in the club.

"I wonder if poor old Daphne knows? Oh well! What the mind doesn't grasp, the heart won't grieve! Isn't that the truth? You know, I can hardly say I blame him. Daphne *IS* past her best, poor thing, and Penny's SO dishy. I always thought old Godfrey was such a crashing bore—but crikey Moses, he obviously can't be—he must have some tricks up his trouser leg, mustn't he? Still waters *DO* run deep, don't they girls?"

Another planter's wife, between sips of tea, kept the scorecard current:

"Well I'll be dashed! Old Godfrey at it again? You know, it's only a few months ago he was banging Georgina. Now it's Penelope! I do see how *SHE* could put lead in his pencil. Don't *YOU*, darling? But, heavens above, what does *HE* have to offer *HER*? To each his own, I suppose. But you've got to hand it to him, the horny old bugger, at his age he can still get his end away! Ha, ha, ha—Catherine, darling, are you Godfrey's next little number?"

The club on Jendarata Estate, which catered to all the nearby UP properties on the Bernam River, did not fit this pattern. Being a community of some twenty-five European staff and professionals, many of them with families, Jendarata's was a large and busy club at one end of a long building by the *padang*, the other end of which housed the estate's operating offices and United Plantation Ltd.'s corporate headquarters in Malaya. The clubhouse segment had a real English-style bar (complete with high stools and a brass foot rail), a comfortable lounge full of leather brass-tacked armchairs and sofas for stag gatherings. Next to it was a wide covered and well furnished veranda where everyone would assemble if ladies were present. Right next to the club were two well maintained clay tennis courts. The women played *mahjong* or bridge on the veranda most weekday mornings. All children's birthday parties were held on the *padang* in front of the club or on the porch in the monsoon season. Compared with other plantation clubs, its atmosphere and clientele reflected a sense of relaxed continental European decorum, perhaps because it also served as the venue for so many family events. All-male drinking sessions were certainly not unknown, but not as inevitable as they were in the model Anglo-colonial club. Danes, however, loved and found many reasons for parties quite apart from Christmas, New Year, Easter, Danish *Fastelavn,* or Mardi Gras, and even Midsummer Night—as if it were not perpetual midsummer in Malaya. Yet they tended to place a higher priority on family life at home, so the club was not the only game in town, unless you were a young cadet bachelor. The latter might occasionally find alternative passtimes involving female attractions in a neighboring *kampong.*

~~~~

The Jendarata-based headquarters of United Plantations were modest, providing only the bare essentials for good communications and efficient management. One very large open space with rich brown teak flooring housed the whole administration (long before the fashionable "open plan" office in the west). There was no air conditioning, but numerous *KDK* ceiling fans whispering overhead and on desk-tops, their sound drowned by the clatter and bell-rings of Olivetti typewriters. The estate manager of Jendarata itself had an isolated area to one side while PB, as *tuan besar* or general manager of all UP's Malayan business, had a similar space, but surrounded by an eight-foot bamboo screen to provide a modicum of privacy. Everybody shared the typewriters' percussion, the monk-like hum of muttering Chinese accountants counting, the rattle of their abacus and the perpetual clang of telephone bells. Heavy black *Chubb* safes lined two of the four walls. A short corridor led to a large fireproof storage room where thousands of files were stored in gray steel cabinets from floor to ceiling, to which access was gained by a ladder tower on wheels, not unlike those in an old college library. It was simple, well organized and very efficient. High performance standards were maintained in a highly transparent environment.

The Company's original oil palm plantation was way up the meandering Bernam River, at Ulu Bernam. It was on this up-river property that United Plantations established Bernam Oil Palms, Ltd. and first planted oil palms rather than rubber trees, as exploding global demand for palm oil started to offer investment opportunities and higher returns than could be earned from rubber. The estate was isolated and very exposed to the jungle of Malaya's long, mountainous spine. The Chinese "commies," based in the jungle since just after World War II, made several unsuccessful attempts to kill the Danish manager and his assistants, but several policemen and troops lost their lives in vicious skirmishes over many months. It was too dangerous for the planters to have wives, let alone children, live with them there. Ulu Bernam was only a few miles from Jendarata as the crow flies, so Ulu was normally reached by a ten minute flight from Jendarata's airstrip in a Tiger Moth or Cessna. The alternative was a very long upstream boat ride taking three or four hours in a launch with armed guards aboard. I tried and loved both alternatives, but actually preferred the river trip through sections of raw jungle between riparian Malay settlements, clusters of little *atap* thatched huts on stilts at the water's edge, slowly chugging our way through the Bernam River's languid flow of thick café au lait. Seeing the jungle and river pass below from a thousand feet was also exciting and deemed much safer, but did not allow one to feel part of the amazing scenery. More disturbing to me than the danger of bandit attacks was the occasional sight of a prowling crocodile, cruising with only its snout, protruding eyes and nostrils visible, breaking the water's smooth surface just twenty feet from Malay children frolicking in the shallow, opaque water by the river bank. The danger of bandit ambush could not be ignored, but was relatively unlikely given the firepower on board the UP launch. It was an adventure, an exploration of virgin jungle terrain and lowland villages interrupted only here and there by the odd Chinese enterprise growing rubber trees or coconut palms on a small scale. Wherever there was *kampong* life, there were endless bananas palms, primitive little rice paddies and a few oxen or buffaloes trying to escape the steaming heat. Some vegetables, the odd coconut palm and indigenous fruit trees would provide modest yields to supplement a diet of fish somehow lured and caught in the muddy river water.

While the emergency had little impact on Jenderata's club life, and although family life continued relatively undisturbed, it did get in the way of free movement. *Mor* wanted to take me up to Cameron Highlands in the mountains, where UP had for decades maintained a cottage for staff recreation, high above the oppressive heat of lowlands. Up there, the air was cooler, refreshed by morning or post-rainstorm mists hanging over every little jungle valley between the taller hills. A week or so up there would have allowed us to catch our breath nicely. When John and I were little boys, the cottage, which was open to all staff, had been an escape from the unrelenting humidity and disease of Jendarata and its sister estates. John actually started boarding school up there in a small convent when he was barely six years old. In 1949, however, the danger of insurgent attacks from their bases in the surrounding jungle was too great. The single lane jungle road from Tapah in the foothills leading up to Cameron Highlands remained an open invitation for insurgents to ambush travelers.

It was in the Cameron Highlands that Malaya produced most of its tea. The industry could never quite compete with India, Ceylon, or China, but Malayan tea was popular domestically and in selected southeast Asian markets. The terraced plantations on verdant slopes opened expansive views to the soft contours of misty hills and let the gentler sunlight of the higher altitude cast slanting patterns through the scattered shade trees. The misty scenery, steep slopes, soft light and tranquil atmosphere could remind you of old prints from the Li River region in Guangxi province so favored by Chinese artists of yore. The bandits deprived us of revisiting this magical mountain refuge.

The same threat prevented an intended trip to Port Dickson, a bucolic seaside village on the Selangor coastline of the Malay Straits, where regular family seaside vacations had taken us in pre-war days. The minor roads in Selangor, like the one to Cameron Highlands, were subject to ambush.

Apart from their Chinese squatter friends on whom the communists in the foothills relied, their support in terms of food and vitals came from the indigenous *Sakai* or *Orang Asli* population in the jungle. This was not because these simple people had any political affiliations or aspirations, but simply because they had skills vital to the bandits, and were brutally coerced to use them for their benefit. The very same *Sakais* had helped Europeans who fled into the jungle to escape the Japanese in 1941 and 1942. Today the informed world understands the *Sakais* or *Orang Asli* want to be left in peace in the rainforest to pursue their preferred way of life. They have absolutely no interest in "development opportunities" and "quality of life enhancement," let alone "cultural exchange programs" pressed upon them by earnest NGOs. The do-gooders would do much better for the population of Malaysia and their own feel-good needs if they were to concentrate on fighting malaria or promoting universal access to clean water.

The habitually placid Malay population did finally get angry over the atrocities of the communist insurgents, particularly when the leaders of the emerging nationalist Malay movement sensed that the Chinese communists could indeed prevail, and they could block their own aspirations for a Malay-led independence deal with the Brits, including *Bumi Putera* provisions to protect and promote ethnic Malay interests. So, suddenly one morning in July 1949, every Malay male on the estates, in the *kampongs* and along the roads leading into Teluk Anson had a *kris* tucked into the waist of his sarong or pants: a *fatwa* had been issued by the *imam* of every mosque across the sultanates of Malaya. The Muslim population had been committed to killing every Chinese communist bandit. Abdul the gentle, pious *hajb* was suddenly fired up, at least verbally if not in terms of intended action. A deep frown over his troubled dark eyes signaled quite unfamiliar anger as he told of the *imam's* invocations.

> "*Orang Melayu* will protect you, Flemming, and *Tuan Besar,*
> *Mem Besar*—and all the *orang puteh*," he said. "We will help
> stop the communists, kill all *jahat punya orang China*, [evil
> type Chinese]. Insh'Allah! Malaya is not for o*rang China*,
> Malaya is for o*rang Melayu* and our friends."

The elite nationalist leaders easily persuaded the Malay Muslim clerics that their congregations had to be inspired to support their independence aspirations, which would be usurped by a victorious communist regime. The problem was that the complacent Malays, unlike their Arab and Indian counterparts, had never confronted a situation in which that kind of *fatwa* was relevant. Not even the occupying Japanese forces had induced any such religious call to action. The ordinary Malay has never liked confrontation; he was never a warrior in centuries past, nor did he now harbor great aspirations to succeed in industry and commerce. This was a challenge for the nationalist Malay elite, who aimed to control the country and its economy after independence. The communists spent no resources on disrupting ordinary Malay life because Malays never got in their way. The communists were quite right: in response to the *fatwa,* the Malays did no more than display *krises* tucked safely into their *sarongs,* never to be drawn

The communist uprising lasted well into the '50s, with the British and close allies slowly getting the upper hand. New Zealand and Australia contributed importantly with troops and supplies. Nationalist Malay leaders worked with colonial administrators, eventually persuading the native Malay population that their interests were at stake as plans for independence were developed. An amnesty for members of the MNLA was attempted, failed, and then withdrawn. Gerald Templer, working the Briggs Plan, stepped on the MNLA's air pipe, slowly choking them for lack of food and munitions. The long, bloody struggle ended as Templer exhausted the communists, who lost the rationale for their "war of colonial liberation," as *Merdeka*, independence for Malaysia, was defined. However, it was not until 1958 that the MNLA signed the formal, final surrender documents in Teluk Anson.

~~~~

In August 1949, I embarked again on a voyage aboard the usual four-masted East Asiatic company boat, this time the *M/V Selandia*, yet again bound for Liverpool. The shipping company had a predilection for naming ships after Danish islands or regions, using their Latin names from antique cartography: *Selandia* for Zealand, *Erria* for Aeroe, and *Jutlandia* for mainland Jutland. I was excited because this time I was traveling solo to join big brother John at school in England. Partly because of the excitement, and partly because I was so familiar with family separations, I was neither nervous nor upset at leaving my parents. A new chapter was opening. Life aboard East Asiatic's passenger-freighters presented nothing to fear, and without parental oversight it might even open new opportunities for adventure. The dockside farewell, however, was emotional and tearful. I was leaving Abdul, and we both grasped the realities; we understood the enduring implications. He wept as unreservedly as I did.

> "*Salamat jalan*, Flemmin'!" he whispered as he clenched my hand in both of his, wishing me a blessed journey, "and may Allah bring you back to Malaya as a mature and learned man. Grow strong and wise! *Salamat jalan*, Flemmin'. I*nsh'Allah!*"

> "*Salamat tinggal, Hajh Abdul!*" was my grateful response as I wiped my tears away, wishing good fortune to my mentor and friend as he stayed there in Malaya.

There were no hugs, no three kisses administered to my two wet cheeks. Abdul just cupped my pink right hand in his two brown ones and squeezed very tightly.

Mor and *Far* had no more concern over my departure than I had. They were indeed relieved to see me leaving a very dangerous Malaya. They were more concerned that I was so upset at leaving my old friend. I never saw Abdul again. By the time I returned to Malaysia half a century later as a tourist with my wife Judy to revisit Jendarata, he was long gone and nobody knew the whereabouts of his long married daughter, Fatimah, nor the fate of Abdul's wife, Raihana.

That brief Malayan sojourn in 1949 had been crammed with experiences, which taught me some of life's indelible lessons at a formative time in life. They made a very deep impression. Many childhood recollections were cemented and quasi-memories of pre-war years at Jendarata were crystalized. Those months left me with love and respect for the gentle Malays and their Muslim life structure, their disciplines under what I had experienced as Islam with a smile, the benign Islam of mutual respect and honor shared by hundreds of millions of Muslims around the world. Six decades later the barbaric hijacking of this religion has exposed many westerners to their very first awareness of Islam, leaving them only with the media's images of violence, fear and hatred of savage, bigoted, bloodthirsty *jihadist* animals. That is quite understandable, but not acceptable. The vast majority of Muslims want only peace and a chance to pursue happiness within their own culture and faith, including a commitment to being good neighbors and exhibiting warm hospitality, in the famed tradition of desert nomads. Populist media have here again exploited the horrors of *jihad* without providing full context, all in commitment to sensationalism as they chase ratings and advertising revenue.

The industrious Chinese population's approach to life, hustling sense of enterprise and opportunism molded urban life throughout Malaya, driving trade, industry and commerce as much as British colonists. The

Malayan Chinese, beyond the colonial government, were the greatest force for economic, social and even cultural progress in the country. The Malays were beneficiaries, and yet they were wary of Chinese power and jealous of their success. This tension was a major component of Malaysia's *bumi putera* affirmative action policies implemented upon independence, giving preference to Malay "sons of the earth" in every sphere of business and government. As most affirmative action schemes, this has steadily led to escalating corruption and economic dysfunction.

I still have memories of dark-skinned Tamils, usually unskilled laborers, chewing beetle nuts through their ceaseless chatter, interrupted only by jets of crimson juice ejaculated through gapped, red-stained teeth. This image is a product of personal memories of Jendarata's labor force, not founded on broader knowledge of India's southern population. I remember Telegus as office clerks and domestic servants, usually a shade lighter in skin color than most of their Tamil neighbors. Sikhs were the impressive and dignified guardians of the traffic and civil order on the streets of Malaya, tall, handsome, bearded, and brilliantly turbaned. The pale-skinned Punjabis seemed to work the side wings of commerce as borrowers, lenders, and currency dealers.

Malaya helped me learn at an early age that no country's enduring viability or progress is served by a given group's sectarian philosophies, rules, religions or beliefs—it is the enterprise and initiative of disparate individuals free to work within a respected and maintained civic order that fuels progress. The British colonial model, warts and all, had provided many of the infrastructural necessities, which allowed a diverse community to evolve and progress. Neither revisionist history nor politics can ever take that away from the Brits. Independent, nationalist Malaysia did not make optimal use of what had been inherited.

I had developed an early disgust for social pretense and snobbery among westerners. Watching my father and his colleagues at work, my deep admiration of personal integrity, industry and energy took root as I came to understand the social and commercial implications of the UP enterprise and the dimensions of its effect. This experience and these memories played their role in later years of learning.

Malayan memories have lingered and featured large in later, more adult perceptions. I had sensed the extraordinary dark drama of black equatorial night against the audio backdrop of the shrill nocturnal voices of the tropics. Uncontrollable fear of proximity to death persists at a subconscious level sixty years later. The theater of Malaya's monsoon downpour and monstrous thunderstorms has never left me—never matched, even in Africa. The chromatic paradise of Malaya projected by the country's fauna and flora, its heterogeneous people, its jungle, its seas and fabulous coastlines—the magic Malayan palette of colors, aromas and scents had collectively captivated me, as had its people.

During those few months I had my one and only experience of living at very close quarters with my father at work. That had a huge impact; I was able to appreciate the discipline, energy, dedication and reserved empathy for people he applied to his leadership role. These few adolescent months between the unreal world of evangelical boarding school in Denmark and a fresh start at school in England had jump-started my preparation for adulthood. The mind had been opened by experiences seldom presented to a pubescent schoolboy. The Malay interlude was a very unusual but inspiring departure point from which to embark on a new chapter in the process of growing up.

Photo Gallery
1920s – 1949

This period, from Flemming's birth in 1936 to his start at Gresham's School in early 1950, covers early childhood in Malaya, the evacuation from the Japanese invasion, the family's Australian sojourn and the return to Denmark after the war to boarding school there before revisiting Malaya in 1949.

PB, newly appointed division manager in his bungalow on
Sungei Bernam Estate
Circa 1920s

Mor and Far, newly wed, back from Denmark on Jendarata Estate
1930

Jendarata and United Plantations headquarters from the air
Circa 1930s

Ulu Bernam Estate boat dock and palm oil processing plant
Circa 1930s

Flemming's christening party, Jendarata
1936

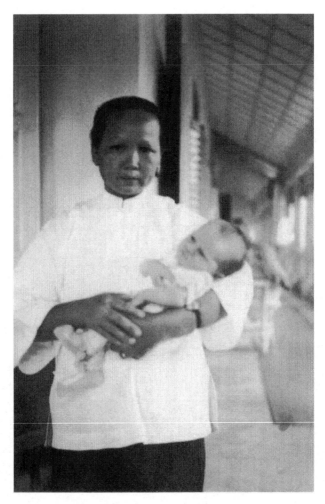

Flemming with *Amah*, Jendarata
1936

John and Flemming on holiday at the beach, Port Dickson, Selangor
1939

Mor, Flemming, *Far* and John outside the general manager's bungalow,
Jendarata
1939

UP's cottage in Cameron Highlands, set in tea plantations
1939

Fatima, Abdul Rahman's daughter
1941

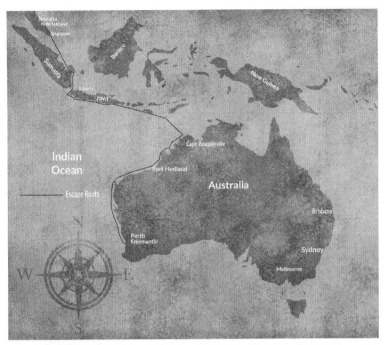

Escape route to Australia

The yellow-brick rental, Macedon Avenue, North Baldwin, Melbourne
1942

Geelong Grammar School, Corio, Victoria, Australia
1944

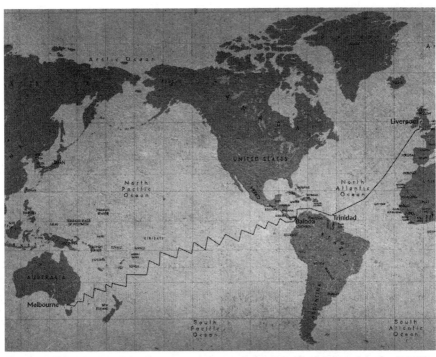

Dominion Monarch's route crossing of the Pacific and Atlantic (1945)
(The erratic route line in the Pacific Ocean illustrates the evasive zig-zag
route taken to avoid detection and attacks)

John, *Mor, Far* and Flemming
1947

Mor and Flemming embarking M/V Jutlandia in Antwerp, Belgium bound
for Penang (Flemming in Haslev Gymnasium school uniform)
1949

Flemming in sarong, Malay suit and songkok
1949

Chapter VI

Public School Politics

"The school's raison d'être was the mass production of gentlemen."
W. H. Auden

ADOLESCENT MATURING WAS accelerated on the month-long solo voyage from Penang to Liverpool. Life among forty friendly passengers was enriched by a US Air Force mom, Mary Haywood Vance, traveling with two nubile daughters, Susan and Dinnie, aged 18 and 14 respectively. This attractive trio dominated social life aboard *M/V Selandia*, and they took total charge of mine. I was totally bowled over by Dinnie, my first ever serious crush. Mother Mary was an athletic, attractive woman en route home to San Antonio, Texas, with her girls via a European vacation. Her husband, a full colonel in the US Army Air Corps, was serving out the last months of his assignment in Saigon.

Susan was a well-endowed, freckled honey-blonde of 18 years going on thirty. She gave rise to a serious vendetta between two bachelors on board. The loser was suicidal by the end of his voyage. He was a fresh-faced young Englishman bound for home leave in England after a first posting abroad with Fraser & Neave in Singapore. He abandoned ship prematurely in Genoa, vanquished in his quest for Susan by a more experienced Danish shipping man, who had spent a few colorful bachelor years in the fast lane of Singapore's social life. Ole Nissen and I shared a cabin except when I was locked out. My access was barred whenever he entertained Susan, usually during siesta time at sea; but I had no problem at bedtime because mother Mary followed her older daughter's every movement with increasing vigilance as each evening wore on.

Dinnie, at 14, was an enchanting, lissome athlete—an excellent swimmer, her mother told me—with long, Nordic-blond hair falling to her waist and quite suggestive curves for her age. The four-week encounter at sea was a lot hotter in my imagination than in fact. However, long after the voyage ended she wrote me lengthy anecdotal epistles during the family's European vacation and then from home in Texas for a couple of years.

A few weeks after disembarking in Liverpool, the three Americans visited John and me at Gresham's in Norfolk, where they caused irrational excitement among 450 sex-starved boys and the younger schoolmasters. John was as excited as I was to welcome them, as he had caught more than a glimpse of Susan disembarking in Liverpool and was not unmoved by her gushing ways and feminine charms. All three toured the institution in tight blue jeans and sweaters—avant-garde in those days, especially in that English boarding school setting. The younger masters were either rendered speechless or stumbled over themselves, competing to give eager accounts of the school's history and explaining the many academic, cultural and sporting facilities.

"You see, public schools, as they are called here in England, are in fact private schools, ha-ha-ha! And the schools that are truly public are called state schools, or grammar schools, which is rather convoluted, don't you think? So silly, isn't it, ladies? You Americans are so straight forward and PRACTICAL!" exclaimed a young Latin teacher. "Our own public school has been private since Sir John Gresham founded it in 1555. London's Worshipful Company of Fishmongers—you know, the old trade guild in the city, or a livery company as they are now called—later financed its expansion. Indeed, ladies, they still help us with our finances after these four hundred years or so—that's ever since dear old Columbus found you chaps on t'other side of the pond … just think of that! … ha, ha, ha! Now isn't that a hoot?"

"It sure is!" exclaimed Susan, engaging the young man with her big, blue eyes, "How cute!"

The American girls gaped admiringly at their surroundings and greeted everybody they ran into. In uncharacteristic animation the old Chaplain's cheeks took on color as he showed the women around the Church of England Chapel, pointing out its simple altar, 20th century stained glass and long rows of tiered oaken pews facing the center aisle. He could not stop his eyes flitting back to the curvaceous topography of their sweaters.

"You see, the Church of England is really a big inclusive tent. It spans the Anglican church complete with quasi-Catholic ritual and accoutrements—you know, like smoky incense, water sprinklers, and little bells—but no whistles in this case! Ha, ha, ha! They also wear rather fancy garb, and their parishioners cross themselves and genuflect in Roman style. We do things differently here, though. As you can see, ladies, we like to keep it a little simpler. Just look at our plain altar," he said as he smoothed down the simple white linen with his hands, "and my plain old black frock! Even my bishop doesn't wear a purple bib or funny skull cap, ha, ha! The Anglicans are *high church*, and our style, if I may use the lingo, is *low church*. Our Church of England en-compasses all of that. To each his own, we say. That's the beauty of it, the C of E really is a big tent. I think your chaps over there are called Episcopalians, isn't that so?" With a last quick peep down the deep cleavage of Mary's V-necked sweater, the chaplain said, "I'm *SO* tickled that you came to see us."

Dinnie lingered long in my schoolboy dreams, an infatuation kept alive by her bland letters from San Antonio telling me of swim meets, proms, July 4th parties and going to ball games with her dad. She even sent me photo's of herself in swimsuits, which certainly did not shorten the infatuation.

The voyage took in Madras, Colombo, and Bombay to pick up cargo rather than passengers, then Aden before heading north into the stifling heat of the Red Sea and on through the Suez Canal. With my American mentors, there were trips ashore, all of them brief and very touristic. The dockside Tamil chatter, jets of crimson beetle juice and clamor of markets in Madras took me straight back to Jendarata—the same excited, staccato voices, the same spice-laden smells, the squabbling gesticulation. Temples and museums *ad nauseam*, but also some spectacular days on immaculate white beaches adorned with overhanging coconut palms and casuarinas providing shade between dips in the duck-egg-blue ocean. Lunch outside Colombo was on the seaside terrace at the luxurious Galle Face Hotel. From there we had a long car ride into the interior hills and Candy's tea plantations. Ceylon's sparkling array of precious and semi-precious stones, particularly the blood red rubies and spectacularly blue sapphires further entranced the American girls.

As we gazed down from the deck railing at the ship's bow waves and wash, the Indian Ocean was a royal blue, matching the sapphires of Candy, sun-drenched and calm. Only cavorting porpoises and occasional squadrons of flying fish disturbed the polished surface of the sea as they took off, skimming over hundreds of yards of water before their airborne adventure ended in a salty re-entry splash.

All forty passengers were, by then, at ease with each other, relaxed and in high spirits, having made their various affiliations to form cliques for the duration of the voyage. Traditional ocean liner parties and games were the inescapable daily routine. There were the usual shuttle quoits, deck tennis, fancy-dress parties and gambling evenings with volunteer croupiers at the roulette tables. The ship's culinary offerings were spectacular, based on the best of Danish cuisine. The Americans were, at first, hesitant when confronted with marinated herring, unpeeled shrimp or the stronger cheeses, but were soon enthusiastic fans; the array of roast crackling pork, meat balls, sausages, pates, and terrines needed no persuasive introduction.

Aden was arid. The desiccated gray Yemeni mountains formed a perfect amphitheater around this natural deep water harbor. Its central stage was home to a large military settlement and a myriad of Arab traders. The town was the destination of desert trade routes from every nook and cranny of the Arab peninsula across to the southern reaches of the Red Sea. The Royal Navy's huge Aden base was strategically placed near the mouth of the Red Sea, opposite the protruding Horn of Africa. From here the British guarded the southern approaches to the Suez Canal, the Indian Ocean's western reaches and all the associated marine trade routes first established thousands of years ago by Arab traders. There was little to tempt passengers ashore, however. The shabby Arab town, which hosted a few Royal Navy families outside the base, did not have the magic of Asian markets and bazaars, nor multi-cultural population to add charm and color. Hidden deep behind the rocky coastline, as explained by *Selandia's* skipper in his best colloquial English, lay Arabia's vast wasteland of mountains, rock and desert, "Miles and miles of bugger all, surrounded by miles and miles of bugger all." The view of Aden from *Selandia* gave no clue to the complex Arab culture, tribal tensions, or warrior history of the territory. However, the busy harbor life offered some entertainment: Our vessel was surrounded by hundreds of waterborne Arab peddlers and smalltime merchants competing for our attention at the top of their voices. Beyond them a steady procession of graceful *dhows* slipped quietly by, en route to or from the Red Sea or distant tropical fisheries in the Indian Ocean, perhaps the Seychelles or Mauritius. Trade with East African ports and the Maldives was busy. It was in that very harbor that *Al Qaeda* 60 years later struck one of its deadliest blows at the destroyer *USS Cole*, as two terrorists steered a high-explosive suicide bomb in the shape of an outboard skiff into the ship and blew a fifteen foot section out of the armored steel hull. The crude but carefully planned attack jolted US naval confidence in the Persian Gulf, crippled the US Navy's state-of-the-art fighting machine, and killed over a dozen American sailors.

As we reached the Suez Canal's southern mouth, the *gulli-gulli men*, comic commercial magicians of Egypt's ports, clambered aboard to take the short ride from Suez to Port Said. Young hazel-skinned boys in loin cloths with close cropped ebony hair would launch themselves into elegant swallow dives from the lifeboats on our top deck into the opaque green harbor for British half-crowns or two-shilling coins thrown over the railings by admiring passengers. With amazing skill and speed they would dive to slice through the water before the coins melted into the depths, which grew murkier and less transparent with every six inches of depth. The *gulli-gulli men* themselves were talented magicians and comedians, who performed their tricks on deck. One of them, *Hussein the Holy*, produced a lovely big orange, which was checked every which way by surrounding passengers and found to be absolutely perfect and completely intact, before he ordered me to cut it exactly in half, right there on the deck, handing me his razor-sharp dagger in front of everybody. I dissected the orange with extreme care and precision, and, there, neatly embedded in the pithy white core of the orange was a shiny silver six-penny bit. He quickly retrieved his coin, and demanded more money for "me fantastic *gulli-gulli man*," flashing his ivory smile from ear to ear under his equally impressive black moustache. He then made a micro palm tree grow from six inches to a foot in two minutes, all the time covered under a big white sheet of cotton before revealing that it was growing from a red beach bucket placed on the deck, full of wet dirt. It was a perfect one-foot coconut palm firmly rooted in loamy soil.

"Bravo, bravo, bravissimo!" the *gulli-gulli man* shouted, applauding himself with gusto as he pranced around the deck, fez on head, and draped in a long white robe. "*Zehr Gut, Herr Doktor! Voila, Monsieur le Professeur!* Hooray, kind sir, and God save the king! Very clever *gulli-gulli man* make Egyptian *bonsai* coconut palm grow double size in two minutes! Ha, ha, hee, hee! ... now I need more *dash* right now, please, more money now for next incredible-special-amazing-magic! Please kind sir! More tips, *dash* for *gulli-gulli man's* many tricks—I have many children, sick mother, dead father and many miseries. Please my kind sir! Britannia rules the waves! God bless you all! *Insh' Allah!* Jesus, Moses, and Allah all very great, all good friends! Give me dash for more best *zehr gut* magic *magnifique! S'il vous plait, monsieur!*"

This constant stream of multilingual gibberish continued until our dear joker had coaxed another handful of half-crowns out of his naïvely mesmerized audience.

Fortune tellers and Persian rug peddlers came aboard. Merchants offering diamond rings and tigers eye broaches, hustlers touting lamb kebabs, sweet sticky dates, jars of olives and sugared coconut candy glistening in the sun. It was a busy commercial scene on the decks of *Selandia* as she eased slowly through the Suez Canal. The canal itself was not remarkable, except for the dimensions of the empty golden-pink desert stretching to the horizon behind the ragged nomad settlements along the waterway itself. A few passengers chose to take triangular overland car trips from Suez to Cairo and the pyramids, then back to the ship in Port Said, rather than endure the canal passage in blazing, breathless heat. They missed the *gulli-gulli man's* magic and charm. It was their loss.

Upon arrival in Genoa after a rough Mediterranean crossing, Susan Vance's vanquished English suitor disembarked, driven to distraction and unable to endure another day of Ole Nissen's accomplished seduction of Susan. Then after passing through the Straits of Gibraltar, a misty rain curtaining off any view of the rock, the Atlantic delivered its predictable Bay of Biscay gale-force-9 storm for three full heaving days. As the winds finally began to drop and the sea to calm, I opened the cabin's porthole to take in some fresh air. Within minutes there was a stormy petrel perched, visibly exhausted, on the rim of the porthole. After a short pause, as if to catch its breath, the bird hopped a couple of feet onto the wooden frame of my bunk. Desperate to help the beautiful bird, yet worried about scaring the poor thing to death, I slipped carefully out of the cabin to seek advice. A steward recommended a diet of milk and bread be left on a saucer in the cabin. It worked. After half a day the bird had apparently regained strength and departed quietly, again through the open porthole. She had impressed me indelibly with her elegant, sleek white and smokey-gray body, small maroon webbed feet, orange beak, large black eyes, much bigger than a seagull's—and long 25-degree-kinked wings of a tern, the tips of which crossed each other as she folded them behind her. An exquisite creature of the ocean, energy restored, was again ready for the challenges of the Biscaye.

What would have happened to her, had *Selandia* not crossed her stormy path as she ran out of energy? Where was she going anyhow? Where was she headed for now?

Soon we were cruising north into the Irish Channel, on the home straight before making the turn east toward the Mersey River estuary. John was to meet me in Liverpool, and sure enough, he was standing there on the dock as *Selandia* slipped into our berth. Another emotional dockside experience sprang to mind as I recalled the day in August 1945 when the Dominion Monarch delivered our family and five thousand others to Liverpudlian safety. It was a happy experience, in contrast to the 1940 monsoon departure from Singapore, which had *Far's* lonely figure disappearing into the gloom.

John had been given two days leave of absence from school to oversee his little brother's arrival and escort him to Beeston Hall, a tiny boarding school a few miles east of Holt, where I was parked for some weeks before I could join John at Gresham's at the beginning of the next school term. When it finally happened, Gresham's became the tenth school I had attended before the age of fourteen. This itinerant schooling experience instilled a capacity to adapt in a changing world, get along with and respect disparate people and deal with unfamiliar surroundings. Children can and usually do gain from being exposed to this kind of sink-or-swim experience, at least to some degree. Navigating uncharted waters can be an edifying experience. Today's increasingly protective approach to raising kids in the western world rarely allows that. The coddled schooling environment of later generations doesn't appear to have improved children's ability to cope with a little adversity, deal with the unpredicted, nor to understand that fate doesn't necessarily favor you as an individual before all others; nor does today's environment emphasize the value of staying committed to a deliberately chosen course, even when the wind changes; nor does it do a great job of teaching kids that the real world does not always deliver instant gratification when commitment and perseverance are called for. A less predictable life and less protected circumstances can also help kids realize that their choices, decisions and actions must always have consequences. An itinerant schooling does illustrate that there cannot always be someone waiting to pre-empt your bad decisions, someone to intervene on your behalf and to bail you out from those consequences, should you have chosen wrongly.

The four formative years at Gresham's were a joy—every single term, every year. They bestowed a profound understanding and admiration of the British people and their values. Postwar food shortages were still a daily challenge, and rationing was strictly applied as American aid in the form of grain and beef shipments continued to avert famine in Europe. Warts and all, the British are among the planet's most sophisticated, civilized, courageous and fair-minded of all nations. I was being introduced to England and its people at the time when America's Marshall Pan was sustaining Europe's postwar recovery. It was the time of General Clay's triumph in thwarting the USSR with his Berlin airlift; the release of the Kinsey Report; and the publishing of George Orwell's *1984*. Laurence Olivier's *Hamlet* had taken the world by storm, and Mao Tse Tung's army had advanced as far as the Yangtze River. The USA had led Europe into creating NATO, the one international organization that has effectively safeguarded Europe's security and thus promoted social progress through defensive but decisive military action over the following six decades. That was the backdrop to an extraordinary and invaluable teenage school experience.

Brother John and I overlapped only two terms before he left Gresham's and went up to Cambridge. He was at the top of the heap in the school hierarchy, in authority as a prefect and acclaimed as an athlete. I was the most junior creature around, at the very bottom of the school's totem pole. John treated me with warm sensitivity and care, but only in private. He made sure he avoided any appearance of favoritism in exercising authority as a prefect, an agent for discipline among the boys. He was "Heilmann Major" and I was "Heilmann Minor"—very minor indeed.

Our vacations were spent together in Denmark with various relations, unless *Mor* or both parents were home on leave from abroad. Outside school, John was my constant mentor *in loco parentis*. The times we shared in Denmark were the bedrock of the enduring love we had for each other and also felt for our country through careers unfolding quite independently in different parts of the world. I maintained the Danish, which had become my first language during the five years at school there, and John developed a commanding grasp of the language.

Denmark was in transition during these postwar years. The economy had long been dominated by agriculture, which was the biggest source of the country's exports. In 1950, employment in agriculture was overtaken by jobs in manufacturing as other agricultural countries became increasingly competitive, particularly in the dairy sector where Denmark had led for so long. Overall growth stagnated. Balance of payments, national deficit and budget problems arose as runaway public spending funded the increasingly generous welfare state. The Social Democrats and their coalition partners were in charge, as they were for most of the period from 1929 to 1982, pursuing ever bigger government and state intervention in all spheres of life. Taxation in one form or another was their answer, the omnibus solution. It was almost 30 years before this course was partially reversed by a right-of-center government, again a coalition. There were between eight and eleven political parties competing for the votes in a total population of around five million. Financial stability and economic sustainability had not been national Danish priorities

During the early 50s, we traveled to and from Copenhagen by crossing the North Sea on an old vessel—a Liberty ship built in California during the war—named *M/V Parkeston*, always traveling steerage in tiny cabins with four bunks squeezed into the tightest possible space. The eighteen-hour, overnight voyage would take us from Parkeston Quay outside Harwich on the East Anglian coast to Esbjerg, a small merchant port with a thriving fishing industry on Jutland's west coast. From there we took the train and ferry across the tiny country to the Danish capital. We loved those trips, except in winter storms when the infamous chop of the shallow North Sea would toss the *Parkeston* around like a wolf shaking its kill, making us sick as dogs. On these occasions the eighteen hours felt like a week. On the westward, school-bound journeys we would carry packages of Danish culinary goodies, including our favorite well-matured cheese, *Gamle Ole*, or Old Ole, with its all-penetrating aroma. The smell in our tiny cabin drove out fellow passengers, especially Englishmen, who would seek refuge in the bar or sleep al fresco on deck. This delivered the luxury of extra space for John, me, and our cheese. Summer crossings with no more than a couple of hours of darkness often developed into convivial all-night parties on deck.

Being Danish also marked me as an alien resident in the United Kingdom. Foreigners of all ages had to have an Alien's Registration Certificate, on which police recorded the exact location at which you were authorized to reside in the UK. Quite logically, the rules insisted that any time you left your registered address for more than 72 hours, you were to report your movements at the local police station, and then report back upon return. I did this dutifully at the beginning and end of every school term. Not a moment's thought of unwelcoming discrimination, let alone persecution. I appreciated the privilege of enjoying a great education and life at school in England, and thought it quite sensible that the Brits kept track of foreign guests in their country. In later life, I still question why people get so hysterical about the authorities managing access and keeping track of foreign visitors and residents. If foreigners and immigrants behave and respect the laws of the host country, they usually add value to society; but unfortunate exceptions are inescapable, and they create a need for reasonable surveillance and vigilance. The United States has, for two centuries or more, understood and managed this extremely well as the nation of 350-million immigrants evolved. It is not easy to accept that neither European nor American voters, nor their governments, can manage the immigration issue intelligently in the 21st century.

Gresham's was an extraordinary school, which had long thrived outside the English public school template. The public school system was generally very conservative with a tendency to be elitist in the worst sense of the word, all-male, chauvinistic and often parochial. Their strong academics and emphasis on good citizenship reflected their elitism in the best sense of the word. They strove to be the best in the field of scholarship and spawning leaders. The best known of them included Eton, Harrow, Winchester, Rugby, Marlborough, Stowe, Uppingham, and Oundle. These institutions all conformed to the public school template. Gresham's had not always done so.

That template could never have commanded the same widespread respect in the 21st century's judgement, given its permissive perceptions and political correctness. Corporal punishment such as caning was commonplace; athletic prowess was almost a *sine qua non* for recognition and success in the eyes of the student body and faculty. The prefects had *fags*, which was the unfortunate name for younger boys who did chores such as making beds, running errands and polishing shoes for prefects. In contrast to this deep-rooted English public school pattern and tradition, Gresham's had been, for almost thirty years following the Great War, extremely progressive, led by two visionary and intellectually powerful headmasters, G.W.S. Howson and his successor J. R. Eccles. They allowed no corporal punishment; the errant ways of schoolboys were punished by loss of privileges and personal options, or surrender of free time. Governance was heavily dependent on an honor system. Although it was successful and acknowledged as progressive, this approach was itself subject to some debate because it included a practice of whistle-blowing, whereby boys would inform on others who did not own up to self-serving misdemeanors as required by the honor system. Part of the logic was to place civic duty and the welfare of the community ahead of the individual's personal preferences and perceived entitlements. The rationale was fair enough and in fact worked well, but the system drew critics who cited negative aspects of whistle-blowing, or squealing on fellow students. Howson built a strong emphasis on the sciences and mathematics, where other public schools might favor the classics. The school placed less weight on athletic pursuits and encouraged the arts, serious hobbies and exploration of nature, provided one demonstrated genuine and persistent effort.

As an adult, long after his years as a pupil at Gresham's, W. H. Auden described the system as "fascist," saying it was "repressive and based on fear" which promoted mutual distrust. On another occasion W. H. Auden sarcastically said that the school's *raison d'être* was "the mass production of gentlemen," noting that the development of a social consciousness was hardly part of the curriculum, lest it question the position of the English upper crust. This was probably a very unfair allegation, given the otherwise very liberal traditions of the school and its luminary alumni in the fields of art, science, music, politics, and literature.

Kurt Hahn was the liberal German-born pioneer of progressive schooling and admired the Gresham's approach so much that he applied many of its principles at Gordonstoun, the boarding school he headed in Scotland after being arrested back home in Germany for being a critic of the Hitler regime. (Gordonstoun's reputation was later burnished in many circles when Prince Charles was sent there in the late 60s at the behest of his alumnus father, the Duke of Edinburgh).

To command respect as a worthy member of the Gresham's community in those Halcyon days of the 1950s, boys did not have to be heroes on the rugby pitch or the cricket field, but could instead freely choose to give their time, talent, and energy to acting, painting, music, carpentry or even physical labor in the school's private woodlands. For example, the school's beautiful amphitheater in the private woods, where Shakespeare plays of singular quality were produced, was maintained by pupils who chose not to pursue prowess in sports. The system's over-arching requirement was that boys had to demonstrate genuine commit-ment of their native talents, and thus acquire skills, or hone those they already had. Though it was not widely recognized in England at the time, this approach did produce an exceptionally brilliant mix of alumni, including infamous communists who spied for the Soviets. Among the luminaries of English literature, apart from W. H. Auden, were Stephen Spender, John Pudney, the artist Ben Nicholson, and composer Benjamin Britten. In contrast were Lord Reith, conservative patriarch of the BBC and Christopher Cockerel the less renowned inventor of the hovercraft. On the darker side was one of the famous "Cambridge Five"—communist spies, Donald McLean of Burgess & McClean fame. (Together, they were responsible for the greatest spy story of the Cold War era.)

There can be little doubt that the Gresham's system between the two world wars liberated and nurtured a wide range of native talent and creativity of its eclectic pupils. The contrast in the thinking and careers of Benjamin Britten and Lord John Reith are a great example. Britten's philosophy as a homosexual pacifist and progressive composer living with his lifelong partner, counter-tenor Peter Pears, was certainly unconventional. His brilliant work thrives almost a century later and draws ever growing attention. W. H. Auden was also a homosexual and pacifist. Lord Reith's conservative values and beliefs, which drove his inspiring stewardship of the BBC for more than thirty years, are tragically missing from the TV screen of today. His journalistic principles were known as *Reithianism*. John Reith's would not sit well with the journalistic whores of today's media. *Riethianism* insisted on "Equal consideration of all viewpoints, probity, universality, and a commitment to public service."

Reith thus summarized his abhorrence of the influence of ratings and political bias in radio and television:

> "Somebody introduced Christianity into England and somebody introduced smallpox, bubonic plague and the Black Death. Now somebody is minded to introduce *sponsored broadcasting!*—Need we be ashamed of moral values, of intellectual and ethical objectives? It is these that are now at stake."

These principles were written into the charter of the BBC and later adopted by the American public broadcasting system, but they have since been steadfastly prostituted and improperly buried on both sides of the Atlantic. In the 21st century, British public trust of the once revered BBC has plummeted to sub-50 percent levels, as the corporation's PC policies permit revolting language, obscene violence and sexual promiscuity while rewarding leftist executives with high salaries for pushing "progressive" causes and abandoning objectivity. These same BBC leaders relish painting the American population and all its voters as "gun-slinging, neo-con warmongers and rednecks."

By the time John and I went to school at Gresham's, the leadership, the pedagogic approach and mentoring style of the school had changed radically—and not always for the better. A man named Martin John Olivier had been appointed headmaster during World War II while the school was evacuated to the western county of Cornwall to avoid exposure to Hitler's bombers. Norfolk, Suffolk, and Cambridgeshire were home to key American and RAF air bases. Olivier steadily steered the institution back in the direction of the traditional English public school template. However, he did so without the support of the extant core of teaching staff and house masters recruited during the J. R. Eccles era of the 1930s. Olivier re-introduced caning in his own residential house—or dormitory in US terms—ironically named Howson's for reformist headmaster G.W.S. Howson. He fostered a growing emphasis on sports and athletic performance as a prerequisite for success and recognition in the community and for leadership appointments in the student body. He also weakened exceptionally strong school traditions focused on Shakespeare productions and choral music by imposing himself and his preconceptions on the masters in charge of them. However, thanks to Eric Kelly, my housemaster and mentor, Olivier's somewhat egocentric machinations and deviant style were not to spoil my own enjoyment of five treasured years at Gresham's, although they did have an impact over time. His weird behavior eventually prompted me to play a role in a precocious schoolboy putsch before leaving.

Gresham's was beautifully situated in bucolic Norfolk, just a couple of miles inland from the picturesque North Sea coastline villages of Blakeney and Cley, made famous by painters like Edward Seagoe. Locals said that there was nothing between the Norfolk coast and Greenland, so this seashore could also be dramatically wild. In 1953, a particularly vicious storm drove right in from the arctic. A near-tsunami flooded and destroyed villages and hundreds of homes along the estuaries, marshes and low-lying shore. More than a hundred senior Gresham's boys, foregoing classes, spent two weeks helping clear the debris and devastation, digging furniture and household chattels out of three-foot-deep mud deposited in cottages, barns, and stables. The coastline and life along it only recovered over the following year or so. During the summer months a chilly, moist mist called a sea fret would regularly spoil precious summer afternoons as it blew inland from the North Sea.

The school was surrounded by lovely woods, full of northern European deciduous hardwoods, abundant chestnuts, a few conifers and a thick undergrowth of massive rhododendrons, the likes of which are exclusive to English woodlands. In season, these huge bushes were bedecked in white and hues of pink, purple and rich burgundy. Although at least three of Norfolk's seasons were raw and blustery, the pastel colors of salt marshes and tidal lagoons always beckoned, dotted with idyllic fishing villages and ancient windmills. Rambling walks in rural tranquility during the warmer months took us over heathland hills of glowing gold gorse, bracken ferns and stretches of purple and pink heather. Inland chalky hills, mixed arable and woodland farms offered lovely alternatives. Narrow English single-lane country roads were flanked by tall, dense hawthorn hedges, home to a million songbirds. Two cars from opposite directions called for polite negotiation and reverse maneuvers to allow passage.

In England's pre-industrial times, Norfolk thrived on its agriculture and commerce, producing a vast portion of the country's wool in an otherwise mixed farming environment. Twenty or so miles to the west of Holt, where the land stretching toward Lincolnshire flattens and becomes sandy, a few immigrant Danish farmers had transformed thousands of wasteland acres in The Fens into excellent potato-growing farmland with bountiful yields—a feat beyond the skills and energy of the native gentleman farmers. There were several highly regarded names like Andreasen, Friis and Bruun in West Norfolk farming circles. As a legacy of its prosperous days of yore, the whole county was littered with hundreds of large churches, almost all of which were built of gray, split flint stone closely set in mortar, as were the majority of the humble tenant cottages. Norfolk's landed gentry enjoyed an indulgent social life of *huntin', shootin' and fishin'* on the lands of monumental mansions and estates, including the Royal Family's beloved Sandringham. Chinless English noblemen and absentee landlords in tailored tweeds and cloth caps staged huge pheasant shoots, complete with liquid refreshments imbibed al fresco between drives. Elegant equestrians of both genders sporting their "Pink" would gallop headlong on fox hunts across the countryside, jumping hedges and ditches, hollerin' and hootin' against the cacophonous sounds of hunting horns and melancholy barking of hounds.

Tallyho!

At the other end of Norfolk's social scale, tenant and subsistence farmers, rural laborers, and local shopkeepers led the simple, oft shockingly crude lives of yokels. In the backyard of my memory lurks the sordid recollection of the village fishmonger's sidekick, William, whose job was to cut up and deep-fry potatoes and chunks of codfish to be wrapped in newsprint and sold as fish and chips. Gresham's schoolboys who knew him as *Taitah Billeh* (Norfolk for Potato Billy) reported regular sightings of him unashamedly masturbating amongst the tombstones of Holt's village graveyard, right outside the windows of the Old School House dormitory where sixty boys resided. That was *Taitah Billeh's* lunch break R&R. There were medieval chasms in the way of life and living standards to be addressed in the community around our privileged Gresham's School. To the school's credit, it did so with low-key, effective volunteer programs as well assigned social service tasks in the community. Such practice was not a common English trait at the time.

The schoolboy population of barely 450 was drawn from a cross-section of English society, but weighted with East Anglian boys drawn from England' eastern parts on scholarship. The school's founders had, in 1555, insisted that Gresham's cater to the "educational needs of the rural counties of Norfolk and Suffolk" as a priority. The Worshipful Company of Fishmongers and the school's governors ensured that about twenty-five full scholarships were open only to East Anglian lads every year. Others might get public aid from county or state (national) scholarships. However, that was far from enough to make more than a dent in the region's socio-economic gaps and challenges.

~~~~

When John graduated from Cambridge and left to launch his career in Hong Kong, he could of course no longer act as my mentor. That role was expanded and taken over by my housemaster, Eric Kelly, affectionately known as EGK. By this time, my father had completed a global exploration of agricultural investment opportunities for United Plantations beyond Southeast Asia and had proposed southern Africa as fertile territory. My parents were sent by United Plantations from Malaya to do some serious business development and agricultural pioneering in South Africa and Swaziland, so we continued to be separated by thousands of miles. At the beginning and end of school terms, or when my fellow students went home for occasional midterm breaks, EGK and his family took me into their home in the Old School House, in the middle of the ancient village of Holt. The building, previously one of Sir John Gresham's mansions, was the original schoolhouse when Gresham's was founded in the 16th century.

The coronation of young Queen Elizabeth II on June 2, 1953, was one of the occasions when the whole school went home for a protracted midterm break, this time for family celebrations of the great Royal event. The Brits across the country let their hair down and celebrated in uninhibited style. Denmark and Swaziland were obviously out of reach, so I spent those few days in the lap of the Kelly family, or celebrating with the villagers of Holt. Parades and brass bands, dancing in the streets, a lot of merry drinking in and outside every pub, a "jolly good party for good old Liz." The new queen was all of 25 years old. Free to leave the prim respectability of the Kelly household, out of school uniform, I joined in the village merrymaking. I somehow talked my way into a few beers and struck up a flirtatious relationship with the sister of a Gresham's friend who attended as a day-boy. Their father was the local chemist, owner of the village pharmacy. Our three-day romance was touchingly innocent, but given the English public schoolboys' world of gender segregation, I dreamed for weeks of the coronation celebrations and my innocent little toot with Jessica Scoones. My Danish vacations over the years were always exciting and liberating, but at no other time at Gresham's was there opportunity for such innocent romance.

The coronation celebrations were also an early introduction to English pub culture, with its chatty warmth and chummy ambiance. Locals, whom I knew only by sight, would engage me with friendly curiosity to learn where I came from and why I wasn't home with my parents celebrating the new queen. They folded me into their chats and joke-telling, which evolved into sing-along sessions and drinking songs. I learned a refrain or toast, which I later came across many times in Yorkshire with rugby chums. Pint of bitter in hand, a local yokel would pronounce:

> *"Through the teeth and over the gums—Look out, stomach, here it comes!"*

Cheers, lad!

The main Gresham's school buildings and the other residential houses built towards the end of the 19th century were a mile out of town. "Big School" was a red brick Victorian assembly hall with leaded windows at the center of it all. More modern buildings housed laboratories and a large library. A pretty gray, split flint stone chapel with an unusually steep, high-backed roof and no steeple was reminiscent of a modern Danish A-frame house. It overlooked the extensive grounds and sports fields, all of which were enveloped by the beautiful school woodlands. A manicured Roman-style woodland amphitheater was where the Shakespeare plays were staged. It was the creation of J.R. Eccles in the 1930s. There were four residential houses, each housing 60 to 80 boys, and a separate junior school for those under 13 years of age.

I felt at home in these surroundings and over those formative years learned more from Eric Kelly than I ever realized at the time. EGK was recruited to Gresham's by Eccles in 1928. He was an extraordinary teacher and counselor, always ready to listen and discuss academic issues or the personal choices a teenager has to make. His persuasive advice and guidance was always articulate, quietly expressed with crushing logic. He was never slow to encourage my passion for sports. As an Australian, he was unsurprisingly a devout cricket fan, who staged annual village cricket festivals lasting a full summer week. EGK must have found my lack of interest in the game disappointing, but that never deterred him in supporting my aspirations when it came to rugby, field hockey, track, and tennis.

Another master took a special interest in me, again taking me into his family. John Williams, a towering blond Welshman with a gentle manner and twinkling blue eyes, was a retired army officer, who taught junior level English and coached the school's rugby team. He was no genius as an academic, but being some twenty years younger than EGK he would have slightly different views and remarkable insight as he helped me plot my course. I spent relaxed Sundays with John, his young wife, and two little blond children. The Williams family played the same role for my closest friend Andrew Mulligan, whose parents were also thousands of miles away in Nigeria.

When I was fourteen, after John left Gresham's for Cambridge, a terse telegram arrived at Old School House from *Far*, who was en route from Malaya via London to a United Plantations board meeting in Copenhagen:

> "Coming to see you. Need your undivided attention one
> half day this weekend," the telegram proclaimed. "Please
> reserve accommodation. *Far*"

The absence of greeting and the sparsity of language struck me. I shook in my boots: What grave sin could I have committed? Was this a summons to justice?

Far arrived by train from London that Saturday noon and made his own way to the Gresham's playing fields to watch a "Colts" (under-16 team) rugby match, in which I was playing. I knew he saw me score a *try* and figured that this small accomplishment would not have done me any harm if he had come to reprimand me for something. However, there were no signs of trouble when I saw him for a cozy supper at the inn on Saturday evening; he merely confirmed that after Chapel Service, we would spend lunch and Sunday afternoon together at *The Feathers*, the inn where I had booked him in. I had the deepest affection, admiration, and huge respect for *Far*, but there was no expressed buddy-buddy relationship between us. Yet, there was loving warmth underpinning all our shared times (unless he was for some reason briefly mad at me, and he did have a short fuse). As a younger boy, I would get very clearly expressed direction from him. In my teens, he would spend time asking thoughtful questions about my reasoning behind decisions and choices I had made. He would only rarely challenge my response, possibly because he knew I understood why he was posing the question in the first place—which was guidance enough. I think he saw a lot of himself in me; John took more after *Mor*.

We had a jovial father-son lunch spiced with his anecdotes and a mischievous smile. After some perceptive questions about life at school and my academic progress, we ascended the creaky stairway to his room overlooking Holt's quiet village square dominated by the Old School House at the far end. I still had no idea what lay behind his starkly worded telegram, but all was to be revealed.

No reprimand.

On a little antique desk in his room, three items had been carefully placed: a checkbook on the left, a savings account book in the middle, and a big stack of crisp, white documents edged in gold on the right-hand side. The black text on the watermarked documents was printed in an ornate script. They were British Government gilts (the British equivalent of US Treasury bonds). *Far* quickly embarked upon an afternoon of coaching me in the use and maintenance of a current account, or checking account as it is known in the States, a savings account, as well as managing the process of liquidating or cashing in the *gilts*. The hint of a smile never left his lips, the twinkle in his eye never faded although he was in deadly earnest. He was happy doing what he was doing; he was on a mission and enjoying himself. I was excited by the trust and confidence he was clearly showing in me.

"Let's start with the current account at the bank and this check book. I have put two hundred pounds in the account. You will have to keep that account topped up— just like a good drink, haha—from the funds in the interest-bearing savings account. That too has to be topped up from time to time, but we will come to that."

"The savings account," he continued, "is to be used as a kind of hopper, or a cushion of cash between the gilts and your day-to-day money requirements, which you draw from your current account as you need to. Do you follow me? ... Good!"

"You see, it takes a process and some time to turn the gilts into cash, Flemming—at least a week or two. So you have to tell the bank manager to sell a given number of gilts well ahead of time, each certificate being worth quite a large sum in liquid sterling, which will be deposited into your savings account. You have to anticipate your needs, and then plan your cash flow to meet them. Do you follow me, boy? You know what I mean by cash flow? The savings account is your water well for topping up your current account whenever it is about to run dry. Meanwhile the money in the savings account is working for you, earning some interest. Do you understand what I'm saying? Good!"

He explained how I would have to write letters to the bank manager in London to instruct the bank to liquidate bonds when I saw that my savings account was getting low. No email or online banking in the England of

1950! My bank was to be the Hong Kong Shanghai Bank, its "City Branch" at 9 Gracechurch Street, London EC3. The *Honkers & Shankers,* as it was known to many who had spent time in the Far East, was *Far's* bank in Malaya and became my bank in the UK for the rest of my life. Every now and then I would have trouble paying by check because people were occasionally spooked by the Chinese characters on the checks. The City Branch in London was close to Liverpool Street Station, through which I would always pass on journeys to and from Copenhagen for vacations, whether traveling by sea or air.

> "The bank manager, Mr. Euan McTavish, will be expecting you to call on him for a chat on your way through London for the Christmas holidays," *Far* said. "I have already spoken to him, but you better write to him a week or so before the end of term to make an appointment. Now do you think you have grasped all this?"

I did have a few detailed questions, which *Far* answered patiently before he continued.

> "You're about to take some real responsibility for yourself, my boy, and I want you to be completely comfortable. You will now be looking after all your routine needs and expenses, paying your own school bills, buying your own travel tickets, your clothes, and allowing yourself an affordable amount of pocket money. Flemming, it will be up to you to figure out how much you can spend—you have got to manage your own resources from now on. And these are the only resources you'll have until you earn your own way, son. This is it, my boy. If you have problems of any sort, you of course know I am always there to help—or John can, from Cambridge, because he will now also be in charge

of his own finances for his last two years at Downing. As
you know, I am going to see him tomorrow. But he's
studying economics at a top university, dammit, so he should
not need much coaching—ha, ha, ha! He may even teach his
old dad a few tricks! I never got an economics degree."

Far expanded his thinking behind all this. He explained that after the
war had wiped out the family savings and assets twice over, with the
Japanese destruction of Malaya and the Nazi occupation of Denmark, he
and *Mor* had to start again financially, virtually from scratch. Fortunately he
had his good job, to which he of course returned. Before looking after their
own retirement, they had made John's and my education their first priority,
and after a few years now felt that the necessary resources were in place.
Our education was financed. They could therefore focus on their own
future needs. John was nearly 20 and already at Cambridge with only a
couple of years to go. At 14, the plan said, I had four more years to go at
Gresham's, and then university years to follow, always assuming I would
make it that far and did not flunk.

"So, Flemming, *Mor* and I can now start looking after our
old age, our retirement needs. You and John will take
charge of yourselves and your expenses." said *Far*. "However, *Mor* and I will invite you out to see us for nice family
holidays with us, whenever we can if neither of us are in
Europe—that way we can be sure to see you for your
holidays at least once a year. But listen, my boy, you and
John have to understand there are some conditions we have
defined for the two of you. There are strings attached to
this arrangement!" he chuckled. "That will come as no
surprise, I'm sure! Here they are, so you know what the
rules are, depending on how things turn out. I mean how
you do at school and, hopefully, at university later. You

have to earn your way, which includes doing well at Gresham's, getting into university, and then graduating with a decent degree. And I mean an institution of repute, and a degree that will qualify you for making a decent living! You see, Flemming, there are always consequences to whatever you do, whatever you choose. If you cannot live up to the plans and provisions made for you, the rules call for change in our understanding, revision of the conditions I have laid out for you. I'll explain."

Before he proceeded, *Far* patted me on the back of my hand, which was resting on the pile of gilts. He looked up at me, smiling through the tears suddenly welling in his eyes. He then stood up to give me a huge bear hug in total silence.

When he finally released me he got back to business, explaining that if either John or I were to flunk, fail in whatever way, or simply cop out on our studies, the funds remaining in our hands were to be split three ways: a third each to the sibling and the parents, leaving a third in our own accounts. On the other hand, if things went according to the plan for each of us, all the way through university graduation, "At some institution of repute," as he put it, my brother and I were to split our remaining funds evenly between us. *Far* had carefully estimated the costs ahead of the two of us respectively, allowing for 2% inflation per annum, for eight years ahead in my case.

> "Once more, Flemming, you're now in charge. I've told you that *Mor* and I will always be there to help, but don't expect that help to be financial. As far as money is concerned, this is it."

It was a painstaking and loving business model. I learned over the following decades that *Far* had given a lot of thought to his role as a father under the extraordinary circumstances of a war-torn world, which upset the best laid plans of conscientious parents around the world. As a priority, he not only wanted to secure our education financially, but he devised this arrangement in order to prepare his sons for a world of personal responsibility and economic realities. He did this by facilitating access to the best education we could possibly absorb, by buying life insurance policies inexpensively for us when we were but toddlers, and much later by sending us the odd check in support of grandchildren's school expenses whenever he and *Mor* felt they could afford to do so. *Far* had realized the war years and then his job had separated him from us and prevented him from being a father in the home.

Within a few months of this episode, the course of the family's post-war journey went through yet another dramatic change. After his decades of leadership in Malaya and his global exploration seeking geographic diversification for United Plantations, PB was asked to launch his own recommended venture in Swaziland, which came to be known as UPSA—United Plantations South Africa, based in Pretoria.

His accounts of journeys up and down the length of the vast African continent were fascinating. Leaving Europe, he departed from Southampton on a *BOAC* flying boat, which took five days to deliver him and about fifty other passengers to Johannesburg after luxurious overnight stays in Malta or Alexandria, Khartoum and Lake Victoria before landing on the Vaal Dam to reach the Golden City. They flew from nine o'clock in the morning until late afternoon or early evening, spending nights in splendid waterfront hotels after an evening of serious cocktails and a gourmet dinner. *Far* related that these very social journeys often spawned long-term friendships with fellow passengers, and just occasionally short-term romances.

Three years later John, with a degree in economics and law under his belt, sent me 124 pounds sterling from Cambridge, and then took off for his first job in Hong Kong. That was half of the 248 pounds he had remaining, left from his fund delivered by *Far* some two years earlier. Eight years on, I had 28 pounds left at graduation and dutifully sent John his check for 14. *Far's* plan worked very well and his estimates of average inflation were proven sound. His two boys got the benefit of the best education we could possibly put to work, the best we could handle. *Mor*, ever anxious that we should never unnecessarily suffer hardship, would occasionally be extra generous with birthday and Christmas presents, different luxuries we would never dream of buying ourselves. For my part, I enjoyed two fabulous vacations for the account of my parents in South Africa and Swaziland during my schoolboy and undergraduate years. They were "holiday trips on the house," as *Far* designated them He had made sure that my mentor, Eric Kelly, knew exactly what was going on. EGK was astounded, but quietly admired the unusual scheme. He never once enquired as to how my stewardship of the funds was going. He probably felt that was outside his role *in loco parentis,* and that the real parents had that under control.

EGK had at least as much influence over my emerging personal values and priorities as did my parents or big brother John. Later, as an adult, I had mentors and friends who influenced me enormously, but none as much as Eric Kelly. We grew close in a very non-intimate way, not quite at arm's length. I never at any stage called him by his Christian name. It was always Mr. Kelly or Sir, and then EGK after I left school. He was a stocky Australian with strong craggy features, smooth white hair consistently trimmed and combed straight across his head from a parting way out on one side. He had deep-set blue eyes under heavy silver brows, which almost bridged a long straight Greek nose. He exuded a benign, dignified calm. He was never in a hurry. An avid gardener, he worked hard physically all year round. EGK was softly spoken and deliberate in his language, always preferring the persuasive subjunctive over the imperative. Outside the classroom and away from Chapel, he was very rarely parted from his pipe. He came across as pensive in an unworried, relaxed way—yet always alertly observant. He had a quiet, dry sense of humor, which he used with great effect to make his point in the classroom or as a personal counselor.

He read economics at University College, Oxford, and upon graduation married Doris, a refined slip of a Welsh girl, whom he met on vacation, hiking the mountains of central Wales. Enormously well read, he was a liberal man in many senses of that horribly overused and misused word. Liberalism in the British sense stands for belief in the essential goodness of man, the autonomy of the individual as he takes responsibility for himself, and for the protection of political and civil liberties, including property rights and equality before the law—all within the limits of only essential government intervention. From EGK I learned that the mark of a truly liberal man is his willingness to listen with genuine will to understand, showing respect for another man's point of view. How many "liberals" in the American (political) sense do you know to be good listeners? EGK told me he never came across a true liberal who raised his voice when making an argument!

In the American sense of the word, he was on the liberal side of the political center; no socialist by a far cry, he had a very strong social conscience and personal sensitivity to the plight of the underprivileged of any given community. He clearly believed society should provide a sustainable safety net financed by the taxpayer to avert the worst of injustices caused by imperfections in our systems of education, government, commerce and industry. He balanced this with a loathing of self-pity, despising dependence on government handouts, or addiction to charity from any source. EGK had an equally strong commitment to free market capitalism and its unfettered movement of labor and capital. He advocated international trade which, he insisted, was the planet's engine for growth and economic development needed to fuel social progress. He defined free movement of manpower and skills as the international *division of labor*, letting competition direct the distribution of labor and indeed capital to where it could be optimally put to work. The creation of incremental wealth was vital, he would explain, to generate the enduring surplus required to finance the elevation of impoverished communities to freedom—meaning access to education, employment, and relative prosperity. The practice of confiscatory wealth redistribution, in any of its myriad forms, was but an obstacle in the way of long term social progress. EGK would have got on well with Walter Bagehot, 19th century editor of the *The Economist,* who described himself as a "conservative liberal" and "politically between sizes."

EGK was the first to draw my attention to Abraham Lincoln's much cited position on the subject of the redistribution of wealth:

"You cannot help the poor by destroying the rich.

You cannot strengthen the weak by weakening the strong.

You cannot bring about prosperity by discouraging thrift.

You cannot lift the wage earner by pulling the wage payer down.

You cannot further the brotherhood of man by inciting class hatred.

You cannot build character and courage by taking away people's initiative and independence.

You cannot help people permanently by doing for them, what they could and should be doing for themselves."

We talked about these things a lot, both in his study by the fire while Doris knitted quietly in her armchair, while strolling on the Old School House playing fields and indeed in the classroom, where he taught history and economics at the university entrance level. He suggested that only flawed, politically perverted economics make assumptions that all humans are equally endowed or identical in their capacities, but he truly espoused the quest for equal opportunity for all mankind, especially equal access to education and training, security and freedom of choice. Equality before the law was obviously a *sine qua non.* The paramount goal was to provide access to the tools that allow people to become self-sufficient and contributing citizens. He was also quick to demonstrate that collectivist calls for "freedom" could never promote enduring social or economic progress without respect for property rights and religious beliefs of the individual.

EGK's principles and ideas became lifelong reference points. Half a century later I was to see many of these principles at work to good effect in New York's inner city, where the practices and programs of a very effective social services agency—the Jacob Riis Neighborhood Settlement— provided an escape route from poverty and destitution in the public housing projects. Riis Settlement was also a wonderful example of an effective partnership between the private sector and multiple layers of government. Eric Kelly's ideas struck a fine balance between fiscal conservatism, socially liberal concepts and promotion of democratic free market capitalism.

The global setting for life at Gresham's in the early 1950s was still one of recovery after World War II. Britain's Conservatives, led by Churchill, returned to govern after defeating Clement Attlee's campaign for a mandate to complete the Labour Party's 1945 socialist manifesto. Food supplies were slowly being replenished, allowing the termination of sugar and tea rationing by 1952. America's $13.3 billion (about $120 billion in today's money) aid program in support of Europe's rebuilding expired. In America the National Security Agency was born, the Korean war was still raging and Churchill announced that Britain had an atom bomb, which was later detonated on a remote Australian island. The US entered its formal Peace Treaty with Japan just after Eisenhower beat Adlai Stevenson in the presidential race. Marshall Josip Tito of Yugoslavia was the first reigning communist leader to visit England and the world's first commercial jetliner, the elegant De Havilland *Comet* made its maiden flight from London to Johannesburg. Science in the laboratories of Cambridge revealed Crick's and Watson's double helix structure of DNA. Danish Christine Joergensen became the world's first transsexual woman after an operation. King George VI died and Queen Elizabeth II married Prince Philip. Literature and show biz was also breaking new ground as Winston Churchill won the Nobel Prize for his historical and biographical writing, Agatha Christie's "Mousetrap" started its 60-year run, Ian Fleming's first James Bond novel was published and BBC television launched its "Panorama" series. In the

United States, NBC's "Today Show" had its debut, and still runs today. Doris Day and Dinah Shore, Ray Charles and Fats Domino were the royalty of pop music, while Miles Davis and Oscar Peterson were rulers in jazz. Benjamin Britten's music was establishing his position as a major classical composer. Queen Elizabeth's coronation celebrations in the streets and pubs of Holt were my only direct experience of these happenings, but education at Gresham's rarely allowed current events of import to go unnoticed or without commentary.

My schoolboy career was in some respects a success, although far from impressive academically. It took really hard work in the classroom and in my own little study at the Old School House to get competitive results. Academic performance was very directly related to diligence applied. Nothing came that easily to me, except perhaps geography, English and French. The system narrowed the field of study to three or four subjects during the last couple of years while preparing for university application. Those two years were marked by a demanding protocol of unsupervised work, almost half of the available school hours. Residential house rules were set aside to creep out of the dorm room at night, to work at the books or write papers in my study downstairs, against a soft background of classical music from my collection of 45 RPM records. The public school system's practice of early specialization and independent study prepares its pupils well for university.

My mathematics were an absolute calamity, thanks in part to two terrible teachers; but there must also have been a black hole in my own native talents. The worse of the two, an unctuous man, had a bald pate, poppy lime-green eyes burning through circular metal-rimmed glasses, shiny purple cheeks, and an explosive temper. He showed zero tolerance for my slowness, or my muddled struggle to comprehend basic algebra—I never got to calculus. Arithmetic was a lesser disaster. Geometry's visual aspects helped me a little, but the algebra part was catastrophic. My ineptitude irritated the teacher to a point where his cheeks took on a deeper magenta hue as he publicly chastised me, driving me to trembling panic.

The man destroyed whatever latent capacities I might originally have had. He rendered me severely challenged for decades, even in my early exposure to business accounting and finance. It took the first years of my working career to recover partially from this huge handicap. The man's surname was Colombé; the *accent aigu* over the "e" at the end was said to indicate derivation from a French word pertaining to pigeon shit. I readily embraced the theory. Paul Colombé was, in my mind, indeed a pious shit, with a genealogy involving something far worse than some poor pigeon's alimentary canal. I was to cross swords with him again later in my student years.

Academic performance in other areas was about average, except for English and economics, in which I outperformed marginally. The sciences were downright weaknesses, thanks to my math handicap. At sixteen, I approached the crucial examinations known as GCE, "General Certificate of Education at Ordinary Level," also known as "O Levels," which would be the measure of how far, and where, I could go in higher education. Olivier, in his "Headmaster's Comments" (part of the regular end-of-term report card) sounded a dark warning. Venomously, three months ahead of the crucial exams, he wrote that my "success in the GCE is doubtful." His message was that I did not have much chance of gaining admission to Cambridge or Oxford. The headmaster's warning may unintentionally have been salutary. He really got my gander up, and I trembled at the prospect of not making it to "an institution of repute," as *Far* had put it when explaining the rules he had established for our financial set up. Olivier played some part, no doubt, in putting my nose to the grindstone in no uncertain way. I ended up scoring the second best GCE performance recorded among the 100 boys in my year. I even passed "Elementary Mathematics," without which Cambridge and Oxford would have been out of reach. The other three subjects absolutely mandated by these two universities were English Language, Latin and one of the natural sciences—in my case biology.

That effort laid the foundation for admission to Cambridge a couple of years later. Thwarting Olivier provided deep satisfaction as a mutual loathing was developing between us. Success at the "O Level" exams earned a gentle pat on the back from EGK and a conspiratorial chuckle over my ill-disguised glee at sticking it to Olivier. Eric Kelly as house master had the responsibility of reviewing my progress every term and giving my parents a written commentary in another section of my report card. He never commented on the headmaster's early prediction of my academic demise. He limited his comments to my role in the Old School House community. Olivier's comment in the following term's report damned me with faint praise. He almost congratulated me on "a surprisingly good performance."

"You little bastard," I thought aloud, "surprising to whom? Fuck you!"

~~~~

With these important exams behind me, my parents invited me for the first time to visit them in South Africa for the long summer vacation "on the house." PB had by this time focused the activities of UPSA on developing citrus fruit groves in Swaziland, where 3,000 acres of raw Swazi bush was now being converted to production of oranges, grapefruit, limes and lemons on gravity-irrigated land. UPSA had aborted an early entry into the softwood plantation industry, fortunately selling its holdings to Barclay's Bank and Anglo American Corporation for significant gain.

Far and *Mor* had a very modest apartment in Pretoria, overlooking a park with a long view through eucalyptus trees, palms, and a variety of Proteas to Sir Herbert Baker's imposing neoclassical Union Buildings, the executive seat of the South African government, set high on a *koppie* overlooking the city. They split their time between Pretoria, with its government departments and easy access to the financial hub of Johannesburg, and UPSA's Ngonini Estate in the northernmost corner of Swaziland.

Armed with the Scandinavian Airlines System ticket bought for me, I flew to Copenhagen for a night before the long journey to the other end of Africa, which would start early in the morning. The flagship of the airline in 1953 was one of SAS's brand new Douglas DC-6 Skymasters, with its impressive four propeller engines and long range. Before boarding, passport control was conducted by a uniformed official, who moved from one passenger to the next in a beautiful lounge furnished with Kaare Klint and Hans Wegner chairs, sofas and coffee tables. Open sandwiches were offered along with the appropriate Danish beverages, courtesy of *Carlsberg* and *Aalborg Spritfabrikker.* On board, the stewardesses wore sexy duck-egg blue uniforms with accessories in rich burgundy, very high heels and shiny nylons, all of which was riveting at age seventeen. There were no male flight attendants. Only the purser, in white shirt and navy tie, navy pants and burgundy jacket was male. The flight plan to Johannesburg involved stops in Rome, Khartoum, Kampala on the way to Johannesburg's Palmietfontein airport. It was scheduled to take 26 hours—a luxurious treat, a pampering adventure, bewitching service, fine food and drink, all enjoyed in great comfort and tons of leg room. International long distance SAS flights were all single class in those bygone dreamy days of air travel. After less than a couple of hours' flight in sunshine and smooth summer air, the DC-6, named *Thorbjorn Viking,* approached the Swiss Alps. The summer view from the low cruising altitude of the day was taken straight from a fairy tale. A panorama of sharp gray alpine peaks topped off pristine white, and between them the softly cozy valleys were deep blue or verdant green, depending on whether brilliant sunlight reached their grassy meadows and woods, or they were buried in deep alpine shadow. Then literally, out of the blue, the plane lurched precipitously to one side, dropped about a thousand feet like a ton of lead, and in a split second hit a new mass of dense air, as if it had struck a giant concrete slab. The drop sent some passengers (who were not strapped in) and most of the cabin crew crashing into the ceiling of the fuselage; the steep angle tipped over a metal fixture in the galley releasing a river of red wine and bordelaise sauce down the aisle between seats. Crashing crockery and cutlery. Screams of terror. Moans of pain. Just as quickly, the plane then reverted to normal flight mode as if absolutely nothing had happened, while the uninjured stewardesses picked themselves up, brushed off their uniforms, straightened their caps, and proceeded to help three or four passengers and a couple of their colleagues who had been hurt quite badly. A broken collar bone, a fractured arm, a concussion, various bleeding cuts, a lot of bad bruises and a lot of jolted nerves. The mess on the floor of the aisle was mopped up and calm restored as the DC-6 rumbled steadfastly on its way toward Rome, passengers and crew alike regrouping and thanking their lucky stars that they had just dodged some kind of bullet.

Upon touching down at Rome's old, pre-1960 Ciampino airport, it was announced that courtesy of SAS, we would have a day of sightseeing and the best of Rome's culinary offerings while the *Thorbjorn Viking* was cleaned up and checked out from stem to stern. Switzerland's turbulent alpine air had delivered a surprise opportunity to experience the glories of Rome, from historical monuments and splendors of architecture to its marvelous Italian cuisine. SAS ensured that there were no holds barred as we ingested Rome in scorching Italian sunshine. Just before midnight the DC-6's skipper plunged the throttles forward to propel its contented passengers down Ciampino's single runway for a delayed take off, the implications of which had been signaled to each of the three ports of call ahead. I imagined the frustration of an excited, impatient *Mor* getting the news from Jo'burg's SAS office.

The long flight south down the length of Africa was spiced with eye-opening vistas from under three thousand feet as the Skymaster approached landings on its gentle glide path or climbed on her slow ascent angle after takeoff. The Sudanese desert confluence of the Blue and White Nile rivers at Khartoum, the two miraculous lifelines of cruelly parched Sudan, Lake Victoria's vast sheet of water interrupted only by the scattered Sese Islands as we climbed out of Kampala, the huge expanse of the Vaal

Dam as we descended over mountainous yellow mine dumps into Jo'burg's Palmietfontein airport at journey's end.

My first series of adventures and exploration in South Africa had been launched. I was warmly greeted by my parents and welcomed by smiling South Africans of every ilk, who were always hospitable and friendly, irrespective of race, culture, or creed. Much of the exploration was to be by car, traveling enormous distances by European standards.

PB's company car was a pearlescent green 1949 Buick with a great toothy chrome grill, which had been his trusty friend for several years and over many thousands of miles as he had explored the southern subcontinent of Africa. Her name, quite appropriately, was *Passe Partout.*

Within a day or so the family was headed east from Pretoria across the *highveld,* Transvaal's dry grassy plateau, on the main road leading to Lorenco Marques in Mozambique over grassy undulating hills and small towns, where Winston Churchill had chalked up his Boer War adventures. The road ran dead straight and dead east before descending through an escarpment at Machadodorp into the *lowveld* bush region and Nelspruit, near the southern boundary of the great Kruger National Park. Ngonini Estate was our destination, so the route took us close to the Mozambique border before turning south at Komatipoort onto a rutted dirt road toward the Swazi border gate. No immigration control at this gate, just a sleepy old Swazi who sprang to attention, saluting us with a toothless grin as he was enveloped in *Passe Partout's* billowing dust. Ngonini was set in the serene Lomati river valley flanked by bare, bulging domelike hills, on which small clusters of stunted bushes, a few cattle, and the odd Swazi *kraal,* meaning a native cattle pen or brushwood enclosure surrounding a community of primitive round mud huts. Dotted around the *kraals* were scratched patches of rusty soil where *mealies* or corn struggled to survive. The only significant vegetation grew in the river valley along the banks of the Lomati, where there was sufficient water to sustain larger eucalyptus, casuarina, and marula trees. Several hundred acres of newly planted citrus groves had been carved out of this peacefully raw terrain, where absolutely nothing had happened for hundreds of years, other than an occasional tribal skirmish. The plantation had brought a veneer of civilization, economic life and opportunity to almost one-thousand Swazis. There was now a village, a school, a soccer pitch, clinic, residential compound and a three-mile canal to facilitate gravity irrigation. There were packing and sorting houses, well-kept roads and a simple general store. The aggregation of people had even drawn competing missionaries in pursuit of Swazi souls and conversion opportunities.

The staff's living quarters, including the managing director's, consisted of a string of modest but well built houses arranged in a crescent along a hilly ridge overlooking the Lomati valley below, with the majestic hills as a backdrop. Each house had a lush, well-watered garden where bougainvillea, golden laburnum, crane lilies, and even proteas thrived around lawns of tough Kikuyu grass. R&R facilities including a pool and tennis court were clustered around a white-washed, thatched *rondavel*-type clubhouse. A *rondavel* is a residential building based on native African construction techniques. It as normally oval or round, with walls of whitewashed mud or bricks, treated hardwood windows and doors, all capped by a thick thatched reed roof. The floors are normally smooth, red-stained cement or slate slabs.

In between the buildings and beyond the citrus plantings off the dirt road, the bush was left to itself, replete with scorpions, lizards, and the odd black mamba, all of which were to be avoided. Guinea fowl, blue cranes and korhaans were conspicuous members of the busy *low-veld* bird life. Various antelope, but mainly impala, duiker, klipspringer and the odd springbok populated the bush and browsed freely when not chased by some predator.

Swaziland's agricultural resources were sparingly developed and there was very little industry beyond some downstream businesses driven by crops of sugar, rice, pineapple, citrus, and softwood timber. The country's scattered population of less than 300,000 was rural, basically illiterate and untrained, but seemed happy to survive on subsistence farming around primitive villages in the bush. The way of life was starkly tribal, characterized by King Sobhuza's absolute sway in all matters outside the jurisprudence of the British colonial government. UPSA's Ngonini development was welcomed and applauded throughout this tiny nation, as were their later plantations at Big Bend and Mkewani, which were closer to the capital, Mbabane, and the commercial town of Bremersdorp. While labor was plentiful, it required major investment in education and training—and a good measure of patience. Swazis do not live by any timeclock. They know tomorrow is another day.

The Swaziland vacation included three-hour drives over the gorgeous rolling hills for visits to Mbabane, the rustic capital where colonial administrators and King Sobhuza II lived in the royal *kraal* surrounded by a dozen or more wives. Visits to the village of Pigg's Peak, a one-horse town in the hills above the Lomati valley were more frequent as its general store was better stocked than the one at Ngonini. PB also had a close relationship with the CEO of a vast softwood plantation enterprise, Peak Timbers, based there. On a shopping visit, I discovered that the Afrikaans owner of the local gas station, cum auto and body shop, doubled as the district's issuing authority for driver's licenses. I saw an opportunity there. Aged just 17, with *Far* irresponsibly looking the other way and *Mor* blissfully unaware, I added eight months in order to cheat my way to a driving test, which the gas station owner was pleased to arrange. I was shown to an old bare-bones jeep, exactly like the vehicles I had learned to drive in Malaya four years earlier.

> "Yes, man, no! It's not a big deal, eh? Take that jeep over ther', drahve her up to the top off the hill, rraaht bah the stor', turn arround and kom raaht beck hier agen. Then beck her into the garrage so Ah ken see you drahve in rreverse, man … and Ah'll hev your lahcense rreddy, rraaht-awai-in-a-jiffy. No big deal, boetie! It'll be faif pounts … thet's all!"

With that Swazi license, I talked my way into an international driving permit at the Automobile Association's offices in Pretoria, and with the internationally recognized license, I procured a Danish driver's permit in Copenhagen eight months before I reached the Danish minimum age. I later happily drove around Denmark as a seventeen-year-old, which did impress the girls.

From Swaziland, the family took a long weekend in Lorenco Marques, capital of Portuguese Mozambique, at the elegant Polana Hotel on the Indian Ocean shoreline. The imposing building's three wings embraced gracefully arched palms and an enormous terrace in the middle of which there was a large luminescent blue circular pool. The property was set at the very edge of a high cliff, which dropped straight to the sea. The Polana was a corner carved out of the Amalfi coastline and transposed to the sub-tropical southeast African coast, its imposing white-washed structure capped by heavy terracotta tiles, tall arched windows, and hundreds of cantilevered wrought iron balconies overlooking the sparkling ocean. The hotel oozed opulence, yet was barely a mile away from abject African poverty.

Lorenco Marques' handsome central boulevard, lined with ornate jacarandas, belied the squalor lurking but one block away, on either side of this stylish thoroughfare. On the surface, everything reflected the best of Portuguese colonial tradition, its façade so carefully preserved by the regime of fascist dictator Oliveira Salazar. Seafood perfectly fresh out of the Indian Ocean; chilled Vino Verde, which brought a prickle to the tongue; curried prawns peri-peri with ice-cold Laurentina lager; police in pompous uniforms with pretentious gold epaulettes and medals galore; siestas deep into the afternoon; romantic late night dining and evening strolls along the well-lit, flower-scented boulevard. Behind this fragile frontispiece, however, Portugal's heavy-handed dictatorship had done little to improve the lot of the urban population or, for that matter, the tribal Shangaans to the west or Shonas further north. These indigenous tribes spanned the border, spilling into South Africa and Southern Rhodesia, providing easy passage for the embryonic revolutionary movements of the sub-continent. In hindsight, the Lorenco Marques scenario illustrated why Portugal, despite being a founding member of NATO struggled so long to finally join the United Nations in 1955.

Before returning to Pretoria, a long and spectacular detour was taken through the Kruger National Park, driving 220 miles from bottom to its very top through much of its 4-million acres. This gigantic preserve is a strip of *low-veld* bush, on average less than 30 miles east to west, with the eastern edge running along the Mozambique line from the Komati River valley all the way up to the Limpopo on the Rhodesian border. The chosen entry point was the Malelane gate east of Nelspruit, where many of the tourists from Johannesburg would start their adventure. Days were spent looking for game, which was only made more exciting by the fact that the count for the day depended to a degree on luck, given the vastness of the preserve. July and August are the best months for game spotting, as the bush foliage is at its thinnest and least opaque after bone dry months of winter. Over five days of driving very slowly in search of game, passing through camps with names like Crocodile Bridge, Punda Maria, Skukuza, Mopane and Olifants, we reached the northern edge of the park. The depleted Limpopo River in the middle of the southern hemisphere's winter is far from being Rudyard Kipling's "great, green, greasy" flow; but all manner of game, from elephant to hippo and warthog, from lion to kudoo antelope and zebra, gather to drink from residual pools in the muddy river bed—particularly as the sun rises or just before sundown. The camps offered basic but spotless accommodations, usually in the form of white-washed, thatched *rondavels* with polished *slasto*—a kind of brown slate—or red polished cement floors. Meals were simple but good, lubricated by Riesling wines, beer and other drinks brought in with the luggage in *Passe Partout's* ample trunk. Crystal clear starlit nights were disturbed only by chilling rumbles and growls of a predator celebrating a nearby kill, or a hyena's impatient protest as he waited for access to a big cat's vacated kill. The luxurious private game resorts and fancy lodges of the 21st century do not win on every count when compared with the simpler, less pampered safari experience of the Kruger Park in the 1950s. "Luck of the game" took on literal meaning in terms of what animals you saw. It was left very much to nature's roll of the dice in the huge preserve, where the explorer would set his own route, driving his own car, and making his own choices. You somehow felt closer to the real African adventure, in which patience and good fortune played their full role. The Kruger Park offered no private game rangers operating in constricted areas where wildlife is placed for impatient westerners; no converted Hummers or plush Land Rovers complete with cocktail bar at sunset to satisfy busy Americans "doing Africa" in seven days.

The world, in 1953, knew Johannesburg as the golden city at the center of South Africa's fantastic gold-mining industry, a busy modern metropolis with American style high-rise offices and apartments, urban grid system, broad one-way streets, and a sophisticated financial hub built around the stock market, which drew investors from around the globe. Super-rich, mining magnates and mineral moguls thrived there, living in the best of the luxurious leafy suburbs a little north of downtown Jo'burg. However, multiple visits to Johannesburg exposed more of the dark underbelly of white South Africa's progression toward legislated apartheid, the exploitation of Blacks as well as the police state practices. The Nationalist Party, which had been in power since 1948, was feeling its oats. Vast Soweto's gaunt bareness, stark misery and crime were not yet obvious to someone visiting the central city or the attractively landscaped suburbs, but it was easily reached and exposed if you were curious enough. The black Alexandria shantytown and mixed-race Sophiatown were close to the city's center, more accessible, a little less gruesome in their presentation of deprivation and poverty-stricken despondence. The cultural and ethnic mix in Sophiatown was in fact intriguing as it was home to many "alternative" artists, musicians, writers and even politicians until apartheid's forced removals or resettlements wreaked havoc on the population in the early 60s.

Soweto, which was to become known worldwide, derives its name from the township's location to the southwest of Johannesburg proper. The original housing project was a product of the early Native Urban Areas Act written into law under the regime of General Jan Smuts's United Party and was then expanded to accommodate mandatory mass resettlement initiatives. The legislation determined where people could live depending on race. Soweto was a vast and depressing agglomeration of displaced families and migrants from rural areas. Infinite rows of small, squalid brick and concrete boxes built into a grid system of dusty dirt streets divested of vegetation, serving as home to hundreds of thousands of people living without power or indoor water supply. The population was a crucial source of black labor for Johannesburg's industry and commerce, so the government did invest in public transport for its needed commuters, who were otherwise deprived of services, access to adequate supplies and adequate retail outlets. Poverty, lack of education and violent crime combined to make life dangerous for residents and visitors alike. However, just as the government wanted, this dark underbelly of society and life on the Reef was largely out of white society's sight, and thus out of mind.

This first South African vacation was edifying to an extent. Given all the excitement of seeing an African country for the first time, immersed with my parents in the western ways of white man's life in the Union of South Africa, I did not fully appreciate the sinister political and social developments being introduced by the nationalist government. The overt actions and protests of communist and revolutionary activists and their organizations had yet to surface. The unfettered liberal press reported accurately on legislative and political moves, but there were, at the time, few dramatic strikes, riots, sabotage incidents or threats to provoke outrage in the media—English or Afrikaans. On the surface, rural African life was simple and very basic, but seemed neither tragic nor burdened by dramatic hardship as one caught fleeting glimpses of brilliant white smiles on ebony faces, pink palms waving happily, welcoming greetings of "*Yeboh, nkosi!*" (hello boss) from Shangaans, Xhosas, Swazis and Zulus by the roadside, or

"*Dumela, baas!*" from young Tswana and Suto boys herding their two or three cattle on the dusty high-veld grasslands. Somehow, the typical African's acceptance of the circumstances, his patience and cheerful nature, all delayed my recognition of the evil gravity of creeping apartheid at work. On the other hand, the everyday confinement of urban blacks to the most menial and dangerous mining jobs, to subservient and impoverished lives, did make a lasting impression and gave pause for thought. Soweto and the other township scenes left indelible impressions and concerns.

The SAS flight home to Copenhagen was again an experience of luxury, this time without turbulent mishaps to interrupt the thrill of being the object of flattering attention from smiling blonde stewardesses in their tight skirts and nicely fitting burgundy blouses.

Back at school, things went better for me socially and in athletic pursuits than they did in math and science classes. Kelly appointed me to prefect responsibilities and then eventually to *House Captain,* which automatically made me a school prefect with authority throughout the schoolboy population. In my final year, I became head boy—*School Captain* in Gresham's lingo. Olivier was not at all enthusiastic about this, but he was boxed into that appointment by my seniority as a very young house captain, so there was nothing the headmaster could do. There was no love lost between us.

The English system of prefects, warts and all, was a good one for a number of reasons. It was a true merit system because the elevation to prefect rank was unsustainable if the promoted boy could not command the respect of his peer group. Neither exceptional prowess in athletics or the arts, nor outstanding academic performance, could alone qualify a boy to be appointed prefect. Citizenship within the community was more important, as were signs of leadership capacity. The system gave the selected boys a sense of elevated responsibility. It also taught teenagers to accept authority when fairly exercised, and some of them to exercise authority fairly if selected to wield it. Leaders were fostered and leadership skills were honed. The system was also extremely efficient in terms of staff productivity, since a major part of the necessary supervision of boarding pupils outside the classroom was done by prefects, not by paid schoolmasters. The prefects basically supervised the non-academic lives of students in terms of community discipline and organized recreation in the houses. They also had ceremonial duties at house and school levels, such as reading the lesson in chapel or making community announcements. I personally struggled with terrible nerves when reading aloud in public, stumbling and making utter nonsense of the simplest New Testament prose. Reading the lesson at *Matins* in Chapel required hours of rehearsal before facing 450 boys, masters, and parents. The experience always left my shirt sodden with perspiration. This phobia of speaking or reading in public persisted and took years to overcome.

A single-breasted navy blazer with three gold buttons, grey flannel slacks, white cotton shirt and navy school tie embellished with silver grasshoppers constituted the uniform. The blazer's breast pocket was adorned with the arms of the Worshipful Company of Fishmongers, a complex shield involving heraldic keys, fish, and grasshoppers—hence the silver critters on the tie. The uniform ruled out sartorial narcissism and teenage attention seeking.

Highlights of my life were the team sports, whether representing Gresham's in external competition against other schools, or in the sharp intramural rivalries between the residential houses. Rugby became my favorite game, partly because of a partnership and close friendship with Andy Mulligan. A truly exceptional talent, Andy eventually went all the way to international rugby stardom, playing *scrum half* for Cambridge, Ireland, and the combined British Isles' "Lions" on tours of the Antipodes. Andy made me look ten times better in my position at *fly half* than I really was at this game. The western hemisphere, with the exception of Argentina, knows relatively little of rugby, but it is a huge sport in Europe, South Africa, Australasia, Japan and the Pacific Islands, surpassed only by soccer on a global basis. It is little short of a religion in South Africa and New Zealand. In the world of Rugby, despite his below-average stature, Andy and his Irish compatriot, Tony O'Reilly, became celebrities, almost deities, in Ireland. At school, Andy Mulligan captained the First XV, and elevated Gresham's rugby to a much higher level than previously achieved. Meanwhile, he and I had become soul mates and very close friends.

Field hockey was another strong program at Gresham's, taking the school team to the annual Oxford Hockey Festival, where it was regularly among the top three in the nation. All sports played an important part in my school life. As years passed, the interest in athletic pursuits lived on; while capacities dwindled with age, interest in sports never faded. Exposure to new cultures and national traditions introduced new sports, but the role played by rugby was never matched. Fond recollections of past participation and performance no doubt flattered actual accomplishments. My favorite T-shirt as a senior citizen is one which appropriately declares that *"The older we get, the better we were!"*

Meanwhile, there were rumblings and problems emerging in aspects of the school's extra-curricular programs along with disagreements within the faculty. Governance problems were barely beneath the surface. In the final year at Gresham's, a low-key rebellion came to the boil and a very small group of schoolboy leaders took unusual steps. It was a term after the headmaster had reluctantly appointed me *School Captain*. My two closest friends at the time, Andrew Mulligan and Napier Russell, were both captains of their respective houses and thus also school prefects. Andy was in Olivier's house, Howson's, where the headmaster obsessively attempted to micromanage every aspect of his life and tried to dig into areas of his personal life, where he had no business. Olivier's obsession with Andy manifested itself in perverse ways. At night, he would occasionally delve into Andy's life away from school by sneaking into his study to steal access to his diaries or journals. In these he read of teenage crushes and adventures with girls during vacations. This prompted Olivier to admonish him as a "vain poseur." The headmaster desperately wanted Andy to excel at everything; on the other hand, he could not stand the fact that Andy had good relationships with everybody else in the school, be it schoolboy friendships or a naturally warm relationship with other masters. In fact, Andy did excel in many aspects of school life, and he was popular with his peer group and staff alike. Beyond a couple of occasions when Olivier found reason to cane him, this perverse behavior never manifested itself in any physical way; it was all about Olivier's obsessive quest for control over Andy's life. It drove the boy to despair as his nature was otherwise light, bright, and keen to enjoy life's every offering. He would seek opportunities to spend free time with me at the Old School House, a mile away from Howson's, where we could freely talk things through and he could unload his concerns. We also exchanged views and experiences regarding Olivier's meddling and damaging interference in the school's rugby, choral and Shakespeare programs, usurping the role of the uncommonly talented masters in charge of them. We eventually started to explore ways in which we could possibly cause Olivier's removal.

Andrew was a tad shorter than average height, with a light athletic build, mouse-blond hair hanging over one side of his brow, a high-bridged pug nose and deep-set, humorous blue eyes. His mouth was always poised for a chuckle or a belly laugh. He and I had an awful lot in common. As in my own case, his parents were based thousands of miles away; his were in Nigeria. His father, Hugh, was a medical doctor and high-ranking researcher working for the British Colonial Service on tsetse flies and related human sicknesses in West Africa. Andy joined me on several vacations with my extended family in Jutland and Copenhagen, sharing wonderful times including teenage parties and chasing pretty girls. Andy, an accomplished watercolor painter, spent time capturing the lovely Lake District landscapes of Jutland. At Tammestrup, we would go bird and fox shooting with my cousin Peter. My musical cousin could immediately join us in a raucous trio causing the woods to reverberate with rugby songs, renderings of "Bread of Heaven" or Cockney ditties. Andy was also a linguist who spoke not just French, but Urdu from an early childhood in India, and a bit of Ibo learned in Nigeria. He attempted Danish, but quite understandably soon gave it up:

"No point in learning this ugly bloody language, spoken by a paltry five million people in this tiny country and a dozen educated Eskimos in Greenland. It has no lilt or charm to it like Swedish or Norwegian. Danish just sounds like the last of the water gurgling as it drains out of the bath tub. Sorry, Flemming! Waste of bloody time ... no thanks, *Nej tak!* Everyone here very sensibly loves to speak English anyhow!"

By his late teens he was a brilliant mimic, raconteur, and extrovert extraordinaire, who captivated any type and size of audience. He would charm the knickers off any pretty female who crossed his path. He was an enthralling character and a treasured friend.

The close friendship with Andy introduced me to his older sister, Shelagh, and via her to an appreciation of emerging British jazz and a passing interest in Formula I racing, mostly from the distant fringe and vicarious thrills of television. Shelagh was the most stunning woman I had ever set eyes on. A classical Celtic beauty with nut-brown hair, astonishingly blue eyes rimmed by the long black lashes of an antelope, immaculate skin and finely sculpted features; she had a perfect athletic figure, and, to cap it all, the brightest and widest of ever ready smiles. Her bubbly personality and breathtaking looks opened any door through which she cared to pass, so in her mid-twenties she moved among British celebrities, particularly in the theaters of jazz and auto racing. Sterling Moss, Mike Hawthorn, and Lance Macklin were good friends, and the whole group was close to the elite of British jazz. Old Etonian trumpeter legend and cornerstone of the English jazz Humphrey Lyttleton, trombonist Chris Barber and his sometime wife, Ottillie Patterson, the renowned blues singer. Lyttleton's career exploded with his hit *Bad Penny Blues*, and he went on to record with Sidney Bechet in the United States, where Louis Armstrong referred to him as "that cat in England who swings his ass off." Collectively they brought American jazz to Britain.

Shelagh Mulligan eventually married Lance Macklin, who tragically died in a crash very soon thereafter. She later remarried Anthony Montague-Brown, who was for some years Winston Churchill's private secretary.

My other close friend, Napier Russell, was a very different character: a smooth boyish face, which rarely needed shaving, slim and tall, narrow shouldered with a languid gait. He was a wistful dreamer endowed with more native athletic talent than evident intellect or energy. Napier exuded charm and warm sensitivity, spoke softly and kindly through a small tight mouth, which would quickly break into a surprisingly full and winning smile. Napier had a quiet, dry sense of humor, which caused him to chuckle a lot but never allowed a belly laugh. His athleticism made him a very elegant cricketer and talented defensive field hockey player; but he lacked the explosive energy, drive, and speed called for in rugby. Napier also spent a vacation with me and my relations in Denmark, although his parents lived near at hand in Sussex, in the boring retirement backwater of Bexhill-on-Sea. It was during a Danish vacation with Napier that I first met and fell for Helle Groenbech, who became an important part of my romantic life through undergraduate years to follow. One of Mor's old friends from her nursing days had thrown a party for "the English schoolboys, so they could meet young people in Copenhagen." Napier and I had a lot of fun together and were good friends, but he was never quite the soul mate I found in Andrew Mulligan.

Napier's housemaster, Max Parsons at Woodlands House, was, like Eric Kelly, recruited to Gresham's by J.R. Eccles in the 1930s. Max hated Olivier with a passion and shamelessly made no attempt to hide it from the boys of his house. He was less discrete than EGK, at times verging on the subversive, given that he was a housemaster and thus a senior member of the school's faculty. Brian Johnson, another senior prefect in Woodlands who had been appointed a school prefect, had with Napier and Parsons been discussing the possibility of doing something to challenge Olivier, or preferably get rid of him. Max was set on discrediting the headmaster, but he was biding his time and never, to my knowledge, let his scheming spread beyond a few trusted alumni and the prefects in his own house. It was in our last summer term at Gresham's that Andy and I learned of these conversations from Brian and Napier and realized that our thinking and embryonic plans regarding Olivier largely overlapped. There was a shared concern that Martin John Olivier's behavior had become increasingly weird as the years went by, and that he was a threat to the values and traditions of the school, not to mention some of the boys in his care.

For fifteen years, the school's renowned Shakespeare productions had been in the hands of Hoult Taylor, head of the English department at Gresham's, a genius at teaching literature. Taylor had a nationwide reputation for this schoolboy program, which Olivier simply could not bear, so he pulled rank to inject himself and interfere. The pupils were soon confused, and the standard of productions quickly tanked. The headmaster took roughly the same tack in wrecking the school's fine choral tradition. It had been in the brilliant hands of Hubert Hales, an emerging English composer and head of music at Gresham's. The history of the music program went all the way back to the better known British composer, Walter Greatorex, (who had taught at Gresham's) and to the famous Benjamin Britten. Olivier all but usurped Hubert Hales' role too. Obviously, Taylor and Hales could but lose their magic touch as the headmaster assertively imposed himself. These outstanding performing arts at Gresham's soon withered on the vine.

Even more alarming was the headmaster's Machiavellian inquisition into the sexual explorations and experiments of dozens of pubescent and teenage boys throughout the school, commencing with boys in Howson's, his own house. Nobody knew how he got started, but he would interrogate dozens of selected boys, one-on-one, probing their friendships and relationships with others. There were stories of distressed boys being admonished by an excited Olivier for confessed relationships of which he, for one reason or another, disapproved. He would then cane them, sometimes with bared buttocks. I personally did not know, nor had I reason to believe, that the behavior of those boys amounted to anything serious, let alone homosexual practices. Nor did I care. I was not particularly bothered by the thought that pubescent boys might indulge in some sort of mutual exploration of their developing young bodies. However, Olivier clearly did have a strangely active interest. As prefects who were distantly aware of this apparently perverse interrogation, Andy, Napier, Brian, and I started to share serious concerns, swapping notes on what we were hearing—sometimes in detail related by the younger boys. Eventually, we decided to talk the whole thing through among the four of us. I told EGK about it for the first time. Kelly had himself observed the destruction of the Shakespeare and music programs, especially the agony of his close friend, Hoult Taylor. He was quite evidently appalled to learn of our story about the Olivier inquisition. However, he was, as always, deliberate and measured, saying only enough to emphasize the need for responsibility and caution in any move we might contemplate regarding the governance of the school. I accepted EGK's warnings, but took them as tacit encouragement, as he gave no direction to cease and desist, nor suggestions as to how we might proceed. Andy, of course, did not have the same luxury of sharing, as Olivier was his housemaster. Max Parsons, according to Napier and Brian, was less cautious than EGK. He actively encouraged Napier and Brian to promote a plan of action, but to his credit, left the planning to the four boys. We were convinced that the school, as a whole, as well as individual boys, were being seriously affected, so the solution had to be some sort of action causing Olivier to be removed. Never short of words or opinions, Brian Johnson, rather pompously proclaimed,

> "Olivier's behavior is showing signs of escalating dementia!
> He's going to bring the school down. He must go!"

Dementia may not have been the right diagnosis. We suspected that sexual deviance was at work somewhere in the strange mix of Olivier's machinations and obsessions, although we never put our suspicion into words uttered beyond the four of us. After swearing them to confidentiality, we talked to the two other school prefects, Tom Whittle and Richard Tilson, (there were six in total), but while they expressed no disagreement with any of our views, they refused to have any part in developing a plan of action. Their reluctance and their reasoning were probably no different from those of half the teaching staff: they did not want to be involved in a public and potentially nasty controversy. The younger school masters were all Olivier recruits and thus tended to be supportive of his tenure, whereas the most senior members of faculty were veterans of the J. R. Eccles era and were admirers of his philosophy and principles. They understood and valued what the school had been in its Halcyon days. However, while the latter group was concerned, it was not eager to act, as they were well into the second half of their careers, with jobs, pensions and their families' welfare at stake.

Olivier's idiosyncrasies were not confined to his bizarre interest in pubescent boys' personal relationships, his jealous intervention in Hoult Taylor's Shakespeare productions, or the Hubert Hales' choral program. He had a poseur's narcissistic sense of drama. In fact, he was said to have declared to one parent:

> "My cousin, Laurence Olivier, may have the looks, but I have the thespian talent, the profound vision of drama and sense of theater."

He immersed himself in the production of schoolboy plays presented in his own house, eagerly demonstrating how different parts should be played. He would micromanage events like rehearsals for the procession of 450 boys into Chapel for the *Speech Day* service typical of public schools. He relished his role in full academic regalia at the podium in the school's woodland amphitheater, moderating the institutional annual *Speech Day* review by the chairman of the governors, including a prize-giving attended by parents and local dignitaries such as the Lord Bishop of Norwich and the Lord Lieutenant of the county.

The headmaster would oversee the rehearsal from his perch on the Chapel's outside balcony overlooking the cricket field. He directed every detail as the procession approached the main chapel door, through which the boys would file to their appointed pews inside. Olivier spoke with a very heavy lisp, lubricated by excess saliva whenever he became excited. When one poor boy got a tiny bit out of line, or if Olivier perceived that a boy was not taking the rehearsal very seriously, he would, in a frenzy of emotion, thrust his arm out at a Hitleresque angle and scream at the assembly while the staff stood by, speechless.

> "Sshhtop!" he yelled. "Sshhtart again, right from the very sshh-tart. All over again, right from the sshhtart, pleash! … Thish ish totally unaccsheptable! Jonessh Minor, you musht take thish work sheriouhsly! You are being quite irreshponshible. Report to my shtudy at noon, Shimon!"

MJO knew every single boy's full name. The whole school wondered whether young Simon Jones—Jones Minor—would get caned, perhaps with his pants down. The rehearsal of the *Speech Day* procession would start anew, being repeated and choreographed to perfection at the cost of hours of class time.

At other times, the headmaster would be on the touch line—the sidelines in rugby terminology—during the school's home matches, yelling encouragement or admonition at boys from his own house playing for the Gresham's team, thus getting in the way of the poor coach's directions. Andy would be especially embarrassed and distracted by Olivier's commentary and directions addressed at him personally.

Whether Martin John Olivier was in some way driven by suppressed homosexuality will always be a question in the minds of many who observed him over the years. He was married in his mid-fifties to a middle-aged, bony caricature of a school ma'am, who taught physical education at the nearby Runton Hill School for Girls. This obviously sterile union did not prove much of anything to anybody. Poor Nancy Olivier, ever timid and expressionless, seemed devoid of human emotion in public, yet content enough to be a glorified housewife to the seventy boarders of Howson's.

At age sixteen to eighteen in the British education system, one had to focus on just three or four fields of study with a view to qualifying at "A" or advanced level of the GCE for higher education. Economics, French, and Geography were within my scope and capacity at this standard. The brightest boys would span four subjects at Scholarship or "S" level, which would help qualify them for scholarships and grants in support of university education. "S" level performance was also a huge leg up for admission to the best universities. We worked in class up to seven hours, four days a week, and half days on Wednesday and Saturday. We studied alone for as many hours as we had in the classroom. In addition, we had two to three hours of study every weekday evening in our own studies. It was during these two final years that one could enjoy academic and athletic experiences to their fullest, when recognition and rewards for accomplishment and leadership were at their peak. The learning experience became exciting, while sports introduced an esprit de corps and great fun. The camaraderie was warm and wonderful. The three long vacations between terms provided opportunities to emerge from the protective Gresham's shell and learn from life's realities, and also to experience the normal two-gender world and broader horizons. This was particularly the case for me, spending vacations with relatives in Denmark or with *Far* and *Mor* in South Africa.

In the early summer of 1954, at the very beginning of our last term at Gresham's, all four conspirators gathered again on a balmy Sunday afternoon to take a long walk around the playing fields and through the beautiful school woods. Wild azaleas and giant rhododendrons here and throughout East Anglia's woodlands were at their peak, the slanting sunlight penetrating the green canopy above to illuminate the brilliant pinks, purples and whites of the blooms. We took in and shared the gorgeous surroundings, noting how privileged and fortunate we were to be there. A mutual attachment and intimate fellowship had developed between the four of us.

We knew it was time to do something about Martin John Olivier if we were not to leave it until it was too late. The end of term and our time at Gresham's was less than ten weeks away, after which our potential impact and leverage, whatever it might be, would quickly erode. We again revisited the question of whether or not we were overreaching, taking ourselves too seriously. The alternative was to leave what we saw as a nasty, festering problem, which would clearly affect the school to which we owed so much, to the detriment of younger pupils and later generations of Gresham's boys. Who else would step in? The four of us were not driven purely by noble aims and altruism. I had grown to loathe Olivier with a passion. Andy angrily yearned for revenge after four years of MJO's attempted micromanagement and interference. Brian and Napier shared our common concern for the school's good, but were no doubt also influenced and spurred on by a vindictive Max Parsons. On the other hand, there were signs of tension and distress in several other quarters. It had become evident, particularly among the most senior boys, that the faculty was divided between Olivier's younger recruits and the senior masters, who still espoused the principles of Howson and Eccles. We surmised that the latter group were themselves divided as to how the issues should be addressed. I personally knew that the situation was freely discussed between EGK, Hoult Taylor, and one or two other members of the old guard, who were by no means in solid agreement. Napier and Brian told us that Max Parsons was now beginning to talk to everybody who would listen, including other masters, parents and Woodlands' alumni. There had been rumblings among groups of "old boys" or alumni, but again, as we saw it, there was division and no cohesive initiative to be expected from any given group. We did not know what parents generally knew or thought, but our own parents had all given us moral support from afar. Andy's father had in fact confronted the headmaster some time before, questioning him on some problem Andy had chosen to share with his dad. There was no reason, however, to think parents generally would or could be agents for change.

The four of us, at the end of several hours of debate on that sunny Norfolk afternoon, solemnly agreed we would ourselves try to be agents for change. Thinking back, these many decades later, it is not difficult see how our actions could be perceived as little more than the product of four precocious youngsters, overly impressed with themselves and out of their depth. Could one blame anybody who might ask, *What the hell did these kids know about running a school? Who did they think they were?*

But on we pushed ahead.

The consensus was that I was to seek audience with the chairman of the school's board of governors, most of whom were members of the Fishmongers in the City of London. The govenors' chairman, Weston Backhouse, was a successful city-based merchant, tea taster and trader by profession, and a prominent member of the Fishmongers' large philanthropic organization. I wrote him a "private & confidential" letter, requesting time in his office for the four of us on the day we were to leave school, at the end of June 1954. I wrote that while the request might be unusual, it came from four of the six current school prefects, who were loyal to the school. We had deliberated for months and were seriously worried about major issues concerning Gresham's leadership and direction. We had struggled for months with the question of how to deal with the situation and now felt that the best way was to discuss the situation discretely with the chairman of the governors, who could decide whether the matter should be taken further. Nothing was written about who might know of our intentions.

Backhouse was quick to write back tersely, agreeing that the request was indeed most unusual and, without further comment, he declared he would be away on business in Belfast the day we wanted to meet him. That was that.

The four of us thought Backhouse was hoping we would simply go away, so we agreed I should write again. This second letter was a little more insistent, pointing out that the four of us lived in different parts of the world and would find it difficult to reconvene after leaving school. We would, however, be pleased to find a way to meet him during the days immediately following the end of term, even if that meant postponing arrangements to rejoin our families, two of us living abroad. It was explained that we would then be scattered, with two of us going up to Cambridge in October and two going off to do national service in the military, somewhere yet unknown.

Once more, Backhouse responded promptly with via note from the Secretary of the Board of Governors on his personal writing paper, this time agreeing to receive us in his office on the date originally requested, as soon as we could get there after the school train arrived at London's Liverpool Street Station. He claimed the chairman had changed his plans for the Belfast business trip. From the enclosed directions, we could see that our rendezvous was off Throgmorton Street just a few hundred yards from the station, in the heart of the City, London's financial district. The four of us registered the weight of the situation we had created for ourselves and embarked upon a series of very deliberate planning sessions. We had some weeks to decide how we would approach the big meeting, what the division of labor should be, carefully preparing ourselves for allocated roles. We understood that there could be no turning back; it was now a question of sink or swim.

Just weeks later, when final exams and many fond farewells were done, the day was upon us. My parting with EGK and his wife was not difficult because I had by then heard that I was admitted at Downing College, Cambridge, and would be there for the coming years, only eighty miles away and within easy visiting range. Almost half the school was assembled at Holt Station for the departure of the chartered train to London or to say last goodbyes. Olivier was darting up and down the platform as the school train was prepared. He was totally preoccupied with his emotional farewells to Howson's boys, including poor Andy. The headmaster, of course, had no inkling of what was ahead of us all. Andy, Napier, Brian, and I were all helping staff get the younger boys aboard and their luggage loaded. Andy had a particularly awkward moment parting company with Olivier, which he described as "acting out a bizarre dream and then waking up relieved that it was actually happening." It was a tense scene for all four of us, finally relieved by the train's whistle as the little locomotive struggled to tug the fully loaded rail cars away in a cloud of steam. Four formative years of school in rural Norfolk behind us, we were on our way, in every sense of that phrase. The locomotive's whistle sounded another three long hoots, one for each of the chartered carriages as the train picked up pace. On the platform, smiling schoolmasters alongside the tear-drenched headmaster waved their former wards goodbye.

As the train rolled through Brentwood in the Essex outskirts of London nearly three hours later, the four of us changed into *civvies,* out of school uniforms into sports jackets, discarding the school tie for neckties of choice. This may have been driven by a sense of liberation or perhaps a self-conscious ritual of transition as we sensed our emergence into a more adult world. English schools did not stage the equivalent of American high school graduations to mark that transition. We were probably just very anxious to look as adult as possible for the potentially recalcitrant meeting ahead of us.

Within fifteen minutes of arrival at Liverpool Street Station we had navigated our way through the labyrinth of narrow city streets and lanes to Weston Backhouse's office in an imposing gray granite building. A doorman stationed at the massive oaken entrance to the edifice ushered us upstairs and into a dark wood-paneled room. It had a high molded plaster ceiling and shiny brown brass-tacked leather armchairs placed around a giant mahogany desk, the writing surface of which was perfect green leather framed by an embossed gold pattern, complete with hand blotter, brass stands for ink and pens. Backhouse himself rose from his chair as we arrived, as handsome and imposing man as could be expected of a scion of the city. His full head of white hair, deep-set blue eyes, a high bridge to his straight Greek nose, his collected manner and erect posture all suggested a man of gravitas.

"Well, boys!" he said in his *basso profundo* after a curt nod for greeting, ordering us to sit down in the chairs arranged in a crescent facing him. "Tell me now just what it is that you might have on your minds. What brings you here? Who is first man up?"

"I think I am, sir," I said. "However, I first want to thank you for seeing us today. We realize this was an unusual request. But then we do have an unusual situation to tell you about."

Backhouse barely nodded.

Then I embarked upon a carefully rehearsed presentation of my assigned aspects of the Olivier affair, prompted by notes held in my quivering hand. After a minute or so, I was abruptly interrupted.

"After all this time, Heilmann, don't you know well enough what you want to tell me?" boomed Backhouse. "Why do you need those notes, boy? Just tell me what's on your mind, tell me the way it is. After these several weeks since you wrote me, you must all be pretty clear what you are here for. I am not here to listen to a lecture. Please get to the point!"

"We have all four prepared notes, sir, for good reason," I explained with my heart pounding as I tried to stay calm. "We very deliberately set priorities, so that we could be sure not to waste your time with trifles and repetitions, and so that none of us would raise issues that didn't merit your attention. We have worked to avoid the unimportant and irrelevant. With great respect, Mr. Backhouse, may I suggest that we planned this carefully between the four of us? We chose to share the presentation of our concerns, as each of us has some differing views on the priorities according to our respective experiences of the headmaster's actions."

A long, terrifying silence followed as Backhouse stared at the glossy green leather surface of the desk in front of him. He then rose slowly from his chair without uttering a word, turned his back to us and started walking to the back of the room.

"Just wait one moment, gentlemen, please! Do remain seated."

Backhouse disappeared through the frame of the heavily molded door. We had just been promoted from being four "boys" to "gentlemen." We all wondered what was coming, exchanging anxious glances, but not daring to breathe a word in his absence, convinced he remained within earshot. After only a minute or so, the imposing chairman of the Gresham's governors returned to the office, heaving a wooden crate of beer and five old pewter mugs.

"Now, gentlemen, we will get down to business. I'm sorry I barked at you, Heilmann. You can now sit back, all of you, with or without your wretched notes! And let's talk. I'm getting the picture. I sense you are responsible chaps and have thought this thing through. It seems pretty serious, whatever it is. And I appreciate that." He paused and then turned again to me saying, "Heilmann, you had more to tell me, by the sound of it. I don't think you had finished, had you?"

Having gulped gratefully at my Newcastle Brown Ale to cure my dry mouth I resumed my segment of our story, focusing on Olivier's strange inquest aimed at the youngest boys in the school, as well as his intervention in Hoult Taylor's Shakespeare productions.

In less than two hours all of us had made our respective contributions. Andy's was the most dramatic and compelling demonstration of the situation Olivier had created, given his proximity and his direct experience in Howson's, right under the headmaster's nose. Andy had been in the direct line of fire, exposed to his housemaster every day, a fate the rest of us had avoided. Without ever interrupting or asking questions, the governors' chairman sat listening intently, his eyes under seriously furrowed brows trained on whoever was speaking. He showed no emotion, making an occasional note when each of us was through. Napier was the last man up, and when he finished Backhouse immediately proceeded to wind up the session without expressing opinions or reacting specifically to any given point, but with soft-spoken friendly words of warmth. He said we had indeed been very responsible, consistent and factual, so he took us very seriously. He said he appreciated our determination and good manners. He would now consult his colleagues on the board of governors. He did, however, acknowledge that he had heard "some rumblings" from various "Gresham's people" about the situation at the school. He never came close to suggesting how he had addressed or dealt with those earlier rumblings.

"The whole matter is of course extremely delicate," he said, "and the school could be terribly damaged if this episode is not handled sensitively, strategically, and with great caution. I cannot over-emphasize that, gentlemen, and I know you understand because you have been admirably discreet up to this point. Now we all have to be terribly discreet going forward."

Backhouse commanded us to remain silent on the matter. He implored us not to talk about it with any master or any schoolboy friend we might have left behind us in Holt.

"Above all, for goodness sake, make no comment to the press, or other strangers for that matter, should you have the misfortune to be hounded by those bloody tabloid people. The same goes for any approach made by the press with questions about this meeting. You are not to discuss this matter with anyone—certainly not before you hear again from me. Please let me have your word on that, gentlemen!"

We, of course, pledged silence. However, I explained that from Cambridge I would be visiting Eric Kelly and his family in the autumn and must be free to talk openly with him. The special relationship I had with EGK was explained, and the chairman of the governors agreed to the exception, provided I gave him some time, at least until I went up to Downing almost three months later.

Weston Backhouse bade us a formal, yet warm, farewell, this time shaking us by the hand as he thanked us for our trouble and wished us luck as we moved onto the next phase of our lives. He gave us a fleeting smile and with his right forefinger pointed to the door in evident dismissal. He again turned away and started loading spent beer bottles back into the empty beer crate. Despite his words, none of us ever heard from him or saw him again, but his impressive persona was etched on my mind for life. A man of gravitas, indeed.

Or so we thought at the time.

Feeling emotionally battered, the four of us made our way, believing that we had precipitated something big. We had no reason to doubt we had brought anything but new news to the chairman. We had no idea that a group of OG's, meaning Old Greshamians or alumni, had approached the governors nine months earlier to call for a change in the headmastership. This in turn had caused the governing body to dismiss Olivier, only to withdraw the termination after Olivier mounted a personal and very dramatic protest campaign involving an alliance of younger staff supporters and a selected group of friendly OGs. After much frantic communication and passionate lobbying, he managed to get himself reinstated. So without knowing it, we had in fact re-opened a can of worms by introducing new information of more alarming impact. We had re-ignited a crisis, which the governors, Olivier and others involved had assumed consigned to history.

Over sixty years later, a pro-Olivier OG wrote a letter to the "Old Greshamian Magazine" in defense of MJO, citing a 1954 letter sent by a handful of alumni (mainly from Howsons) to all OGs, encouraging them to signal "a debt of gratitude and loyalty, and we feel the Governors owe him one too." So it is clear that the hard feelings and factional differences persist to this day.

Apart from saying fond goodbyes to each other, I do not recall how the rest of the day was spent. Strangely, there was no attempt at any form of celebration at the time; we certainly didn't dive into the nearest pub for a party. I believe I went back to the grimy Liverpool Street Station hotel to wait for a boat train to Harwich, where I would embark on the *Crown Prince Frederik* for the overnight passage to Esbjerg and the Danish summer.

I never saw Napier again, and various attempts Brian and I later made to find him were fruitless. We did hear stories that he ran into problems with drugs, but that was never more than hearsay. The Old Greshamian Society also lost track of him.

Andy, who was off to Nigeria to see his parents (until he was due to be back to take his place at Magdalene College, Cambridge) remained a lifelong friend with some family ties between us, as he married a distant Danish cousin of mine. The tight schoolboy and undergraduate friendship was a long and lasting one, but distance and separation eventually took their toll as decades went by. His brilliant international rugby career, a vast network of associates linked to top level rugby, his time spent in sports journalism, and the PR business all caused our paths to diverge for reasons other than just geography. Andy eventually settled in Washington DC, at first working for the European Common Market, later the EU in a senior public relations role until, for some reason, he left. When we met from time to time, he would always avoid discussion of our careers, but I am told that in order to stay in the USA he declined a promotion to a top European Union PR job in Brussels. He launched an unsuccessful television production project, and then an unfortunate adventure involving a highly leveraged air charter business, which lost significant sums of other people's money, including a rumored one-million dollars from Tony O'Reilly. Tony, as Chairman and CEO of HJ Heinz in Pittsburgh, had to some degree become his sponsor and protector. Andy and his very beautiful wife Pia eventually ended up living in Portland, Oregon, where a son was working in the IT industry. Andy died very tragically, only in his mid-sixties, of an aortic aneurysm. By then our shared memories and adventures sadly meant more to me than the extant relationship. Nevertheless, Andy's place in my heart remains very warm to this day.

Brian Johnson immediately went off to do his national service in the army, and our paths did not cross much when he went up to Cambridge a couple of years behind me. However, we reconnected very happily forty years later, just after Andy died, and rekindled the treasured and enduring friendship. His fascinating career had meandered through development economics, to teaching at university level and dabbling in politics and journalism. When we reconnected, he was living with his wife outside Scansano in southwestern Tuscany, making a living as a landscape painter and designing English gardens for British tycoons, who bought vacation properties in that gorgeous region of sunlight, cypresses, and succulent Sangiovese. We found that while we had very different careers in disparate environments, we still shared views and values, including a taste for good Sangiovese and juicy Morellino wines grown in that area. He is a tall blonde man, with twinkly blue eyes under heavy brows, who speaks jowly English exactly as it should be spoken by a true Englishman of his education and family background. At Gresham's, Brian's brilliant imitations of Winston Churchill were a source of great mirth, and they remain so today. He has always been very British in the best possible way, and in my senior years he reminds me how much I owed Gresham's and its great host country.

Years later, the school commissioned its departmental head of History, Steve Benson, to write the story of the school he served. Andy, Brian, and I were contacted and questioned at length about our time at Gresham's and particularly our initiative regarding M. J. Olivier. Benson got it straight from all three of us in turn, both barrels blasting from all three guns; but he proceeded to whitewash Olivier and the whole affair in an attempt to keep the school's history unblemished at a time when the 400th anniversary of the school was approaching. Benson's account never rang true as he carefully avoided key facts, any questioning of Olivier's record, and the duplicity of the governors' actions surrounding his dismissal. Benson's account did, on the other hand, acknowledge that "the staff appears to have become divided over their headmaster." He wrote that "various matters were brought to the governors' attention by parents, and, importantly, by some senior pupils before Olivier was finally removed."

Brian and I chose to challenge the pussy-footing of the whole affair, reminding the author that three of us had given him details of the damage, pain, and institutional instability caused by Olivier. As a result, Benson sent me a long letter setting out his rationale for his particular version of the tale and wrote that we four boys "were the most central characters in the gruesome drama," and that "all my instincts are with you, Andy, and Brian, and others." Steve Benson was apparently uncomfortable to be thus challenged.

> "I will not apologise for my bending of this saga," he wrote,
> "I had to be aware that Olivier's widow was still alive, and
> that he had his supporters. Furthermore, I did not want to
> give any press reviewers a cause célèbre, which would have
> overshadowed the great triumphs of Gresham's."

In what seems like a capitulation, Benson said that what the four of us had done was clearly the right thing to do, and actually cited my own expressed view that Olivier did indeed

> " ... destroy himself as he proceeded to destroy the traditions and values of Gresham's by reversing what Howson's and Eccles had put in place to make Gresham's special."

Brian, writing separately to Benson, pointed out that

> "The decision to dismiss MJO on the basis of the facts presented and verified, at such an historically important moment in the school's history, does say a great deal for the abiding force among at least many of the staff of the school, and old boys (not to mention the governors) of the ideals of the Howson/Eccles era."

For many years after the Gresham's days, as the world generally moderated its interpretation and understanding of homosexuality, I struggled with the thought that there could have been a collision between the sexuality of the headmaster and the single-gender boarding school environment. Could it be that the environment or the public school system itself inadvertently caused confusion or nurtured latent homosexuality? As for the boys, could it be that spending eight months of each adolescent year in an all-male environment could nudge a young boy's sexual experimentation, and then his preference, in the direction of homosexuality? That complex postulation certainly did not jibe with me or any of my close schoolmates. However, it is a fact that at different times several renowned alumni, such as Benjamin Britten, Stephen Spender (who was unhappy at Gresham's and left early to go to another school), and W. H. Auden were all known for being homosexuals or bisexual. The term "gay" had not yet

been invented. It was never a secret that Stephen Spender, through three
marriages and multiple affairs with males and females, plunged back and
forth between homo—and heterosexuality, so the question is a complex
one and not necessarily invalid. In an abstruse letter to Christopher
Isherwood, another bisexual literary cohort, but not a Greshamian,
Spender wrote:

> "I find boys much more attractive, in fact, I am rather more
> than usually susceptible, actually. I find the actual sexual act
> with women more satisfactory, more terrible, more
> disgusting, and, in fact, more everything."
>
> Ref. John Sutherland, 2004, "Sir Stephen Harold Spender," Oxford Dictionary of
> National Biography.

How's that for complexity? Would the adolescent Spender have grown
up to a different adulthood had he gone to a coed day school at home in
the rather social, up-market neighborhood of London's Kensington where
he was raised? Such extrapolation is, of course, dangerous and not very
useful. Taken together, the sexual orientation of just three alumni artists of
the 1930s, the fact that there were few obvious gays among the 450
Greshamians of our day, and then the Olivier affair, lend neither credence
nor validation to any theory or claim. On the other hand, the question is
not necessarily invalid either. By the time two of my sons went to
Gresham's School in the 1970s, the institution had been coed for some
years as a fast growing percentage of female boarding pupils had been
introduced over the previous years. Adolescent romance at Gresham's, to
the extent it was allowed to bloom, was evident and heterosexual.

In October 1954, when Andy and I went up to Cambridge, almost
three months after the Backhouse meeting, reporters from *The Times* and
The Daily Telegraph had checked the dates we were expected to arrive at our
respective colleges, and they were encamped outside the Porters' Lodges of
Magdalene and Downing, ready to pounce.

The story was out.

The Fishmongers had announced that Olivier was dismissed with effect a couple of months later at the end of the current Michaelmas term, without further explanation. The absence of comment or reason certainly caused speculation. Gresham's teachers, alumni, parents, and pupils across England were hounded for details, but very few people knew what had happened, and none would tell if they did. The circle of insiders who knew how badly the Fishmongers under Weston Backhouse had bungled their first run-in with Olivier was small and tightly discreet. It was years later that Andy, Brian, and I learned that Backhouse did not live up to his impressive façade, that he was a man of far less gravitas than we had perceived. We, however, had honored our side of the deal made with him: In answer to the reporters' many questions, each of us independently, with precocious solemnity, declared that we had "No comment!"

Happily, the Olivier affair was a short-lived subject of interest in the British media. The school's reputation was not materially damaged and under a new Scottish headmaster, a star of rugby football and a sound pedagogue named Logie Bruce-Lockhart, Gresham's prospered as a source of quality education and preparation for admission to the better British universities.

The education at Gresham's was totally different from what would have been encountered at school in Denmark. The contrast at age thirteen meant a broadening of horizons and called for adjustment and adaptation. Some Danish preconceptions had been challenged, especially in terms of individual responsibility, social values and priorities. It was surely a healthy component of an adolescent's maturing process. English schooling was yet another building block in an itinerant preparation for adulthood.

The Gresham's years also illuminated marvelous aspects of the United Kingdom's singular culture and traditions. Breathtaking English choral music, ecclesiastical and secular, unmatched by any other nation, heard in spectacular cathedrals, churches and chapels across the country. The magic of seventy thousand Welshmen singing "Land of Our Fathers" in near perfect unison at Cardiff Arms Park before an England versus Wales rugby battle. Great national sporting traditions such as Ascot's equestrian glamour complete with morning coats, outrageous ladies' hats and frilly frocks. Henley's colorful regatta blending sartorial excess with world class athletic performance on the Thames. Wimbledon's "whites only" tennis gear contrasting with its manicured green and traditional champagne, strawberries-and-cream off court. Five-day cricket matches against Commonwealth countries at The Oval or Edgebaston ending in a draw, having brought the country's industry and commerce to a standstill. The Oxford and Cambridge Boat Race bringing a million Londoners, whether they be alumni or not, to line the banks along 4.2 miles of the Thames between Putney and Mortlake as sixteen of the planet's best oarsmen gave their all for their university's honor. Sold-out audiences at Sir Thomas Beecham's summer *Proms* celebrating popular classical music at Royal Albert Hall. The West End on— and off—Shaftsbury Avenue and Covent Garden, crucibles of British drama and opera. Parades and processions of colorful military precision, pomp and circumstance laced with royal fanfare as young Queen Elizabeth II communed with her loyal subjects, genteel white glove waving from a gilded carriage. Parliamentary debate peaking in entertainment value at Prime Minister's Question Time—Winston Churchill's 1953 invention, which gave MPs direct access to him in the House of Commons every Tuesday and Thursday. Poppy Day when around forty million Brits, in rare national cohesion, wore bright red cloth poppies in buttonholes or on bosoms to remember their fallen in two world wars.

Europe's postwar collectivist concepts and socialist leanings were on the march well into the 50s. The sociopolitical thrust in Denmark was stubbornly focused on building an egalitarian welfare state, where unconditional entitlements and personal gratification trumped sustainable social and economic progress. Danes recovering from Nazi occupation wrote and talked about their sacred freedom while building big government, which steadfastly reduced the individual's freedom of choice. Personal enterprise and risk-taking were certainly not priorities of Europe's collectivists, including the UK's Labour government. In contrast, the system at Gresham's called for individual responsibility, placed the longer term needs of the community ahead of the individual's immediate gratification, and yet encouraged personal choice.

Chapter VII

Bedders, Bumps and the Backs

"I find Cambridge an asylum, in every sense of the word."
A.E. Housman

THE CLACKING DIESEL engine of a little black London-style taxi
sputtered under its testing load. Burdened by the weight of a huge cabin
trunk, two large suitcases, and me, it struggled from the Cambridge rail
station down Regent Street, and then reeled abruptly through the heavy,
black wrought iron gates carrying the arms of Downing College and
gratefully pulled up at the Porters' Lodge just inside.

The anemic East Anglian sun was low in the early October sky, casting
a soft autumnal glow on the sandy-pink, gold and beige limestone of
Downing's clean neoclassical buildings, which form the huge rectangular
"*quad*," the heart of the College. Framed on three sides by these imposing
residential ranges was the immaculate expanse of lawn, carefully spaced
horse chestnut, beech and limes trees set along pebbled walkways. Ionic and
Doric colonnades marked the two major buildings of the *domus* at the time:
the Master's Lodge where the head of the College resided with his family,
and Hall, where students and fellows dined communally every evening. The

Master's and Fellows' gardens were home to an exotic array of decorative trees, interspersed with all manner of flowering shrubs, late seasonal blooms glowing in the sun. Bells tolled from the sky-piercing spire of the neighboring Catholic church, breaking the insulated stillness of this enclave in the southern reaches of the urban academic phenomenon that is ancient Cambridge. The setting was almost theatrical, absolutely removed from the banal practicalities and bustle of the real world outside the iron gates.

That luminous autumn afternoon was the genesis of a singular experience, the inception of an extraordinary process of learning and growing, away from mundane distractions, removed from ordinary people doing ordinary things in the ordinary world of realities. It was the beginning of a new chapter, in which the brilliance and eccentricities of British intellect and Anglo-Saxon culture were to unfold. Cambridge is a setting that only changes physically and organizationally at glacial pace over centuries, yet daily spawns incessant mutations of human knowledge driving man's capacities forward. This collaborative federal institution generates transforming innovation and discovery at a pace rarely matched elsewhere in the world. While its buildings, garden settings, and traditions are exquisitely English, the university's population is richly diverse, drawing thousands of students, scholars and researchers from countless countries on every continent. Cambridge quickly invades the far reaches of your soul and settles there for all your living days.

In the year 1800, the college was founded according to the will and testament of Sir George Downing, third Baronet, who had died almost a century before. Building commenced so late because of his avaricious widow's persistent attempts to keep his whole estate for herself. In pursuing her obstructionist strategy, she employed unusually aggressive lawyers to plead her greedy case. From the *College Foundation Stone* of 18 May, 1807, one learns that

> *"Downing College in the University of Cambridge was ordained by the will of George Downing of Gamlingay, baronet of the same county,*

who furnished her munificently with wealth in the year of salvation
1717. At length the College was established under royal charter by the
best ruler George III in the year 1800. These foundations of the
building were laid by the Master, Professors and Fellows that it might
proceed successfully with a view to the cultivation of religion, and the
knowledge of English law and medicine and in promoting the right
instruction of free-born youth."

So this was it, here and now. The time had come for "the right in-struction of free-born youth," a youth named Christian Flemming Heilmann, a nervous arrival in Cambridge after years of anticipation. Ex-pectations had been sharpened by impressions gained on occasional Cambridge visits to see brother John while he was in residence. More ex-posure to its spellbinding ambience was gained on trips to play rugby or field hockey for Gresham's against our arch rival, the Leys School on the southern outskirts of Cambridge, a quarter of a mile from Downing.

While formative years as a schoolboy at Gresham's were pivotal, life as a Cambridge undergraduate was to be nothing short of transformational. I lived it to the full and loved every week of every term and every year. Years of keen exploration and discovery, often wincing at the enormity of my own pathetic ignorance and naïvete. Years of grappling with new concepts, absorbing some yet learning to challenge others. I was exposed to men and women of vastly differing intellectual capacity and ambition—the astoun-ding brilliance of teachers and more normal, but still disparate, peer-group students. Eric Kelly's definition of a liberal mind was constantly invoked as Cambridge presented endless opportunity to respect new and opposing views and gaining from curious listening. An itinerant schooling brought unusual opportunity to explore and learn en route, but here was a mind-boggling range of the world's best thinkers, converged in one small town, under the inclusive academic umbrella of the university.

How fortunate could one be? And what responsibility did that extraordinary good fortune bring with it? Would I make it? What if I couldn't? How could I be sure not to let my parents down ... they had given up so much to afford me this opportunity? How would I live up to their expectations and those of my teachers, and brother John, who had graduated ahead of me? The excitement was not unadulterated, not untouched by fears and doubts.

In terms of immediate practicalities, the first order of business was to check in with the college porters, who showed me to my rooms and carried in my possessions. My suite was number five on the second floor of M staircase in the south-facing North Range on the quad. There was a starkly Spartan bedroom with flimsy cotton curtains barely covering the grey steel frame window and a relatively comfortable living room cum study with a small gas fire and two huge sash windows opening to a magnificent view across the grassy quad to the distant Catholic church spire. Downing's tranquil *domus* stretched before me, marked by The Paddock and a row of Victorian town houses at its southern extremity. The room contained a large brass-studded brown leather sofa and two matching armchairs around a solid oak coffee table. Minimalist comfort with an all-male patina. Shoulder-high oak paneling on three walls, but bookshelves to the ceiling over and either side of the gas fire's mantel making up the fourth wall The room's dominant feature was a plain light oak writing table, upon which stood an iron table lamp with a broad white linen shade, and tucked into it a very upright wooden chair with a high slatted back and no seat padding—a hint that hard work and many waking hours lay in store. Down a barren sandstone hallway, I found the kitchenette equipped with one laboratory-type gas ring, a cast-iron kettle and a frying pan, then the ablution facilities—all shared with three second-floor M staircase neighbors. The clean elegant lines and grandeur of William Wilkin's and Sir Herbert Baker's neo-classical exterior architecture somehow belied the rather monastic undergraduate living quarters within.

Basic daily comforts of life in college were secured by cheerful, ever-caring *bedders,* who would make beds, organize laundry and dust our rooms.

Some of these folksy townswomen would even wake slumbering
undergraduates in their care with steaming cups of milky, sweet tea.

> "C'mon, dearie, you've missed yer nine-o'clock, you 'ave!
> Now get on wivvit! Rise 'n shine, m'dear! It's a loverly dai
> fer studyin' ... sow c'mon, luv, owt you get from under
> them-there covers! I knaow you've got a ten o'clock
> leckchah. Up ya' get!"

The *bedders* were crucial to many aspects of college life, for they not
only saw to domestic hygiene, but most of them could be called upon to
exercise career-preserving discretion from time to time. Under college rules
women were expressly forbidden anywhere on the *domus* after 11:00 PM.
Being caught with a lady guest as morning arrived would, without exception, warrant punishment of life-changing impact; *rustication* if you were
lucky, or even being *sent down,* depending on flagrancy of the circumstances
     In quaint Cambridge vernacular, arriving at the university is termed
going up. Conversely, departing Cambridge is, quite logically, known as *going
down.* However, if the departure is both permanent and involuntary, one
has been *SENT down* for some rather serious misdemeanor. End of prom-
ising Cambridge career. The punishment for a serious, but not terminal,
transgression is removal from residence in Cambridge for a specific period
of time (a few weeks or a full term, for example) termed *rustication.* Being
rusticated is seriously expensive. It causes failure to spend the mandatory
number of nights in residence to complete the required date-stipulated
academic term in Cambridge. Graduation absolutely requires completion of
a minimum of nine academic terms in residence. So, in effect, rustication
means a fine equal to the cost of a full extra term in residence before
counting the value of time lost.
     Brother John had very nearly fallen prey to this ancient and strictly
enforced rule. At the end of one term he had sneaked away from
Cambridge two days early to get home to Copenhagen for some special

celebration with his sweetheart, Inge-Marie. His absence was somehow detected by Downing's chief porter—an officious, scrawny little man with beady eyes and sharp hooked nose named Alf—who reported it to John's tutor, the acclaimed and very popular international lawyer Clive Parry. The morning after he arrived in Copenhagen, he received Professor Parry's telegram ordering him to return at once, so he could register the requisite number of nights in college before the academic term officially ended. The alternative was to lose the full term of residence! The episode involving an extra round trip air fare back to Cambridge made a huge hole in John's otherwise carefully managed budget, but the alternative would have been career-ending, that is his Cambridge career! His budget could never have coped with an extra full term at Downing. A year or two passed before he told me or our parents about it, but a major lesson had been learned and passed on to me before I went up to Downing myself.

As a freshman, while still clinging to some beautiful egalitarian ideas and leftish views on social issues, I accepted generalizations regarding intrinsic rights of people and the duty of government to secure them, without giving much thought to what it took to sustain those rights as defined. Neither experience of life under the Danish welfare state nor years at insulated Gresham's were among the best of places from which to get a sense of life's true economic conditions, although being put in charge of my own finances had helped. Reading economics and law was soon to improve comprehension and kindle respect for some home truths in matters financial or fiscal. Idealistic preconceptions developed at school and during privileged teenage years were soon tested. New realities were introduced to the internalized debate; new elements were added to the existing mix of idealism, compassion, personal bias and the attendant naïveté. Serious questioning evolved. Topics and preconceptions concerning such issues as religion, equality of man, structural options for systems to secure civic order and governance were all opened to question. Freedom of choice as it relates to individual responsibility, ambition and effort in relation to just reward, and even the cost of risk were newly considered. History's lessons and new knowledge displaced some alluring but unsustainable idealism. Religious and political dogma was challenged and omnibus solutions—so often vulnerable—were shot down as perceptions matured.

It seemed that improvement in the overall plight of man on the planet Earth was fueled by economic enterprise and innovation working within a sustainable civic system. Where man's native ingenuity and his individual aspirations were allowed to flourish they seemed to outperform collectivism and excessive central control. Enabling and promoting economic and social self-sufficiency became the mission, the priority; and therefore the challenge was to facilitate equality of opportunity, equality of access to the tools necessary to that mission. History demonstrated that hard economics, not soft social theory, underpinned progress wherever it was accomplished on a sustainable basis through the millennia.

~~~~

Most of ancient Cambridge along the banks of the idyllic little River Cam had remained untouched by industry or commerce. Its spectacular and varied architecture reflected the evolution of the university born 750 years earlier. Architectural style reflected its growing number of member colleges as it evolved into the extraordinary federal collegiate institution that it is. Only Oxford, founded some sixty years sooner than Cambridge, has a similar collegiate structure. In fact, many will say that for the first three hundred years of its history, Cambridge was totally outshone by Oxford. Dr. David Starkey, the Cambridge historian of later years, mischievously provoked and teased the Cambridge establishment by claiming that until the reign of Henry VIII

> *"Nobody who mattered ever went to Cambridge, not a word that ever mattered was uttered there, and not a single idea worth having was ever conceived there."*

A different view comes from alumnus Steven Fry, famous for his eclectic career in English literature, drama, journalism, comedy and broadcasting. At the grand New York gala celebrating the University's eight-hundredth anniversary, he reminded 600 *Cantabs*, as Cambridge alumni are known, assembled in Gotham Hall that their university was founded in 1209 when a handful of academic malcontents arrived in Cambridge to found their own new institution

> *"… having fled that shithole, Oxford."*

In 1954, any thinking freshman had to be properly humbled by this singular community, its brilliant history of transcendence, its legacy of knowledge, wisdom and its constant innovation. You can but succumb to unquenchable thirst for understanding and the relentless challenge of the status quo taking place around you. Alison Richard, as vice-chancellor 50 years later, said:

> *"Cambridge is a place where people cross boundaries—academic, intellectual, social and geographic—making connections in surprising ways to achieve remarkable results."*

The university's goals and purpose continue, as ever, to be quite simply stated:

> *"The mission of the University of Cambridge is to contribute to society through the pursuit of education, learning, and research at the highest international levels of excellence."*

The institution's stated core values are no more complicated than the mission:

> *"Freedom of thought and expression; freedom from discrimination."*

Better than other universities, Cambridge and Oxford seek to live up to these principles by encouraging and promoting, if not demanding a questioning spirit and mindset via an uncommonly intimate inter-relationship between its teaching, scholarship and research, which enhances the appetite and ability of its of students to continue learning throughout life.

An astonishing aspect of Cambridge undergraduate life is the absence of immediate pressure from supervision because there were almost no checks on a student's everyday life, social and work habits. No compulsory attendance at daily lectures, or classes, as they are called in America. No mandatory study hours or daily demands. The only opportunity for a tutor to know how a student was doing was feedback from the weekly or fortnightly *supervision* (tutorial) in each segment of the subjects being read. The tutor would be told by the supervisor in question if a student went astray in terms of delivering acceptable papers or attendance.

My own undergraduate years brimmed over with fun and social adventure. I do not recall that academic demands were terribly arduous, except for the torture of the two frantic months before *prelims* (preliminary examinations) at year end. Exam results at the end of my first year would bear this out. My performance was commensurately unremarkable—inarguable mediocrity by the standards set by the institution and my peer group.

Failing *prelims* meant being sent down; failure was career-ending. The pressure and torment of the last term as a senior before *finals* were almost unbearable. The whole of undergraduate Cambridge went into lockdown. Every single student prepared for the exams knowing the results achieved would characterize his or her academic and intellectual worth for the rest of his or her life. By the time I reached the final law exams for my degree, I had improved time management and discipline, just enough to be placed a smidgen north of mediocre.

Cambridge University is a federal, truly collegiate and very complex institution. The university "owns," appoints and runs the faculties, the central and specialty libraries, all the laboratories, and the institution's common facilities, assets and programs. The University defines the curricula, sets academic standards, and manages policy; it ensures the integrity of all academic work, writings and research; it sets the exams, officially evaluates all academic performance, writings and research; it awards all degrees; it, selects, adjudicates and funds all Ph.D. projects; it appoints all professors, lecturers and readers; it manages all interface with the world outside Cambridge and the university's relationship with government and sources of public and private funding. Each Cambridge professor, lecturer, reader and researcher, and every single student is either a *fellow*, a *senior member* (post-graduate) or *junior member* (undergraduate) of a college, of which there were eighteen in 1954 and thirty-one in the early 2000s. The university is ultimately ruled by a huge, central council representing all the colleges and the university's central institutions. This complex and cumbersome constitution has evolved over eight centuries of hotly debated compromise in a ceaseless quest for independence and democracy among the colleges. Unsurprisingly, administrative decision-making tends to be glacial. The challenging leadership role of the vice-chancellor calls for strength of will and being a deft, persuasive politician. The University's "head of state" is a ceremonial figurehead titled Chancellor. He or she is theoretically elected by the still-living population of Cambridge graduates holding an "honours degree." In reality, a recent chancellor's election drew only a paltry four thousand votes, of which there was nary a nay. The opposition didn't show, and a plurality rules.

However, the University itself has no students. As mentioned, every member of the university, at every level, is a member of a college. The colleges are quasi-autonomous, self-governing academic communities ruled by their respective governing bodies of *Fellows*, who are also known as *Dons*. The master or head of the college is *primus inter pares* among the fellows. It is the college that takes direct responsibility for the academic and social welfare of its undergraduates. While the University defines and offers the courses of study taught by its faculties, it is the colleges that direct the studies of individual undergraduates via an extraordinarily intimate process of teaching. College tuition is an intensive complement to central teaching at the university level. One supplements the other. Depending on the particular strengths and specialties of the fellows at a given college, it is often at the college level that the most effective teaching is done. Thus a college may develop recognized strengths in one or more academic disciplines. For example, Downing is today particularly strong in law, the sciences, and medicine. If perchance an undergraduate is reading Central Mongolian Philosophy or Ancient Nordic Philology and his college lacks capacity to teach in that particular field, it is the responsibility of his college tutor to place him or her somewhere else in Cambridge with a properly qualified teacher.

Junior members (undergraduates) of a college each have their tutor acting *in loco parentis,* meaning that tutors have a protective role beyond academics, through social and disciplinary oversight. Meanwhile, *supervisors* give intimate teaching of specialized component studies. If the degree subject is law, specialties such as criminal, personal property, constitutional, international or contract law, etc., would be taught by different *supervisors* teaching in groups as small as four or five students. The intimacy of teaching in such small groups was so highly valued that if college *dons* deemed the demand from junior members threatened this intimacy, students would be assigned to supervisors outside their college. Weekly or fortnightly papers would be submitted and then discussed in the *supervision* group. This meant that whatever the quality and pace of the courses, the intimate teaching at college level could make the best of the student's individual capacity. For example, I personally thought the university lecturer in Constitutional Law was a crashing bore, and so chose not to attend his lectures. However, with the help of his renowned text book and the personal interest of my Downing supervisor in Constitutional Law, I managed the subject quite adequately. That's how it worked—the system assumed the undergraduate's sense of responsibility, so there was no spoon feeding. The system certainly promoted the very best in the brilliant, yet also recognized that any given student's talent was finite and so it nurtured those who might be less brilliantly endowed. A rare lack of responsibility on the part of a student would eventually be tracked down by the tutor with consequent admonition. In extreme cases, rustication could be the result. This extraordinary collegiate approach is the reverse of the welfare state approach to education, where uniformity of capacity is so often assumed, so that academic objectives and standards tend to be diluted or lowered to the level of the lowest common denominator. The colleges of Cambridge and Oxford were and still are intellectual hot-houses to which the best, the elite of the academic world, flock if they can.

I initially read economics, and found my university lecturers in economic history and macroeconomics boring (Eric Kelly had groomed me well in these subjects at Gresham's), so again I simply made sure to read their set books and worked through the curriculum with my more inspiring supervisors. One of them was a softly spoken young fellow, Malcolm Fisher, of Jesus College, who later became a protégé of the great Milton Friedman of Chicago University. Dr. Fisher mightily reinforced my emerging understanding of capitalist free market ideas and their role in enduring social progress. Today's body of supply side theory had not yet been refined or even thus named, but Malcolm Fisher went on to be one of its acclaimed proponents in the free world. A quietly persuasive New Zealander, he was an oracle to his students, whose teaching was underpinned by argument of overwhelming logic and practical example. He stood out in Cambridge economics at the time, as the university faculty was still dominated by widely held macroeconomic positions of the John Maynard Keynes school of thought. Like a few other unfashionable economists in the Cambridge of the 50s, Fisher challenged Keynesian belief in central solutions to all problems. Others found themselves at odds with Cambridge's still pervasive intellectual arrogance, omnibus solutions, strongly influenced by the Bloomsbury group to which people like Virginia Wolff and Keynes himself belonged.

Career aspirations were soon modified to reflect an evolution of mind-set. Earlier predilections and prejudgments were discarded as new comprehension was gained. Even the ivory tower and insulation of Cambridge could not get in the way of realities in the world beyond. Early thoughts of working in one of the exploding number of United Nations agencies, the World Health Organization, UNESCO or UNICEF were discarded by the time *prelims*—the first round of annual exams—were taken at the end of the first year.

My academic career was far from stellar. The prospect of highly mathematical Economics Part II *tripos* (the final honors examination for a BA degree at Cambridge University) terrified me, so I switched to reading law. This entailed significant time and extra effort to catch up with those who had already read Part I of the law degree in their first year. My chosen areas of focus were basic jurisprudence, International Law, Crime, Contract, Personal Property, Tort, Constitutional and Roman Dutch law—the last one because of my growing interest in South Africa, where the Roman Dutch code ruled (as it did in Ceylon, South West Africa, and Rhodesia). I took international law, not only because of my own background and interests, but also because it was taught so brilliantly right there in Downing College by Clive Parry, the world's leading authority in this area of jurisprudence. He was especially well known for his work in maritime law and its related territorial issues—the very Clive Parry who had recalled brother John from Copenhagen to Cambridge. I went to his jam-packed university lectures, but also had the enormous privilege of being supervised by him, along with four other Downing undergraduates. Parry was not only a great lawyer and teacher, but also a humanist with a teasing sense of humor that attracted young and old. He had a trim, wiry figure and a relaxed, low key demeanor masking his alert interest in the welfare and academic progress of his students.

Criminal law supervisions under Henry Barnes, a fellow of Jesus College, were quite different and an education unto itself. He was a wildly unkempt Irishman, sporting an unruly Albert Einstein hairstyle, heavy white eyebrows, and serious mustache. He reveled in analysis of the goriest, bloodcurdling details of physical crime, employing language that was always colorful and often profane. He was an atheist and very NPC (not politically correct) on the subject of criminals suffering the consequences of antisocial behavior. Barnes believed that the law was there not only to protect citizens and against crime, but also to provide strong deterrence to criminals. He was no eager proponent of the therapy concept in preventing repeated crime. I switched to Barnes from a previously assigned supervisor in criminal law, Garth Moore at Corpus Christi College, because the latter was a narcissist, from whom it was impossible to learn at the required pace. He was a fastidiously dapper homosexual, who looked a bit like Noel Coward and would spend more supervision hours talking about the latest male thespian star of the famed "Cambridge Footlights" review than about crime. The disparity between these two law *dons,* their views on life and teaching, were the starkest contrast you could imagine; but that was Cambridge. The *dons* of a college varied in character and intellectual capacity depending on the makeup of the given college's fellowship. In my day, Downing's fellowship was academically vibrant, driven by some brilliant *dons* among its members. Apart from Clive Parry, there was Frank Leavis, who was the leading critic and thinker of English Literature of that era, with an enormous following throughout the Anglophone world. He was a literary counterpart to the Bloomsbury Group, whom he characterized as purveyors of dilettante elitism. The master was Sir Lionel Whitby, a nationally acclaimed physician and hematology researcher, who developed the sulphonamide antibacterial group of drugs.

Frank Leavis basked in adoration and loved having undergraduates, Ph.D. candidates, and literary critics at his feet, which they literally were— sitting in large groups on the floor of his sparsely furnished Downing rooms. He was a standout eccentric in dress and conduct. A balding thespian with remaining wisps of white hair drooping to his shoulders, he wore white shirts unbuttoned to his navel to expose a hairy mat under his wide-open Donegal tweed jacket. Leavis' sartorial preferences were in bold conflict with a world where ties and three-piece suits were generally de rigueur among *dons*. His transport around Cambridge was a decrepit, very upright old bicycle with elevated handlebars to which a large wicker basket full of books was strapped. He propelled himself at the lowest possible speed at which gravity allowed a bike to remain upright. He staged a ridiculous daily spectacle as he peddled across the quad in slow motion to hold court in his rooms in Downing's West Lodge. The academic world was not wholly divested of vanity and narcissism.

But that was Cambridge.

I never quite understood the fuss Leavis created in the literary world by launching a vicious ad hominem attack on C.P. Snow, the English novelist. Years later I read Snow's riveting novel, "The Master," about the internal politics pertaining to the election of a new master of a fictional Cambridge college, and I finished none the wiser. Frank Leavis, however, was a giant figure in English literature and its interpretation. He championed rigorous intellectual standards and was thus at odds with the intellectual elitism of the Bloomsbury group.

Not all *dons* were seen as academic heroes. As a freshman, my tutor was a youngish Ken Norman, Ph.D. in Central Asiatic philology, a taciturn man of scholarly distinction, but with the emotions of an amoeba. He had a long, thin, serious face that appeared distant and unengaged; his mouse-colored hair was cut very short back and sides and he had dark, deep set unresponsive eyes behind steel-rimmed glasses. My tutor's interests and priorities in life were not remotely relevant to my prosaic aspirations: academic, athletic or otherwise. I actually had little to do with him, but that was doubtless a function of my academic mediocrity and the fact that I rarely transgressed to a degree warranting his attention. In contrast to this sterile relationship, I had respected friends in Clive Parry and another senior law don, H.C. Whalley-Tooker, Esq., who was the senior president of the Downing College Rugby Union Football Club, in which I was active.

Brilliant teaching and improved effort on my part improved my performance over the years to a *Lower Second* grading, or "II-2," in final exams. That left me (and the quality of my degree) at the bottom of the top half of Cambridge law graduates of 1957, but it did secure the *Honours Degree* nomenclature, which is no big deal as everyone is awarded one except those who score grades at the margin (earning an "ordinary" degree based on second-chance, retaken exams, or an "aegrotat" degree allowed because of illness at examination time).

~~~~

Life outside Cambridge during vacations was steered by deep roots and tight bonds to family and Denmark. *Mor* and *Far* were in distant Swaziland and South Africa, where I spent my last long summer vacation before my final year. Otherwise, I continued the pattern of the Gresham's years, spending vacations between relations in Copenhagen and at Tammestrup. The vacation spent in Swaziland and South Africa, however, was to have an impact on my evolving career plans.

A month of the time in South Africa was spent with brother John and Inge-Marie in Northcliff, a middle class Johannesburg suburb tucked under a massive rocky bluff, where jacaranda trees proliferated. I worked as an intern in the office of PB's Johannesburg law firm, and was placed under the wing of a young lawyer, John G.F. Lang. He was an affable, distinctly podgy fellow standing some six-foot, four-inches tall. He had a mischievous face, beak of a nose, and prominent chin reminiscent of Punch, with a curl of long brown hair hanging permanently over his right eye. His mannerisms suggested he was a school-boyish prankster, extrovert, and energetic in a highly disorganized way as he rushed to address the next urgent item on an endless agenda. John and his wife, Brenda, opened their home to me and a happy friendship developed. He was later to play a role in my life and eventually presented some real surprises relating to his mission and priorities in life. Also during that vacation, a chance meeting with a prominent South African financier and captain of industry at a UPSA cocktail party in Swaziland would prove pivotal as I prepared for graduation a year later. Bryan Smither was a banker with connections.

The social life of young white people in Johannesburg's northern suburbs was lighthearted and carefree, especially over the weekends. Parties galore. One particular evening ended as it could only end in apartheid era Johannesburg. About twenty of John's and Inge's friends joined them for an early springtime supper party, dancing outside to gramophone music with plenty to drink. It was the first warm night marking the departure of the high-veld winter, so someone decided it was time for a vernal night-time swim. The problem was that John and Inge had no pool. However, this challenge was quickly resolved by guests climbing a six-foot mesh fence, ignoring "NO TRESPASSING" signs to plunge into the large pool of a neighboring elementary school. Everybody piled in, cavorting like adolescents. John and I, for some reason, decided to address each other in our best Indian accents learned long ago in Malaya, which caused much hilarity and elevated the noise level.

"Isn't dis delectably vonderful, little babu?" John shouted, treading water in the deep end.

"My goodness, gracious me! Indeed dis is delightfully refreshing and so vet! Big babu Johnny, it is svimming here in dis cool pool I could be doing all night!"

"Come on in, my Bengali friends, it's into de vater you should be jumping," John continued as his guests joined us in the chlorine-loaded water. "Jump straight in here for to cool DOWN and sober UP! ... Ha-ha-ha! ... More magical even dan de Ganges! Come on in, my Bengali babus! Share dis exquisiteness vith us!"

All at once, a dozen dazzling lights pierced the night's darkness as a whole squad of SAP officers surrounded the pool armed with their heavy nightsticks. A neighbor had called in to report that the *Europeans-only* school had been invaded by "a bunch of rowdy non-whites, who are disturbing the peace." As the situation became clear to the police, they exchanged a few words with John to convey the neighbor's concerns and simply chuckled as they again faded into the night. Had the trespassing, let alone use of the pool, in fact, been done by a harmless bunch of Indians, the incident would have undoubtedly involved some harsh treatment, arrests, and incarceration. The white intruders, however, were just left to climb back over the fence, rendered almost sober by their nocturnal swim.

In Swaziland, a grand reception was held at UPSA's Ngonini citrus estate to celebrate the opening of PB's impressive irrigation canal cum hydroelectric power project, which would facilitate the planting of an enormous acreage of citrus under gravity irrigation. Water from a weir four miles upstream on the Mlumati River was funneled through a canal, not only allowing irrigation of trees below the contour, but at the end of it, residual water dropped almost 500 feet to drive a turbine, which generated all the power requirements of the plantation. It was one of PB's innovative pioneering projects. Despite Swaziland's topography of steep hills and valleys, nobody in the country had previously thought to capture predictable rainfall and river flows for hydroelectric power. The planting of citrus groves and construction of an irrigation canal with raw Swazi manpower in the middle of nowhere was to provide several vivid learning opportunities: Different cultures are driven by different human motivations.

The timing of the canal project's completion was critical to minimizing startup costs and the plantation's early financial performance. If effective irrigation of brand new plantings could be commenced in August at the very beginning of spring before the rains arrived, a whole growing season could be secured, rather than having to wait another year for optimal timing and early growth. When the nescient Swazi labor failed to accomplish the required excavation on schedule, costly delay threatened. PB promptly applied good western and Asian logic, doubling the piece rate paid per cubic meter of soil excavated. He confidently assumed this would accelerate excavation, allowing construction to get back on plan. Swazi logic and Swazi priorities, however, were non-conformist. With glee, the labor force realized they could now earn the same amount of money by noon instead of sundown, allowing them to return home to the *kraal* and drink *marula* beer in the comfortable shade of a marula tree through the whole afternoon, and indeed into the night. PB faced a setback with dire financial implications. So he abruptly reversed course and reduced the original piece rate by 50 percent. Bingo! Swazi productivity immediately exploded, so canal construction was soon back on schedule and completed on time.

And everybody lived happily ever after—or at least for several decades.

The Swazis, with help from their employers gradually learned new ways. They were delighted to have not only a source of income in their remote and primitive surroundings, but also access to housing, basic health care and schooling for children. Out there in the indigenous bush, United Plantations South Africa had brought them to a starting point, which the Swazis, on their own, might have taken many additional generations to reach. Everybody was happy at the arrival of the enterprise and the opportunities it generated.

The 200 guests attending the irrigation canal's official opening included contractors, engineers, bankers, colonial government officials, shareholders and His Majesty King Sobhuza II of Swaziland himself. Sobhuza reigned first as Paramount Chief and then King for nearly eighty years. On this occasion his retinue included none of his eighteen wives, but he was in full sartorial gear: splendid cheetah skin draped across one shoulder, multicolored cotton loin cloth under an ample belly marked by a popping navel along with long decorative pins stabbed into his black super-Afro coiffure from multiple directions. On his left arm he carried a ceremonial shield lined on each side with sable and kudu antelope skins.

I was helping the bar service satisfy the urgent thirst of guests, some of whom were more impatient than others. When I asked His Majesty what his pleasure might be, he said

"Yess pliss! One glasss off best Mr. Harvee's Breestol Crim Sherry, eef you pliss!"

I mistakenly assumed His Majesty was signaling that he would modestly have only a single glass of sherry and hurried off to fetch his royal tipple. I duly proffered a customary shape and size of sherry glass containing three or four ounces of the sweet, fortified wine.

"My goot friendt, young man, ... sah! I say one glasss off best Bristol Crim, and you bring me one bebby's cup, not one glasss ass keintly requestid. Sorrry, diss is verry in-suhfficiaahnt, pliss!"

I scrambled to replace the inadequate ration with a beer-mug of Harvey's Bristol Cream. His Majesty's lips parted in the widest and whitest smile before he quaffed half the mug's contents, about half a pint, in one long draft.

"Aaahhh! Verry goot, sah! Goot weerk! Tenk yu evvaso mutch, yung men! Best Breestol Crim iss mah fehvurit befferidge. Tenk you!"

The bar ran dry of Harvey's Bristol Cream within the hour, prompting the accelerated departure of His Majesty and his all-male entourage along a distinctly weaving path.

Neither this second exposure to southern Africa nor the school boy vacation some years before caused me sufficient pause to think much about the implications of the Nationalist government's emerging policies and legislation. Somehow, the opportunity to contemplate this escaped me, perhaps because I had no reason yet to anticipate any long-term involvement in that part of the world. The Nationalist Party was still in the early days of its forty-five year regime, its leader and prime minister at the time was Johannes Gerhardus Strijdom, who succeeded D. F. Malan. Strijdom shared Malan's deep loyalty to the Afrikaner cause, but considered him too moderate in his relations with the British. The depth of the new prime minister's embedded racial prejudice had yet to be clearly seen as an enduring threat to the dignity and aspirations of the country's broader population. Racism and discrimination was, after all, still par for the course in many parts of the western world and its colonial territories.

~~~~

The continuing vacations in Denmark nourished deep Danish roots and appreciation of the culture, which influenced me strongly throughout my life. By now, I was spending a lot of my Danish days with a serious girlfriend, Helle Groenbech, and her academic family, in the suburbs of Copenhagen. Time with Helle dominated personal priorities, so that I gave scant attention to Danish politics other than to note that the whole system was heavily socialistic. I did observe that any overt signs of personal wealth could tarnish perceptions of a person and his or her reputation. In 1953, the Social Democratic leader, Hans Hedtoft, became prime minister for the third time—the first time, he was forcibly removed from the post during the Nazi occupation, returning to the post after the war for a three-year term before losing it very briefly to centrist Erik Eriksen. Hedtoft extended socialist welfare policies until he died in office in 1955 to be succeeded by another Social Democrat, H.C. Hansen, with precisely the same political philosophy despite threatened national financial crises.

~~~~

In Cambridge, undergraduate life continued to stimulate and spring surprises. Sports were a major determinant of my social life, but so too was the small population of Scandinavian girls in town. Only two of Cambridge's eighteen single-sex colleges were female institutions, so girls were scarce. The gender ratio of the university population was catastrophic from a male point of view.

Helle crossed the North Sea to spend a year in Cambridge, ostensibly studying art at the Cambridge City Technical College & School of Art. Perversely, that added remarkably to my personal popularity, for through Helle I became an unmatched source of introductions to scores of young Scandinavian women studying at the art school, or polishing their English at either of the renowned Davis and Bell language schools in town. These two institutions drew young women from all corners of Western Europe. First dibs in the process went to rugby playing chums in college and beyond. My closest friend in Cambridge was still Andy Mulligan, who had risen to rugby stardom, and through Andy I had many friends among the *Blues* of the varsity team. To a man, they had urgent need to meet my Scandinavian girls.

Johnny Allen, who later played for Scotland, plunged into a torrid affair with a lovely Danish girl, Anne, whose heart he later shattered. She was absolutely crushed when he moved on. However, Anne eventually recovered, returned to Copenhagen, and by happenstance married a second cousin of mine, this time without my introduction. Fifty years later I was visiting my cousin Henrik and Anne in Denmark when I told her of my plan to link up with Johnny Allen in London the next week, to go to the annual Cambridge versus Oxford varsity match at Twickenham. Anne was quite overcome, suddenly blushing as hot tears welled in her eyes. With a furtive glance at Henrik, she stepped aside to make sure he was out of earshot and begged me to convey a loving greeting to Johnny. A week or so later, I honored my promise over a pint with Johnny before the big game at Twickenham, the Mecca of English rugby, only to find that he had absolutely no recollection of Anne—not a hint of recall. I knew that alcohol was not the culprit, as he recalled names of half a dozen other Danish girls from those Halcyon undergraduate days. I never told dear Anne. Johnny was an absolute Adonis even in his mid-sixties, so his memory simply could not cope with the number of conquests made over the decades.

Undergraduate social life was heavily influenced, but not in the least hampered by lack of modern transport in the city of Cambridge. The choice was shoe leather or bicycle. Undergraduates were not allowed cars, unless special permission was granted, usually for medical reasons. Leaving town was an expedition. Only rare two-hour trips to London broke a parochial pattern, which meant that social life was almost completely confined to the idyllic academic setting of the colleges, university clubs, associations and sporting venues. Winter gatherings for afternoon tea and buttered crumpets toasted over gas fires in college rooms. Sherry with a friend before dinner in Hall. A pint at "The Squirt," Downing's favorite watering hole more properly named The Fountain, twenty-five yards from the College gates. "The Squirt" was ugly and smelly, but offered fantastic utility of access and good bitter brewed by Younger's.

A winter afternoon favorite was watching the *Blues* playing against world class rugby teams in leaden-grey drizzle driven by icy wind blowing in, unfettered, across the *Fens* from the North Sea. We gladly froze our feet solid at the Grange Road rugby ground with its quaint little grandstand cum club house and otherwise open concrete-and-steel bleachers. Outdoor life entailed a degree of masochism during the months on either side of the Christmas vacation. Much of my year was devoted to Downing's rugby club and its "first fifteen," which represented the college in intercollegiate competition and, during vacations, on tours in Cornwall, the Welsh coal-mining valleys and West Germany to play local clubs and British Army regiments.

Several Downing undergraduate clubs were prestigious and influential on the *domus*. None had greater impact than *The Griffins*, named for the heraldic beast featured in the college arms. Its members were *blues*, athletes who had represented Cambridge against Oxford, or had featured large in college athletics as leaders or outstanding competitors. It was an elite group, many of whom were also prominent in student government or academic, cultural or other social organizations on the *domus*. A feature of the community at large was elitism in its very best manifestation: elitism in the sense of commitment to being the very best in a chosen endeavor. Elitism thus defined still characterizes the Cambridge environment as it continues to foster ambition, self-discipline, self-assessment and ultimately performance. This notion of elitism is not rooted in the arrogance or snobbery usually associated with the popular use of the word. Members of the Griffins Club, for example, were achievers in the community, student athletes in an environment where poor academic performance could only be attributed to laziness or irresponsible mismanagement of time. In this milieu, elitism is a cornerstone of excellence, performance and progress.

An unusually sophisticated organization for such a youthful community was *The XI Club*, a wining and dining group, which had ten officers and one member. I was the single freshman member, impecunious, ignorant, and no oenophile. Twice a term the club held excellent dinners and introduced very good wines, port, cognac, etc. procured at favored prices from the copious college cellars. It was also an early introduction to quasi-adult public speaking and a lesson in the inescapable effects of alcohol on self-expression and articulation. The morning after dinners was always a challenge, when most members would pass on nine-o'clock lectures, trying to recover with the help of our *bedder*'s steaming cup of tea. Daisy always knew when her help was needed.

Attending debates in the Cambridge Union, where so many British politicians cut their oratorical teeth, was an occasional ad hoc experience for me. Once in a blue moon, the motion to be debated might fit my intellectual capacity, and prick my curiosity. I enjoyed physical proximity to this venerable institution, as my final year was spent in *digs*, a small room on Bridge Street overlooking the narrow slate passage leading into The Union past the 12th century Norman Round Church. The Union, where

tradition and protocol were strictly obeyed, attracted hundreds of the
brightest, politically active undergraduates, as well as brilliant speakers from
the highest echelons of British politics, philosophy, and the arts. Occasionally, someone like Anthony Eden or Harold Wilson would feature in
a debate. It was the pulsing fulcrum of the University's political life and an
incubator of great thinkers challenging the public status quo.

This academic world was an infinitely diverse society. No matter what
your social, cultural or political inclinations were, you could pursue your
particular interests and test their boundaries somewhere in Cambridge.
There were also nooks and crannies where you could find yourself in totally alien territory. The Pitt Club, for example, was home away from home
for well-heeled sons and a few daughters of England's landed gentry, who
spent their weekends hunting with the hounds or beagling (hunting on foot
as opposed to equestrian, behind beagles) in the grassy chalk hills of rural
Cambridgeshire. They were the tweed-clad beaux and belles of the English
counties. To be a member of the Pitt, you had to be very "U"—upper
crust—and your pedigree had to fit.

Mine did not.

Summertime brought a change of scene and sporting attractions: lazy
afternoons watching slow moving cricket matches with friends at Fenners,
the University Cricket Club's serene, green playing field. "Well organized
lethargy," someone called cricket, "with occasional rounds of polite applause
for sudden bursts of surprising athleticism." Matches could be played for
two or three days without yielding a winner. Elegant *May Balls* held with
Cambridge logic in mid-June after the annual exams, lasting the night
through sunrise. Long luminous laughter-filled evenings lounging on the
grassy banks of the Cam, relief and relaxation as the dreaded *prelims* or *finals*
became a gruesome memory. Elegant, pretentious garden parties organized
by arts, drama, or literary clubs, whose members occasionally regarded
themselves socially a cut above their peers, a vulnerable condition in an
environment where pretensions could be dealt vicious blows. The vagaries of
the East Anglian climate did little to dampen enthusiasm. Rainy garden

parties were stubbornly endured, prompting yet another attempt to outdo the weather gods. Formal black tie dinners were frequent and always liquid. The black tie tradition was and remains a part of the social fabric—spawning a sense of occasion, not affectation. Unfortunately neither the sense of occasion nor this garb could always deter ridiculous behavior as the evening wore on. The lifespan of a dinner jacket is abbreviated at Cambridge.

Seasonal crop picking of strawberries or digging potatoes in the flat sandy fields of the *Fens* was a budgetary necessity for some, a social pastime for others, but always fun with a well-stocked lunch hamper and a bunch of kindred spirits. The same could not be said of serving tables in cheap Indian or Chinese restaurants to supplement scarce spending money. The Cambridge cocoon was not entirely divested of life's practicalities.

Summer called for punting on the River Cam with friends. Either down the Cam through the town or a leisurely glide upriver to the enchanting medieval village of Grantchester for afternoon tea and scones, as prescribed by Rupert Brooke. This could be a romantic interlude or a good laugh, depending on the inclinations of the girl reclining on the punt mattress and the navigator's punting skills. The narrow, languid River Cam played a pervasive role in the lives of 8,000 undergraduates and 12,000 graduate students. *The Backs* were the centerpiece of the Cam. They were the enchanting green spaces along the banks of the urban reach of the Cam, where the oldest colleges displayed the quintessential architecture of their vintage. They harbored immaculate grassy courtyards and exquisite English gardens, where springtime is ever magic. Velvet lawns, carpets of daffodils, narcissi, hyacinths and crocuses—millions of them blooming in nature's sequence for those relishing a stroll along the magical banks of the river; lazy parklands and lush meadows nourishing pampered calves and lambs; cherry, apple, plum and other blossoms shedding vernal blizzards of purple, pink and white in the breeze. So many Cambridge icons span or rise from the river's banks: the Bridge of Sighs, King's College Chapel, the Mathematical Bridge of Queens College, Clare's intimate gardens, hundreds of punts lined up for hire at The Mill Bridge, the best remembered pub in town.

The River Cam is also home to the *May Bumps*, which like the May Balls are held in June. The rowing races, along with the balls, crown summer's social and sporting calendar. They constitute a series of extraordinary contests on the narrow Cam's winding downstream reaches outside town, a traditional competition between colleges for bragging rights as *Head of the River*. The races are held over four afternoons and early evenings, which are called *nights* despite the sun remaining well above the summer horizon at the end of the racing. The Cam is too narrow to accommodate two crews racing side by side, so a unique format was devised in 1827, with crews ranked by immediate past performance, one behind the other. The fastest crews are in the first division, starting on the first *night*, according to the order in which they finished *The Bumps* one year before, one-and-a half boat lengths apart for a simultaneous start—a bit like a shotgun start of a golf tournament. Each boat's cox and crew of eight await the cannon shot, the shell tethered to a starting post positioned on the bank. At the cannon's blast, the coxswain drops the chain, and the crew springs to life in pursuit of its quarry just ahead, seeking a *bump*. A *bump* is deemed to have been made when the bow of the trailing boat hits or passes the stern of the boat ahead. The achievement of a *bump* ends the contest for the bumped boat, because it must immediately pull in to the riverbank to let other boats race past. It is a question of bumping the boat in front, before you get bumped by the one behind. If you have neither bumped nor been bumped by the finish line, you have *rowed over* to hold your position on the river unchanged. Scoring a bump promotes your boat one place upriver at the cost of the vanquished crew; being bumped moves you one place back. This procedure is then repeated for three more *nights*.

At the end of the fourth *night*, one First Division crew earns Headship of the River for its victorious college. The whole event is a cross between an aquatic circus involving apprentice-level paddlers of Division IV or V and a contest of acclaimed athletic prowess between extremely gifted oarsmen of the top divisions. Thousands line the riverbanks each *night* to encourage and cheer up to fifty crews. The bends and straights of the river such as *The Gut, Grassy Corner,* and *Long Reach,* are landmarks, which determine the strategic stroke rate and timing of attacks on the stern of the crew ahead. Strategy is all-important and is planned and rehearsed months ahead. The crew at the *Head of the River* has reached the pinnacle of Cambridge intramural rowing, which in turn leads to wild all-night celebrations. The victorious oarsmen or women carry their shell over their heads from the college boathouse through the town's streets and then burn it in a ceremony on college home turf, while intoxicated oarsmen or oarswomen jump through the flames, over its ashes between libations. A crew, in any division, which makes four consecutive bumps *wins their blades,* which means their oars become personal trophies adorned with college arms and the scripted names and the weight of each crew member.

The races are cheered wildly from the riverbanks and pubs along them. Unkempt *dons* remain disheveled in their tweed jackets and crumpled flannels. Undergraduates sport blazers, literally of every stripe, in gaudy boat club colors or white flannel trimmed with silk ribbon, or double-breasted navy blue with gold embossed buttons. Pants of white cotton or linen. English roses giggling with flushed cheeks in flimsy flowery frocks, flaunting cleavage and curves. The crowds are particularly dense around *The Plough at Fen Ditton,* favorite and most fashionable of the observation points at Ditton Corner. This is the perch from which to watch the races if you also wish to be seen and noted. The venerable pub's champagne, gin-and-tonics, numbered Pimm's and Buck's Fizz are consumed in abandon along with endless pints of tepid, flat *bitter.*

Weekends, at any time of year, brought a quickening of the Cambridge social pulse. The noontime arrival of the *Popsy Express,* (ten o'clock Saturday morning train from London's Liverpool Street station) would bring pretty girls, lots of them, to spend the weekend with boyfriends or new male acquaintances encountered at home counties' cocktail parties or perhaps while working vacation jobs. Within half an hour the *Popsy Express* couples would be ready for a lunchtime drink at the Mill Bridge, the punting terminal on the Cam, hard by Queen's College. To launch the weekend

program, the girls from London might be offered a strategic *Devon Cider;*
but those with previous experience, who knew what they might be in for,
might choose an alternative beverage. The harmless sounding apple brew
from Devonshire, served in a large tumbler, was, in fact, uncommonly
potent. The cider could make for good sport after lunch, either in a punt
en route to Granchester or during a quick siesta back in college rooms or
digs. Inexplicably, there was no designated reverse *Popsy Express* taking
girls back to London at the end of the weekend. The explanation might
be that the visiting ladies of London mustered varying degrees of enthusiasm and stamina in coping with the full range of opportunity
involved in a Cambridge weekend, and so retreated at different times in
the course of a Sunday.

Through teenage years, Danish vacations allowed me some experience
of female company in a way unknown to many of my English boarding
school peers. Nevertheless, Cambridge certainly played its part in accel-
erating my social coming of age. At eighteen I was the youngest freshman
in College because I had not served two years of National Service as had
my British contemporaries under the UK draft. During my first summer
term, I was invited to a particularly sophisticated party, at least by undergraduate standards, at Homerton College, which was not yet a part of the
University. It was an independent institution for graduate female pedagogues from every reach of the planet seeking to hone their teaching credentials. I was well taught in the course of the evening's fun and games.
That balmy summer night, under the spell of an entrancing French-
Moroccan blonde from Marrakesh, I was introduced to a number of life's
delectable vices. She had strong teaching skills.

Sadly I never saw her again.

Along with frivolities and a rich experience beyond study and learning,
there were life-changing friendships born, beliefs and aspirations shared,
differences debated and disagreements mutually tolerated. Some bonds of
comradeship were strengthened over the years and others snuffed out.
Preconceptions, bias and established values or priorities were challenged;

new perception was gained and new convictions built on firmer grounds. The status quo was constantly tested over these years.

Early on, there was a challenging encounter with an old school friend, who had become a consummate born-again Christian. He had become hyperactive in a bible-punching group known by the acronym CICCU (aptly pronounced "kick-you") for Cambridge Inter Collegiate Christian Union. He knew from Gresham's days that I had been confirmed in the Church of England at the age of seventeen. Now my erstwhile friend's missionary fervor caused the CICCU activists to pester me persistently, and I initially made the mistake of engaging in debate rather than telling them to get lost. It developed into a long-endured contest. I had by then moved on to question all religion, not just the Church of England, so leaps of faith no longer had a place in my thought process or reasoning. The net effect of their onslaught was to promote even deeper agnostic questioning. CICCU and my Old Greshamian friend actually set me on a path to atheism. The full time score in this contest was Godless 1, CICCU 0.

Some colleges were more diverse than others. Kings, Trinity, and St Johns, for example, were weighted in favor of top English *public school* recruitment, whereas others drew more broadly from British grammar schools and overseas territories, especially in the British Commonwealth. Downing's undergraduate community was socially and ethnically eclectic, which made for edifying crosscurrents, whirlpools of ideas and diverse aspirations. New departure points for evolving values and personal priorities became the catalysis that expanded one's capacity to engage in life after Cambridge.

The British Commonwealth was still the glue that caused many different ethnic groups and cultures to come together. Students and scholars from Southeast Asia, India, Africa, and Australasia easily outnumbered those from the European continent and the Americas. That built-in cultural reach of Oxbridge in the 1950s made the politically manipulated "diversity" of America's 20th century colleges and universities seem manufactured and quite pathetic. The spontaneous diversity of Cambridge and

Oxford was the result of extending some of the world's best education to the whole world's population at large; the diversity was neither engineered nor legislated. Consequently, there was no forced or formula-driven diversity policy, which could result in lowering standards. Nor was the multi-ethnic, multi-cultural mix a product of political correctness; it was diversity spawned by the best attracting the best. No legislative device or political contrivance elsewhere has matched what these two universities achieved. Nothing epitomizes this notion better than the Gates Cambridge Scholarship program announced by Bill and Melinda in 1999. The Gates program annually awarded almost 100 full ride, multi-year grants to forty graduates from the USA and up to sixty from any other country in the world. In Bill Gates's own words, the program seeks to encourage leaders who "can take people with them" in their respective endeavors and communities. The one-billion dollar Gates program administered by Cambridge dwarfs even Oxford's wonderful Rhodes scholarship in scale and reach, although it is much less known and touted. The Rhodes program curiously caters only to the United States, Germany and the current or past British Commonwealth countries.

Despite the many similarities of Cambridge and Oxford, the latter's relative strengths seem inclined to the humanities, with special strengths in the realms of philosophy, politics and the classics; whereas Cambridge might claim to be stronger in the sciences and the applied subjects. An aspiring politician, a philosophy, or Sanskrit scholar may possibly choose Oxford, while the budding bio-scientist, astrophysicist or engineer might prefer Cambridge. This debate on relative strengths triggers howls of indignation and protests from Oxonians and Cantabs alike, both pointing to the danger of "rash generalizations."

The mission and extraordinary fellowship of All Souls College at Oxford uniquely points to that university's emphasis on the humanities. Founded in 1438, its relatively few members are all *fellows*, with at least three years of experience (within or outside academia) after graduating with "first class honours" degrees. About a dozen are elected annually after an ancient two-day process of written and *viva voce* examinations followed by the writing of an essay on a one-word subject such as exceptionalism, diversity, orgy or duty. Election is very competitive. After the initial process, a short list of applicants is interviewed, and, if then elected, they receive a *stipendium* covering up to seven years of further scholarship at All Souls, including fine board and lodging privileges. The fields of study, however, are limited to seven: the classics, English literature, economics, history, law, philosophy and politics. Among unsuccessful applicants, one curiously finds names such as John Buchan, author and Governor General of Canada, Lord Denning the preeminent British jurist, and Harold Wilson, sometime Prime Minister. All Souls is also unique for its quaint traditions. Once every 100 years, the fellows assemble for a lavish feast in College, directly after which they, with flaming torches in hand, parade around the college led by a *Lord Mallard*, preceded by another man carrying a long pole—on the top of which a mallard duck is attached, commemorating a legendary mallard, which flew out of the foundations of the main building when it was being constructed nearly five centuries ago. The mallard was real for ages, but more recently it has been either stuffed or carved from wood. The next celebration led by yet another *Lord Mallard* will be held in 2101. Cantabs cannot boast of an equivalent community; but not many Cambridge graduates have lost sleep over it.

Admission to a Cambridge college was substantially easier to achieve in the 1950s than it is now. The academic standards can hardly be compared, but my own qualifications at the time would fall far short of today's requirements. Sixty years ago there may have been a slightly heavier emphasis on "the well-rounded" applicant who had shown signs of involvement in the community around him. Cambridge and Oxford offered a plethora of academic, research and musical scholarships (sometimes called *exhibitions* at Oxford) funded either by the colleges themselves, by other private sources or by the government; but neither financial nor other subsidies were ever extended for athletic prowess. While accomplishment in sports could feature as a positive element in a college application, admission was not extended to airhead athletes or jovial jocks.

Student athletes had to be at least half-decent scholars. A number of my teammates became acclaimed writers, judges, actors, pedagogues, doctors, captains of industry, international financiers or politicians. Derek Robinson, a Downing rugby player emerged as a Booker Prize-winning author early in the new millennium, and as a respected rugby referee, who also wrote several guides to the rules of the game. John Drake-Lee became a nationally known pediatrician. Several contemporary Cambridge rugby players became household names after going down. Richard Scott, a South African rugby *Blue*, for example, went on to become a Law Lord as Baron Scott of Foscote. He chaired the UK's 1992 government inquiry into British support of secret arms sales to Iraq. Renowned Scottish rugby player, Arthur Smith, earned a degree in math by age 18 and proceeded to a Ph.D. (Cantab) at age 22 on his way to fame and fortune as a financier. Ian Beer, captain of Cambridge rugby, became headmaster of Ellesmere College at the age of 29, and later head of well known Lancing College. I do not, however, recall that any of them won reputations as poets or philosophers.

Secluded as Cambridge was, the community was never unaware of world events, or left totally unaffected. The global current affairs backdrop was always there, influencing students, researchers and teachers at every level. My freshman year finally saw the end of meat rationing in Britain after 14 years of war and a slow recovery. Oxonian athlete, Roger Bannister, broke the four-minute mile for the first time in history. The Irish Republican Army rekindled "The Struggle" with its bloody attack at Armagh. Lord Montagu of Beaulieu and two friends were convicted of conspiracy to engage in criminal homosexual acts, a finding which led to the Wolfenden Committee's recommendation that homosexuality be decriminalized. The 1967 legislation which implemented it ended what had been punished as *buggery* for more than four hundred years. Dylan Thomas's *Under Milk Wood* was premiered in London as he lay on his deathbed. Winston Churchill at 80 years, resigned during his last term as prime minister for health reasons, handing the reigns to Anthony Eden, who famously bungled the Suez crisis before Harold Macmillan took over. American Dr. Jonas Salk first put his anti-polio vaccine to work on 500,000 people in the UK, while Northcote Parkinson scorned government bureaucracy with the publication of his renowned "law" stating that "work expands to fill the time available for its completion." Unemployment ran at only one percent, or close to it. Two of the "Cambridge Spies," Burgess and Maclean, surfaced in Moscow having disappeared mysteriously from the British Foreign Service years before. Humphrey Lyttleton brought traditional American jazz to Britain with his *Bad Penny Blues*. Egyptian leader, Nasser, nationalized the Suez Canal, precipitating the crisis that followed. Malaya, which included Singapore, won independence and Malaysia, was born.

During vacations, Downing's Rugby club tours opened new horizons. A week in South Wales introduced the culture, fabulous choral traditions and the history of the coal-mining region immortalized by Richard Llewellyn. There was nothing very green about these valleys, where the soot and grime of row houses in moribund mining villages lent appreciation of the union movement and its bitter origins. The cheerful lilting accents of rugby-loving miners, generous welcome parties and extraordinarily melodious sing-alongs with the whole community. The local rugby club doubled as the civic center, where ordinary Welshmen shared extraordinary knowledge of literature and poetry. It was Dylan Thomas country, complete with Jones the Milk and Evans the Post.

A tour in Cornwall was an exploration of cozy country pubs, Cornish pasties, scones with strawberry jam and fresh cream for tea. Rugged rugby-playing Cornish farmers and tin miners opened their homes to us. The jagged Atlantic coastline and rolling inland countryside gave new dimensions to "England's green and pleasant land."

The British zone of allied occupied West Germany offered competitive matches against regimental rugby teams stationed in the shadow of the Soviets in East Germany just across the River Elbe. No quaint rural pubs or pasties on this tour. It was all about formal dinners in officers' messes, gleaming regimental silver displayed on brilliantly polished mahogany dining tables, young officers in medal-bedecked mess uniform. Toasts to the regiment, country and Queen, in that order. The loyal toast—vintage port, of course—to the Queen at the end of dinner signaled the moment when smoking was first permitted that evening. After dinner came puerile drinking games, some of them rough, involving physical contact and wrecked dinner jackets or uniforms The cavalry regiments were particularly adept at pomp and ceremony, but not to the exclusion of the silly games led by Sandhurst-educated officers with upper-crust accents. Her Majesty's Government picked up the tab.

The culture surrounding the game of rugby generates an astounding global network of fun-loving men and women, always quick to welcome and support newcomers to their own community. Rugby's popularity is still growing today. Early in the new millennium, the global count was five million players and a fan base of more than three billion people. Four-point-two-billion people watched the 2007 World Cup final. The average American's sadly lacking exposure to this game and its culture has left us the poorer. Unfortunately, our collegiate attempts at building a rugby tradition have generally fallen short because the physical and self-disciplinary demands of the game have not been understood or respected. A few American college clubs, however, have built fine rugby traditions, such as those at Dartmouth and UCAL Davies.

Relationships from Downing years have endured, rekindled by camaraderie, shared respect and many common values. They serve as reminders that engaging in disparate philosophies and priorities of others can only enrich one's own perceptions.

Arjun Puri, a handsome Punjabi mathematician, who roomed two doors down the hallway on M Staircase, was a gentle, quietly spoken and deliberate man, yet fiercely combatant on the squash court. He taught me, by example, that personal crisis and disappointment are not best addressed by outbursts of emotion. Arjun went on to lead the British corporate giant ICI into the world of computers in the UK and India. Richard Porter was the epitome of the best emerging from the English *public school* system: ever courteous, understated, meticulously turned out for whatever occasion, and always warmly engaging. He would bark at imperfect manners and was unswerving in his intolerance of cheating or foul play. He became a successful City lawyer. The consistently cheerful Jos Bird was also a bright fellow, a tease who had a knack for deflating the pompous or pretentious with good humor and attendant laughter. His career as a small town lawyer in Bury-St.-Edmunds allowed him to be a champion of preservation and conservation in rural Suffolk. Michael Neubert, almost six-and-a-half feet tall and slightly stooped, sporting a bulbous pink nose, was the classic student politician and a cornerstone of the Cambridge University Conservative Club. To nobody's surprise he became a Member of Parliament and was knighted. Michael rarely missed a debate in the Cambridge Union and was ever active in Downing's Junior Common Room, the heart of student government. Michael Crouch was a hyper energetic, wild and unpredictable colonial type from Nakuru in Kenya, always in search of adventure and unconventional thrills. He reveled in exploration of the uncharted and loved to confront the unexpected. His career was that of a senior MI6 intelligence officer operating at tribal leadership level in the Yemen before assassination attempts drove him out. He ended up in Western Australia teaching at university level, still undertaking the odd secret mission in the Yemen. Beaufort Pinney, aristocratically chinless and always sartorially im-peccable, was a phlegmatic man of few words until a pretty girl was sighted. Only then would Beaufort spring to action with startling energy and eloquent charm to ensnare the unsuspecting maiden. He was one of a few contemporaries who dropped right off the radar screen; but he probably lives somewhere in the Chilterns or the Cotswolds wearing well cut tweed jackets, newly pressed cords, and brilliantly polished country brogues.

Personal romance through these years was a roller coaster. The schoolboy romance with Helle blossomed and was sustained despite challenges from rivals. Given my tender age, I kept to a rather narrow path through a wide open world of romantic opportunities. At times the relationship with Helle and her year-long presence in Cambridge added to the richness of the whole experience; at others, it caused unproductive tensions and constraints on both of us. Since monogamy is not a natural male state, I certainly had a crush or two on other girls, but those relationships were inhibited by a naïve rather than virtuous sense of loyalty to Helle. She did not always display the same level of constraint when her pretty Nordic looks drew the attention of undergraduates on the prowl. There were quite a few of them among the 12,000 graduates and 8,000 undergraduates in town.

Finals suddenly became a looming reality as the last Easter vacation arrived. Knowing that some work had been neglected, the four-week vacation in Copenhagen was largely spent with nose to grindstone. Back in college for the final term at Cambridge the real agony and terror set in. Sleep was cut to a maximum of six hours a night while coffee and nicotine consumption exploded. Year-end *interim* or *prelims* exams had been taken at the end of each year but *finals*, of course, had the greatest of irreversible consequences. It was too late to make up for procrastination or neglect in years past. Why hadn't one learned from predecessors? Why hadn't one listened to *supervisor*s' admonitions? The dice had been cast. There was suddenly an absolute limit to what could be done in the remaining weeks to compensate for past folly. Options were locked in. The only remaining variable was the amount of revision and catch-up that could be squeezed into the remaining weeks, days, and hours.

Cramming old lecture notes; re-reading convoluted laws of Roman-Dutch intestate succession; memorizing facts and names of cases under-pinning criminal common law; revisiting weekly supervision papers written through the year; plugging holes left by slovenly reading; re-reading inter-national marine boundary treaties; panic-driven extra sessions requested of obliging, usually responsive supervisors. We were all miserable and desperate for the pain to stop. Hellish short nights of tossing and turning, sometimes feeling dangerously fatalistic and indifferent to the outcome!

Downing's usually busy quad turned dead still as a village graveyard— a silence which multiplied the decibels of the booming bells of the Catholic church just across Lensfield Road beyond The Paddock. People cracked up. A fellow law student and rugby mate Mike O'Connor broke down and then went berserk. For weeks he had been wearing earphones through the night, playing tape recordings of his inadequate lecture notes. He was committed to Addenbrooks Hospital, from where he was soon dismissed to be shipped directly home to Ireland. He was later reported to have gone native in the peat bogs of the central County Offaly.

Finally, we sat for the exams over a period of ten days or so.

The system was hardly a healthy one in those days, yet it prevails today. If anything, the tensions are higher now because in today's competitive job markets the grading of the earned degree is much more important, and that grading reflects only your performance in finals—not your work done through the academic year. The Cambridge and Oxford examination experience is a blunt yet invaluable lesson. The sole annual testing of academic performance is the ultimate demonstration that your choices made over time have consequences, many of which are irreversible. The more time wasted during the year, the greater the backlog, the deeper the panic and the worse the trauma at its end.

So it was with painful anxiety that I joined the crowd on the perfectly shaved lawn by the white marble Senate House, in the windows of which graduation results were to be posted at nine o'clock on a sunny June morning. Names were listed in order of merit or grading, starting with the very top of the class. A single grade, based on all papers written, was given for the degree as a whole; results for the individual component subjects were not published. I knew I hadn't failed, but what quality of degree had I attained? Eventually I found "Heilmann, Christian Flemming," on page three, roughly halfway down the *Law Tripos* list to learn that I had got an

Honours Degree at the *Lower second* (or 2-II) level, which meant the lower half of the second class, right in the very middle of the 1957 graduands. I was as happy as a daisy in May.

Like the May Balls and the May Bumps, this celebration was also enjoyed in June. My brighter law friends, such as Jos Bird, got *Upper Seconds*, but none of my close personal friends got a *First* in law. Arjun Puri, however, got a *Starred First* in Mathematics. An *Honours* degree signified that you had not scraped through by the skin of your teeth by meriting only a *Pass* or a *Special*, which are awarded after a second try at the end of the summer. Specific circumstances of illness might justify the University awarding you an *Aegrotat* (aeger is Latin for sick), meaning a non-honours degree without taking exams because of medical incapacity at exam time. So there is a pecking order in the range of Cambridge degrees: First, Upper Second, Lower Second, Third—all *honours* degrees—and finally the less distinguished *Pass, Special*, or *Aegrotat* degrees.

Graduation itself was splendid in typically English style. No nation masters ritual, pomp and circumstance better than the Brits. *Mor* and Helle were in Cambridge for the great day. PB was busy at work turning native Swaziland bush into citrus groves, and John and his wife Inge-Marie were newly arrived in Johannesburg from their sojourn in the Philippines. It was inevitable that *Mor* would be there to witness my graduation. Despite the family's enforced separations, *Mor* held the family tightly knotted by being a communicator par excellence. During all those years of physical separation, it was a rare week that went by without a long hand-written letter from her—usually in the form of an *airgram*—posing informed questions about life at school or university and giving explicit accounts of what was going on in the lives of the other three. She had been in Cambridge for John when he graduated and would not have missed my day for all the tea in China. It was also a big day for her.

Degrees were ceremoniously conferred in groups, college by college, inside the Senate House in the heart of the town, next door to the 13th century administrative buildings known as *The Old Schools*. Graduands wore white tie, dinner jacket, graduate-length black gown down to the knees (undergraduate gowns barely covered one's posterior), a white sheep skin hood topped by a black mortar board with tassel. We assembled in the college quad to be joined by Downing's master and *fellows* in full academic regalia, gowns of vivid colors and mysterious insignia on their sleeves and hoods of every hue, displaying their credentials of academic rank and pedigree. The whole group then walked in procession through the Cambridge streets past other colleges. Pembroke's facade on Trumpington Street, St. Catherine's ugly wrought iron fence, William Wilkens' (same architect as Downing's earliest buildings) golden sandstone New Court at Corpus Christi, then past King's College with its celebrated perpendicular Gothic Chapel on King's Parade, finally arriving at the handsome gleaming Senate House. Inside, the Vice-Chancellor, in all his splendor, was seated on something like a throne, with three cushioned knee-stools ranged in front of him. We, the *graduands*, approached the great man, in lines of three at a time, to kneel before him while he mumbled a Latin recital pronouncing us Bachelors of the Arts. We were now newly baked *B. A., Cantabs*.

Vice-Chancellor Lord Adrian, resplendent in bright scarlet gown and snow-white ermine cape, was also Master of Trinity College. The dual roles were permitted in those days when the University's leadership rotated among *heads of house*—principals of colleges. He later became Chancellor, the titular figurehead of the University. Edgar Douglas Adrian, also known as First Baron Adrian of Cambridge, was an electrophysiologist to whom a Nobel Prize was awarded in 1932 for his work proving the presence of electricity within nerve cells. During World War II, he put his personal values, specialist skills and brilliance to good work treating wounded soldiers for all kinds of crippling nerve damage and shell shock conditions. His astounding feats received scant attention in the media.

The graduation procedure and its minimalist ceremony behind us, the whole contingent, mingling with family and friends, took a sunny stroll back to Downing and a very happy, bubbly garden party offering champagne, sweet strawberries, cucumber sandwiches or scones with clotted cream and jam, and tea in the stunning Fellows Garden. Even the East Anglian weather gods celebrated with us on this occasion. The late afternoon sunlight, still bright, cast deep blue shadows of majestic trees across immaculate lawns, and it illuminated flowerbeds bursting with color. Proud parents, dropping their English reserve, chatted away with strangers, relieved and elated students sensing liberation gulped at the free champagne. There was excited reminiscing, ambitious discussion of future plans, followed by never-to-be-fulfilled promises of faithful communication. These gloriously kaleidoscopic gardens in summer sunlight and the buoyant gathering were happily captured in a fairytale bubble. We were splendidly isolated from the outside world's issues and current problems.

Outside that bubble it was the year Harold Macmillan took over with his firm hand on the British tiller. France returned the Saar territory to the Germans. Adenauer's CDU party won the West German elections, while just next door twenty-two Russian divisions moved into East Germany, newly renamed the German Democratic Republic. The Dutch lifted a ban on Sunday driving imposed to counter a shortage of oil, while their citizens were expelled from Indonesia where their fixed and other assets were stolen—or "nationalized"—by President Sukarno. The USSR extended heavy economic and military aid to Syria, and Mao's signature speech expounded his Marxist ideals in the city we still called Peking. The declaration of Ghana's independence from British colonial rule was the initial breeze, which quickly strengthened to Macmillan's winds of change blowing through Africa. The UK's Medical Research Council affirmed the link between tobacco and cancer. Norwich City Council just fifty miles from Cambridge became the first local authority in Britain to install computers. On April 1st, the BBC's iconic TV program *Panorama* aired an hour-long documentary on spaghetti trees, showing the skills of carefully trained laborers at work harvesting the crop in Switzerland's spaghetti groves—the world's first April Fool's joke played on television. Eisenhower was inaugurated, and his doctrine was put to work in the

Middle East and other areas where the Soviets were a looming threat. The Ku Klux Klan forced truck driver Willie Edwards to jump from a bridge to his death in the Alabama River. The Civil Rights Commission was constituted and the Civil Rights Act followed. Elvis Presley's fame and fortune allowed him to buy Graceland outside Memphis, Tennessee. The Ford Motor company launched its disastrous Edsel. The first Boeing 707 took to its wings, and the electric typewriter had its debut in Syracuse, New York. The Mafia wars were near their climax as their own "dons" of a different ilk were regularly assassinated, while others continued to slip through the fingers of the FBI. The first American combat fatality occurred in Vietnam and Dag Hammarskjöld became UN Secretary General. Bernstein & Sondheim's *West Side Story* hit Broadway. The words "In God We Trust" first appeared on US dollar bills. In Africa, the African Convention was founded and its futile mission embraced in Dakar. Hamad Karzai was born and Jean Sibelius died.

This was the wide world into which the brand new *Cantabs* would be stepping from the Fellows' Garden in Downing.

After graduation I stupidly neglected most of my Cambridge contacts. It took thirty years in South Africa and North America before a personal reconnection with Downing occurred. In the 1980s, I decided to show our sons, Per and Niels, the treasures of Cambridge while on a trip to Denmark and parts of Europe. My wife Judy already knew Cambridge from her visits in the late 60s to see a South African boyfriend, Chris von Christierson, with whom she was an undergraduate at Rhodes University in South Africa. As I walked with the family through those familiar old cast iron gates of Downing from Regent Street, I was stunned by the new splendor of the *domus*. It had evolved magnificently through additions of new buildings to become a neo-classical architectural gem, true to the 18th century vision of William Wilkins and later the great Sir Herbert Baker. Since my day, the three wings of the quad had been made whole by the addition of a chapel, true to the clean, sand stone lines of Herbert Baker. The quad's horse chestnuts and linden trees had grown to add majestic

canopies over the main walkways, framing the view of pristine lawns
stretching to the open *Paddock* and the spire of the Catholic Church
beyond. Exotic plantings throughout the college gardens and along
thoroughfares had matured. There were new Howard and Kenny courts
each with their own intimate gardens. A beautiful, relatively ornate Howard
Building (employing Corinthian columns, rather than simple Ionic and
Doric capitals) for large gatherings and conferences was a major addition
made in the 1980's. Also added was a spectacular new octagonal college
library in pink and gold Ketton limestone, the variety favored by Sir
Herbert Baker and Quinlan Terry the prominent neo-classical architect of
the late 20th century. Ketton limestone offers lovely pinks and gold which
spring to life and glow the moment sunlight touches it.

In published reports on Cambridge developments, I learned that the
academic, cultural and athletic performance of the college had also
blossomed, catapulting Downing into the highest echelon of Cambridge
colleges. It had leaped to prominence on the list of most-coveted colleges
in terms of admitted applicants—undergraduate entry to Cambridge is via
admission to a college, not to the University itself. In my day, Downing
had been little more than an "also ran" among eighteen peer colleges.

Pivotal in this transformation was the charismatic leadership of John
Butterfield, preeminent physician and pioneering teacher of medicine at
Cambridge. He was a promoter of athletics and civic awareness in the
college and throughout Cambridge. His presence and personal approach
to junior members of the college promoted elitism in its noblest sense: a
commitment to be among the best, making the most of native talents
while contributing to the community. The *esprit de corps* of Downing and
the performance of its student body were set afire. The college became a
leader in academic, sporting, and cultural arenas of the university.
Butterfield had been an undergraduate at Oxford, where he had read
medicine and was a triple *Blue* in rugby, cricket, and field hockey—a singular accomplishment. He earned a higher medical degree at Cambridge,
where he went on to become head of all medicine and developed

Addenbrooks as a teaching hospital. He was elected Master of Downing College, Vice-Chancellor of the University in the 1970s, knighted by the Queen, and was eventually elevated to Britain's peerage as Lord Butterfield of Stechford. I got to know him as a warmly engaging man before he died in attempted retirement. He continued to dine regularly in Hall. His appetite for and personal interface with undergraduates and alumni and his interest in their careers was insatiable, so he continued to be a sought-after adviser in college.

Other *fellows* were catalysts for the remarkable metamorphosis of the college. A senior tutor, Frank Wild, had made the college a bastion of the Natural Sciences; John Hopkins, university lecturer in law, was a champion of many stellar legal careers, so many of his protégés now thrive in London's Inns of Court and City law firms. The wish of the founder, Baron George Downing of Gamlingay, expressed in the words on the college foundation stone, has been truly honored; Downing College had built a great reputation in medicine and the law. The Baron's plea for the "cultivation of religion" did not do equally well.

In the summer of 1957, the extraordinary adventure had come to an end. A bittersweet farewell, perhaps, but it was time to leave the Cambridge cocoon for the real world. I had wanted to become a barrister in London, but the system in those days required that one obtain a *pupilage* with "a barrister of repute." It was a kind of apprenticeship and introduction to the role of the *clerks of the courts*, who were crucial conduits to obtaining briefs and making a living in the profession. A barrister of sufficient repute would demand at least 350 pounds sterling up front, and you had little hope of meaningful income for the first year or two as you learned the workings of the Inns of Court and gained the necessary introductions. I had 14 pounds left at graduation, after splitting my residual surplus of 28 pounds with John, and there could never be thought of asking for more parental help. Our parents, having lost everything during the war, had given up so much for our education before considering their own rather modest retirement plans. So I needed to make some money by getting to work, promptly, but only after a final academic summer vacation on my parents' account.

The day after graduation, *Mor*, Helle, and I loaded up my now modest belongings in the old family Austin Somerset and set off on a rambling tour starting appropriately in the low country of Flanders, the land of the Flemings, then on through West Germany, and then home to Denmark. The ferry from Harwich delivered us to terra firma at Hoek van Holland on the continent, where we set course for Koln, across the Flemish delta country, skirting the industrial Ruhr region to the north, determined to reach the Rhine's best scenery and alluring wine lands as soon as possible.

The scenic glory of Germany is widely underrated. Vistas of precipitous vineyards, tiny villages along the banks of romantic the Rhine and Mosel are unmatched around the world. Mosel Riesling vines from manicured slopes rising at a sixty-degree angle from the river at Bernkastel promise the most refreshing, flowery reward to the palate of passing travelers. If you survive the siren calls of Loreley as you head south along the Rhine, the enchanting east bank town of Rudesheim am Rhein beckons and there your wine is poured from tall, longnecked brown bottles as opposed to the equally elegant green glass of the Mosel. The route turned northwest through huge forests, rolling hills, and arable valleys to historic Marburg and its fairytale castle, *Marburger Schloss*, perched atop the medieval timberwork town. Centuries earlier it was a place to pause on the trade route from Koln to Prague; later Marburg was home to the earliest activist Protestants promoting the Reformation. Further north was Kassel, at one time also a beautiful historic city of stern Calvinist philosophy with its attendant harsh judgments. However, in 1943, it was bombed to smithereens by the Allies. The wooded Hartz Mountains, where lovely gorges and lakes abound, are the highest in northern Germany, crowned by the renowned peak named the *Brocken*. It is to this very mountain (called Bloksberg in Denmark) that legendary Danish witches flee death in the flames of bonfires on the beaches of Denmark on *Sankt Hans Eve*, midsummer's night, riding their broomsticks to safety. The border of

Communist East Germany ran only a few miles east of the idyllic mountain villages of Goslar and Bad Harzburg.

On the way home, straight northward toward the Danish border, the scenery changes to heathland in the German coastal plains along the North Sea and the Baltic. An overnight stop in ancient Schneverdingen revealed the town's history of occupations by Swedes and Danes in bygone times of Nordic power. A stopover in Hamburg at the elegant *Hotel Vier Jahreszeiten* brought a refreshing stein or two of good German *pils* while enjoying views of the adjacent lake, a boat trip on the River Elbe, Germany's gateway, via the North Sea, to the Atlantic. We shared glimpses of magnificent riverside mansions and the starchy Arian snobbery of the Hamburg Yacht Club. It was hard to imagine that much of this grand community had once been Danish before 1864, when the Prussians took Schleswig-Holstein. It was even more difficult to realize that almost the whole of Hamburg was a heap of rubble after allied bombing barely a decade before.

A day's easy driving took us up the coastline of the North Sea, past the fancy summer resort island of Sylt, where wealthy Germans from all over the country took their holidays among soft white dunes and sea grass, relaxing in the wide open space of endless silver beaches. North of the border was Denmark's oldest town, Ribe, a Viking settlement from the 9th century, where the first Danish Christians built their church three hundred years later. That church eventually became Denmark's first cathedral, which now stands in the center of the idyllic town, its houses almost perfectly preserved externally from the time of its restoration after a massive fire in 1585. From Ribe it took only five hours to reach Copenhagen and home, crossing the whole country from west to east via the bridge from Jutland to Funen, and the ferry from Funen to Zealand.

My last eight-week vacation enjoyed in Denmark was spent in the bosom of family, this time including both parents for several weeks, and the *hyggelig* Danish environment I had grown to love so deeply. It was the last vacation of more than two consecutive weeks I was to spend in that homeland—or anywhere for that matter.

Chapter VIII

From Bowe Bells to the Brollie Brigade

"I have never let my schooling interfere with my education."
Mark Twain

I HAD BEEN extremely fortunate to be given access to the best academic education my finite talent and intellect could absorb, retain and apply. By far the most important lesson learned at Cambridge was my enduring comprehension of the narrow limits to my knowledge and experience, how little I knew then—and now. Enormous gaps remained in my education and preparation for the real world and the realities of life as an adult, outside the coddled world of academia and away from domestic family care.

At Cambridge, I had not always aimed to be a barrister. During my early, naïvely idealistic days, I thought of teaching or maybe working for the UN, perhaps one of its larger agencies. Over time, with fewer stars in my eyes, and as the questioning of teenage and student preconceptions hardened, some of the naïveté and wishful thinking lost traction. Law, jurisprudence and applied economics studies along with life's real challenges and current world affairs had their edifying impact. Interaction with so many people of different beliefs, traditions and values had spawned new aspirations. Some reasoned understanding of the forces driving technological, social and economic progress emerged. New views on social priorities evolved. The notion that all men are born equal was forcefully challenged by realities because evident inequality, in terms of individuals' native capacities, seemed inescapable. Egalitarianism had generally been displaced by a superior concept of promoting equality of access to all the prerequisite tools for contributing citizenship; improving security for individuals and their property; protecting their right to make choices and ensuring equality of treatment under the law.

Equality of opportunity, access to education and medical care, along with access to other needed tools had taken over as priorities. Attempted policies of social engineering and legislated redistribution of physical assets were discredited. It seemed indisputable that creating access to education and the protection of a sustainable social safety net both have to be funded by society's creation of incremental wealth—yes, by some level of taxes on that wealth! The world's population was increasing rapidly, so the aggregate pot of global wealth had to be expanded, rather than politically redistributed. Studies and observation had demonstrated that when existing wealth is excessively redistributed away from its creators, it generally ends up in the hands of either unqualified people or government agencies, both of whom cause waste and inadequate improvement in the plight of man or the equality being sought. It was seen to rob productive Peter to pay dependent Paul. Abe Lincoln, after all, made it clear: Social engineering in a much broader sense could be productively applied to influence citizens' behavior in necessary and progressive ways. For example, legislation to hinder and discourage anti-social behavior—a needed form of social engineering. Equal treatment before the law is essential; it is neither unrealistic nor unsustainable. Different religions, which aim to influence their believers' behavior for the benefit of the community—another form of social engineering—does not have to be counterproductive. But the use of excessive legislated wealth redistribution in the name of equity is futile, as are so many illogical attempts to mandate that all men and women be equal.

Incremental wealth was understood to be created by adding value to the world's natural, technological and human resources. This broadly meant putting the *factors of production* to work. My mentor, EGK, back in my Gresham's days, had made that pretty clear. Idris Glyn Jones's book, *Essentials of Economics*, had explained how the creation of wealth (*production*) required that resources (*land, labor, capital*), and organization (*enterprise*) be enlisted.

To me, that meant "business," and "industry," and it meant seeking "profits," the big generic evils that dominated the thinking and policies of the left in the post-World War II era. Pennies had begun to drop for me. Personal priorities and ambitions were gradually redefined, new aspirations to succeed both materially and as a contributing citizen emerged. So, by the time it was obvious that the London barrister route was out of reach, going into industry was becoming an attractive and inspiring alternative. Besides, making a living and achieving financial independence were *conditio sine qua non*. No modern-day *gap year* for me: I had to get a job, simply to make a living, promptly. Nobody in my family had significant industrial, legal or banking experience, and my father's career in planting could teach me little, so I was embarking on an uncharted odyssey.

The final weeks prior to graduation had been full of conversations with both peer group friends and mentors about careers and where to start. Obviously both undergraduates and teachers varied infinitely in their views and recommendations. Suggestions ranged from academic or scientific research to the professions, government service to business and commerce. Unsurprisingly, intellectual and class snobbery were not entirely beyond the range of suggestions. One English literature *don* told his protégé that he must not stray from the precious life of letters, that he should not be lured away by vain promises of wealth, power and privilege. A philosophy professor warned against politics and government service, where narcissism and ambition inevitably vanquished ideals.

"Enrich your life, my dear boy, transfigure your life as a *WHOLE*, by submerging yourself in history and the literature it inspires!"

"A lawyer's life is so drab … please don't miss what a real life has to offer … lawyers spend all their energy in futile attempts at curing criminality, reversing self-imposed mistakes or the follies of other men. Soul-destroying!"

"You simply can't go into *industry*, dear chap. You can't consider any place where they actually *MAKE* things. That's a horrible life spent around soulless machines in filthy factories, in dreary cities, where dirty pubs and football games are the pinnacle of social intercourse and cultural life."

"The publicity and advertising world is the place to be. Comfortable surroundings! It's a civilized people business, where ideas count and your education is put to work … and, you know, they throw a lot of marvelous cocktail parties," said a member of the Pitt Club.

The university-sponsored career counseling office took me nowhere. It was not the place to seek a sensible starting point for a career in law, finance, industry or commerce. On the other hand, it was useful and quite effective for brilliant graduates who emerged with *Firsts*, headed for the Foreign Service, the Colonial Office, academic careers, or even scientific research appointments in industry. It was a bureaucratic endeavor that worked well with other bureaucracies. In its work, it confused activity with effectiveness. The Cambridge University Appointments Board's work expanded until its available resources were exhausted, irrespective of results. A living iteration of Parkinson's Law.

Much more useful were the notes I had kept from the Swaziland trip taken just before my final year at Downing. At the cocktail party celebrating the opening of the irrigation canal, which PB had built at Ngonini Citrus Estate, he had introduced me to Bryan Smither, a prominent South African banker and captain of industry from Johannesburg.

After the guests attending the canal opening had departed, including the Swazi king, seated on the floor in my parents' living room next to the armchair in which Brian had parked himself with scotch in hand, I was impressed with this quietly spoken, warmly engaged and interesting man. First, he declared that a Cambridge education was more universally acclaimed than I could ever imagine. He said that my degree would always open doors around the world because everyone knew that neither Cambridge nor Oxford admitted dummies. Second, it became clear to me that he had a passion for engaging young people of whom he thought well, often steering them towards one of the many enterprises in which he was engaged. So I jumped at his invitation to keep the notes he jotted down for me regarding introductions to some business colleagues and contacts in London. Later that evening, my eyes boggled at his list of names, all industry chieftains or leading bankers and lawyers to whom he would introduce me if I chose to follow up. They were leaders of blue chip icons like Unilever, ICI, Thomas de la Rue, Shell, Courtaulds, Metal Box Company, Baring Brothers and Barclay's Bank. Bryan chatted away, discussing South African and world events in a relaxed style, which only confident men can manage. He constantly came back to ask for my thoughts and aspirations. I warmed to the man, and sensed that the feeling may have been mutual.

Back in Cambridge barely a year before graduation, I wrote to each one of the men suggested by Bryan. It emerged that he had already written them notes to introduce me, in case I followed up. This led to a long series of interviews and yet another fascinating learning experience. The treatment given to job applicants varied from company to company. In pleasant meetings at Barings and Barclay's, I confined my efforts to polite conversations, undertaken out of gratitude and courtesy to Bryan, because finance had never really caught my imagination, and I thought my quantitative skills fell short of the requirements ... thanks in part to botched teaching of math at Gresham's. In the course of my career I later got to know Barings quite well and realized I could have enjoyed working with them in the world of mergers and acquisitions, private equity or international banking. I discovered that Bryan was Chairman of Barclay's South Africa, and that he was Barings' representative in the southern part of the continent. He was also on the board of Metal Box South Africa.

It was the industrial world of manufacturing that attracted me at this time, naïvely underestimating the pivotal role of financial institutions in the welfare and progress of the world. I had concluded that companies like ICI, Metal Box, Unilever and Courtaulds were enterprises that added more value to society by actually producing physical products and consumer services, thus creating incremental wealth—generating growth in terms of capital, employment and resources. I recalled with amusement the words of the Cambridge *don*, who had warned against seeking a career in a "place where they actually *MAKE* things!" I was victim to a false perception that people in the financial services industry tended to make too much of their living by simply taking cuts out of other people's deals! Naïve, perhaps, but not totally inaccurate.

The industrial folk had differing styles. ICI invited short-listed applicants to spend a weekend at their countryside mansion, a kind of conference center, where they spied on us to evaluate our behavior in the group, check how we held a knife and fork, and whether we put our elbows on the dining room table while eating. I learned that they noted whether you used the term "napkin" or "serviette." Snobs, I thought. Courtaulds' executives, on the other hand, seemed somewhat superficial in their approach to recruiting, with an undue interest in the pedigree of applicants. I wondered if they, too, were snobs. For some long forgotten reason I was not inspired by De La Rue's business of printing bank notes and playing cards. In fact, Andy Mulligan eventually took a job with them in a PR role. At first blush, I really liked Unilever's strong international emphasis and infinite product range, but they suddenly insisted that I commit to relinquishing my Danish citizenship to become a Brit. They knew I was entitled to British nationality because of my birthplace, Penang, a *crown colony* of His Imperial Majesty in 1936. I had read and believed

Unilever's full-page recruiting advertisements in *The Times*, and *The Daily Telegraph* in which they claimed to be seeking "talent, initiative and competence, irrespective of citizenship, race, color and creed." Perceptions of their internationalism proved to be exaggerated. Their personnel managers were all Brits who wore bowler hats and carried tightly wrapped umbrellas, a City uniform I came to despise. Unilever's interest in a young Danish man born in Malaya, with a refugee history in Australia and partly educated in Denmark, waned abruptly when I made it clear that I would remain a Dane.

Metal Box Company appealed most and captured my imagination. To my mind, they were real industrialists, very people-oriented and had a well-conceived "Graduate Management Trainee Program." Their down-to-earth personnel management communicated well and was committed to a sophisticated training protocol designed to develop a versatile pool of talent. Trainees were exposed to all facets of the business and its complex dynamics over a period of eighteen months, and then tested in an entry-level job deemed to match a given set of talents before assignment to a longer term position with responsibilities. No degree from an elite university or top business school could match the Metal Box graduate program as preparation for the rough and tumble of industry and commerce. It was a real-world extension of academic education.

The interview process consisted of conversations with a range of managers. Reflecting the company's approach to the value of training, the first interview was with the chairman of the board, Sir Robert Barlow, and includeed factory visits for conversations with plant managers, shift supervisors and union representatives. It was clear that the personnel people received feedback from these visits. Fortunately, the process culminated in an offer. Along the way, I had wondered what life would be like in the prosaic packaging business. Food and beverage cans, paint containers, tin boxes, and canisters for groceries and baked goods, aerosols, plastic detergent or cosmetic bottles and toothpaste tubes—these were hardly sexy products. The manufacture of packaging appeared initially to be more closely associated with dreary cities and dirty pubs than comfortable surroundings and marvelous cocktail parties. However, the packaging of branded consumer goods is far from prosaic. It is an infinitely diverse industry, which addresses intriguing aspects of processing and preserving, distribution and marketing of durable as well as perishable goods. Its viability rests on expertise in areas ranging from bacteriology, engineering, materials chemistry, electronics, logistics, financial management expertise, unforgiving quality standards, all the way through to unswerving discipline in hygiene and environmental accountability. The industry's direct and indirect markets are global, which explains why its major players are so international in their deployment and reach. The industry is a little known but essential link in the provision of food and other consumer goods to satisfy the needs of billions, rich and poor, educated or not, and thus an invaluable part of the global social fabric.

I was unaware that Bryan Smither, as a director of Metal Box's South African subsidiary, had suggested to its chairman, John Baxter, that the parent company be told that they wanted to try me out in a Johannesburg job after my traineeship and a stint at an entry level job in the UK. So, once again, I was embarking on a new process of education in the practicalities and dynamics of industry, not knowing I might be on a path to a career in the antipodes.

Eighteen months of real-world exposure and learning started on October 1, 1957. The first factory assignment was for three months in the East End of London, in an old tin box factory located in the Cockney heartland of Hackney, sooty and surrounded by smog-darkened slums, deep in poverty within earshot of Bowe Bells, as a true Cockney locale must be. The grimy brown-brick factory building was a cherished source of work and income for 600 Cockneys, where it produced a wide range of tinplate containers for non-perishable consumer products that do not require processing at high temperatures and pressures. It was a relatively low tech plant using mostly semi-automatic hand-fed machinery, in contrast to the more sophisticated plants where a single production line would make sanitary cans for processed foods and beverages at speeds of 600 cans per minute, overseen by a single person. Hackney had lost much of its industrial base to automation and new technology, which allowed manufacturing to move to more attractive areas. Metal Box's old factory, with its dependence on manual and experience-based skills, was a source of income and hope to its 600 people in an otherwise destitute part of London.

My allotted digs were in deeply blue-collar Walthamstow at the edge of Epping Forest, a twenty-minute bus ride from work. I had a minute room, almost completely filled by a rickety single bed with a mattress shaped like a hammock, a nightstand, a small closet, and one spindly old dining chair. There was no writing table, which meant using the kitchen table downstairs when necessary. The only bathroom in the tiny brick row house was shared by all three inhabitants. My landlords were a married couple born and raised on the very same street, Ulverston Road. The rent was eleven pounds a month, including *high tea* served when I got home at night around seven o'clock (no breakfast, as one had to be on the way to work by six a.m.). The weekly bus fares cost just under a pound. A solid meal at the factory would cost me two shillings and sixpence. The subsidized lunch was an absolute necessity: big portions of bangers-'n-mash or fish-'n-chips with the odd carrot or half a dozen peas thrown in. Alternatively, pilchard in tomato sauce on toast; a hefty ham-'n-cheese sandwich or "French toast" would cost half the price. The half hour *underground* return trip fare from Walthamstow to the West End was half a crown, my path back to "civilization" over a weekend. That's what the *tube* trip cost when I wanted to draw breath on a Saturday, see some of my chums, enjoy a half-decent meal and a few pints of bitter in less drab surroundings. The alternative bus fare was exactly half that, but took three times as long. All of these essentials had to come out of a monthly starting salary of 37 pounds, ten shillings and sixpence after some small deductions. A trainee's life in a preeminent British industrial company was not that of a fat cat. It was an early reality check.

If Cambridge was isolated from the real world, life in Hackney and Walthamstow quickly made up for realizations missed in the ivory tower of academia. It offered unfiltered observation of deprivation patiently endured by people working for a livelihood just above western subsistence level. The indomitable spirit, feelings, and the very essence of ordinary people in everyday life: love, hate, jealousy, patience, courage, stoicism, generosity, fairness, enterprise, tenacity, ambition, cheating, parasitism, crime, sickness, tears, humor, laughter—they were all in the mix. The commitment to community, individual responsibility and mutual caring by far outweighed the antisocial behavior that is unavoidable in communities of deep poverty. All of these, right in my face, every single day for a hundred days. How can education in truth be consummate without some comparable childhood exposure or experience in early adulthood? Even after a wartime childhood and vicarious exposure to starvation, deprivation, and disease in Asia and Africa, this assignment to Hackney was a startling wakeup call. People generally understood and taught their children that arrogance, impatience, instant gratification, selfishness, greed, complacency and self-pity serve them poorly; a lesson sometimes missed in the raising of children further up the social ladder.

After the brief orientation at Metal Box Limited's "Head Office" in Baker Street, the personnel people instructed me to report to the manager of Hackney Branch at 7:30 on a Monday morning, for my first day of work. After checking into my digs on that Sunday night, I made sure I could be at the factory by seven o'clock ... just to be safe! The Cockney night watchman, about to go home at the end of his 12-hour shift, showed me to a chair in a barren hallway outside the branch manager's office. At 7:30 sharp, the man arrived, sweeping straight past me without a glance in my direction. Not a nod, nor a word. He disappeared into his office, leaving the door wide open. He was a stubby, bald man with a monk's rim of heavily trimmed black hair, small rimless glasses, Hitler moustache, wearing a worn, shiny pinstriped suit, starched white shirt, and a plain black tie as wide as a garden trowel. Not sure what to do, I sat tight for a bit and just waited. After all, he could not have missed seeing me on the way in. After 15 minutes, I gingerly approached his open office door and tapped timidly on the door frame. No reaction. His head was firmly down, glaring at a spreadsheet smothered in numbers. After standing stock still for a minute or so, I cautiously tapped again. Barely moving his head, only his eyes rolled up from his sheet of figures.

> "Now, what the 'ell would YOU be doin' around 'ere at this toime of dai?" he growled in his barely blunted Cockney accent.

> "Good morning, sir!" I said. "They told me to report to you here in your office at 7:30 this morning."

Another long silence followed while he returned to the numbers for what seemed an eternity before again looking up at me, this time with head lifted, his face completely expressionless.

> "I s'pose you wouldn't knauw whoy I left you sittin' out there, now would ya?"

> "No, sir, I can't say that I know the answer to that."

> "Well, Mr. Fancy Pants Caaaimbridge gradu-ite, I'm just maikin' it clear that we down't need no bloody gradu-ites at this factory, nor do we need the loikes of you in the rest of the fuckin' company oither. We're doin' roight well as it is, wivout your 'igh-follutin' degrees and theeries. 'Ave I mide myself cleeer? You jus' get your edukited arse down to Alf in the press shop, and ask for the broom. Alf'll knaow the drill. Then you clean up the 'ole bloody shop ... so clean, that the girls can eat their lunch roight off the fuckin' floor.

Understand that, Mr. 'Oilmann? I'll be down there m'self by lunchtoime, to see what your lousy degree's done f' ya on the job ... ha ha ha, and what it'll do for the rest of us 'ere in 'Ackney Branch."

Baptism by fire.

I extricated myself anxiously from his office and made my way to the press shop, asking for directions along the way, but I did not set eyes on the manager again for a whole month. He never showed up, as threatened, that first lunch break, to check my cleaning job on the press shop floor. Nevertheless, his direct influence and direction was clearly evident in every action taken, every decision made throughout the plant. The man was extremely competent, regarded by everyone as hellish tough, but always fair. He was well respected despite his unsympathetic style. Legend had it that the branch manager had worked his way up the traditional ladder, starting work in the factory at age sixteen, when he too cleaned the press shop floor for Alf's predecessor. My decreasingly menial tasks around the factory never really called for any contact with the branch manager's office, but he had obviously defined every element of my training program in his factory.

Alf was the current press shop foreman. He was an affable little Cockney, with a big heart and a messy home-rolled cigarette perpetually hanging on his lower lip waiting to be re-lit. He greeted me warmly with a knowing smile. Alf indeed knew the drill and simply handed me a wide broom with hard steel bristles and a very large dust pan. It was reassuring to know that someone had gone through this before me and presumably survived. First step was to pick up and remove waste tinplate shreds and trimmings from the presses to huge recycling bins. After working the broom, the next task was to scrub the oily film of grime on the blackened wood block floor. After a couple of hours Alf told me to empty the scrap bins full of spent metal sheets from which thousands of container components had been stamped, leaving interesting metal webs with patterns of round and rectangular holes. The branch manager was quite right: the press shop did not need any fucking graduates to fix anything. Everything was working pretty damned well, I thought, as I labored on.

The score of "girls" operating the tinplate presses ranged from chattering teenagers to hefty senior women who looked as if they could bite through a coconut. Every one of them wore a scarf tied tightly around the head, over their ears and knotted in a bow at the front, high over their brows. They giggled, joked, and pointed as they paused to watch me go about my initiation, a routine all too familiar to them. I gave it my all, every bit of elbow grease I could muster, so by ten o'clock it was absolutely impossible to remove one more molecule of grime from the floor. Years of grease, oil and dirty boot leather had left an indelible, sticky-black coating. At the tea break, Alf called me into his cubbyhole office, where two steaming mugs were waiting. He finally lit his expectant cigarette butt and then pulled out a couple of tattered old hardcover books that looked like photo albums. They were operating manuals for Bliss metal presses, machines which came in all sizes and capacities. Bliss machines were the workhorses of the *general line* manufacturing segment of the metal packaging industry, where semi-automatic presses, metal bending machines, and some hand assembly ruled. Alf heaped several loads of sugar into his tea and handed me the spoon, suggesting I should gain some understanding of the machines and the processes they facilitated.

> "Oi'll give you a crack at workin' a couple of 'em durin' ya time 'ere in the shop," he said after sipping his tea and drawing deeply on his cigarette, "saow you moight as well knaow a bit about the kit you see out there. You'll also 'ave to learn 'ow to grease 'em up, and keep them buggers runnin'"

He patted me on the shoulder and returned to the shop floor. Huddled in Alf's office, I spent the rest of the day studying the workings of these simple but versatile machines. I skipped the canteen lunch, as my first paycheck was only due at the end of the week and cash was running low. A hefty *high tea* would be waiting for me back in Walthamstow at the end of my first day in the throbbing heart of British industry. I knew I would not go to bed hungry.

Americans misuse the term *high tea*, having no inkling of what constitutes high tea in the daily lives of millions of Brits. It is the main meal at the end of the workingman's day. Fried eggs, fried bread, fried bacon, sausage, chops, or ham, with *chips*—French fries—and lots of HP Sauce and hot English mustard, along with bread-and-butter heaped with jam out of a large tin. Huge ceramic mugs of tea with lots of milk and sugar. Either grilled tomatoes, cabbage, parsnips, peas or mashed potatoes would represent the vegetable kingdom. High tea in England never had any re- semblance to mid-afternoon tea taken by the upper classes, where elegantly sliced cucumber or tomato sandwiches, anchovy toast, or scones with cream were teatime fare. These are the elegant ingredients of a genteel afternoon tea in the drawing rooms and clubhouses of privileged England, complete with fine china cups held with the right hand pinkie pointed in the air. American social climbers trying to impress tend to get this terminology quite wrong.

My landlady did me proud. I never ever went hungry. She fed me the outrageously high fat, high carb, high calorie diet of delicious British work- man's fare. Mrs. Wiggins and hubby Henry were kind, even-tempered folk, who said very little to each other or to me. She was always humming to herself: *Land of Hope and Glory, Rule Britannia* or *Greensleaves* very softly, ever patriotic and always right on key.

Elgar, Thomas Arne, and perhaps even Henry VIII would have been proud of her. On Sundays, the repertoire would switch to hymns like *Oh God, our Help in Ages Past*, or *All Things Bright and Beautiful*. 'Enry Wiggins was far from gregarious, his nose forever buried in the sports pages of the tabloids, where he would arduously study the horses and league football standings and fixtures, making notes and preparing for his weekly visit to the bookmaker. 'Enry would bet on his selected horses and play the football pools. The anticipation would occasionally prompt him to utter a few words in excitement.

> "Tonoit's me noit for some fun, y' know! Oi reeely fancy this 'orse called *O 'Reilly's Daughter*, so Oi'll 'ave a bit'v a flutter on this young mare tomorra. If she lets me daown, Chelsea mai do it for me in the pools boi beatin' Arsenal. Ya can't winnem all, can you now? But Oi feel real good abaout the mare … and the odds are Ow Kai. Anywaaiy, Oi can't loose anyfin' on a couple o' points o' Fullers at the pub, can Oi?"

These transactions were rituals every Friday evening, his *pink-ticket* of the week, when he had his night out at the Stag's Head with his chums. He would slowly sip two or three pints of bitter at its tepid best in the course of two or three hours.

> "A point 'n haour ain't overdoin' it," Henry would assure me. "And Oi can just abaout afford that."

Henry was the strong and silent type of his peer group, but would have more to say in one evening at the Stag's Head than he would utter the rest of the week at home. Mrs. Wiggins worked at the post office next door, five hours a day, three days a week, spending the rest of her life well within a five hundred yard radius of the row house. Woolworths, the local grocer and the newsstand defined the outer boundaries of her routine life. Closer to home she would chat and drink tea with the neighboring ladies of Ulverston Road, expanding on new tidbits of gossip. She was the only one who never went to the flicks, so she was socially at a disadvantage. The couple's married life, from my observation, was not enriched by much conversation, or by visits from children or grandchildren. From time to time I saw a glint in Henry's eye, staring at full-page photos on page three of the tabloid where scantily clad girls were featured every day of the week. Nocturnal sound effects bouncing about the tiny row house suggested that the physical aspects of matrimony were looked after on Sunday nights after a good weekend of rest and relaxation.

As the first week of training at the Hackney factory progressed, so did my tasks in Alf's press shop. My time was spent recording hourly production, tracking waste percentages, scheduling plain or printed tinplate deliveries from the warehouse and measuring statistically sampled stampings or components with a micrometer for quality control purposes. Every component had to be within tight dimensional tolerances to ensure a good fit with containers or other components. Machine maintenance schedules had to be checked. As promised, on the last day Alf had a press set up for me to operate. He gave me a short demonstration and showed me the stamp-and-release pedal, which advanced the tinplate sheet with every stroke of the press. A batch of components would drop out of the machine into a receiving bin below. After a few minutes, I was ready to go on my own. By this time, the whole press shop had fallen silent. The machines stopped and all twenty women sat dead still on their stools.

In silence, the girls watched my every move until the giggling broke out. I gingerly pressed the pedal to trigger a single stroke of the stamping operation. Escalating hoots from the press shop chorus; more hysterical giggles, as eighteen little tin box lids dropped into the bin below the press. Another bang, clank and the next batch of lids appeared. Then a short series of strokes, so I thought I was doing pretty well, but the girls were now howling with mirth, rolling around on their stools. I couldn't fathom what on earth the big joke was, and therefore simply carried on, increasingly efficient and comfortable with the process, but a little distracted and embarrassed by the antics of the girls.

The whole scene was apparently a well-established ritual performed whenever a trainee completed his week in the press shop: My press had been loaded up with printed sheet for the labeled lids on little Durex tins for retailing premium latex condoms destined for a million pharmacies and shop shelves across the world. Durex was easily the leading British brand of condoms, and only their top-of-the-line product was marketed in little tin boxes. It became clear that this was the cause for hilarity. The girls cheered my accomplishment, some asserting that I must have earned a Cambridge Ph.D. in birth control by condom. The cockneys called them *french letters*, for a reason I never learned. "Tee hee hee!" A nubile teenage girl called me "Flemming, *love*" and quite unabashedly invited me home "for tea and a little bit of fun." More shrieks and guffaws.

> "'E should be saaif enough wif you, dearie!" commented a more mature but voluptuous woman wearing a very tight sweater. "Too bloody saaif for what Oi fink the man needs!—If 'e reely fancies a good roll in the haiiy, 'e betta 'ave tea at 'ome wif meee! Oi've got plenty o' crumpet 'n all!" Turning to me she announced, "You're comin' 'ome wif me then, aren't you, darlin'?"

Production resumed after a few more moments of playful taunts and laughs. But subliminally those few moments caused a distinct change in my relationship with the whole labor force and supervisors in the Hackney factory. A new warmth crept into my relationship with the press shop girls and the interface with people all around the plant. Six hundred cockneys seemed to know I had been through the ringer and took notice of how I reacted. For sure, I had not become one of them, but I was now somehow treated as part of the scenery, not just a tolerated alien presence.

Alf and I became good friends, but the connection sadly did not survive beyond the months spent together in London's East End. Nevertheless, short relationships can be deep and can make a lasting impression on personal views and values. He taught me a lot by example and via his reasoned opinions, usually delivered without any direct attempt at persuasion. Alf set high personal standards and was faithful to solid values rooted in the practicalities of his solid family life and his determination to make progress by working hard and being tenacious. He had strong views on the role of family structure; he had equally strong views on the hypocrisy of politicians publicly touting family values while "fucking the whores and tarts of Westminster."

Alf took me to football on Saturday afternoons and folded me into his group of chums among the tens of thousands at White Hart Lane cheering on the *Tottenham Hotspurs*. Their logo depicting a cockerel atop a soccer ball was everywhere in a sea of navy blue and white. In those mid-fifties days, the fans were as loyal and numerous as they ever would be; there was a deep love and informed appreciation of the game itself, which has not exactly characterized the hooligans of British soccer in more recent times. Our tickets gave us happy communion with surrounding Spurs fans, standing in the packed open stand sipping sparingly from jumbo size bottles of Fuller's, which had to last through the first half of the game. Expert fans screamed profane commentary on the Spurs' mistakes, but the atmosphere was light and convivial, even in the proximity of opposing supporters. There were no fights. If the police were present, they were not noticeable.

Occasionally, on a Saturday night after football, Alf took me on a long, slow pub crawl in the West End, an adventure Alf characterized as a *bender*. His favorite area was south of Oxford Street between King's Cross Station and the streets of Soho near Carnaby Street, where the avant-garde designers of the day were launching a new fashion. Alf would enjoy window shopping, studying the details of goods priced way beyond his means (and, of course, mine at the time).

> "Eh, tike a butcher's at that spivvy coat wiv a velvet collar and lapels, and them there Teddy Boy trousers! Moi boy would love to 'ave that outfit. 'E would be so chuffed if Oi could afford to give 'im suffin' loike that for 'is birfday."

After an hour or so he would be hungry.

> "I'm feelin' a wee bit peckish now. It's time for some grub, Flemmin' ... and the nosh is reeely graait at The Lion's 'ead, and the beer ain't bad niver."

We talked about his family, football, and occasionally politics over a couple of pints. In the context of current welfare legislation and unemployment benefits being debated nationally, Alf expressed his views on society.

"We just aain't all maaide equal, so why the fuck pretend we are? It's the saaime in the bloody jungle, aain't it? Only in the jungle nowbody's pretending—the big toiger just gobbles up the little monkey, and nowbody's one bit surproised! The cleverer monkeys keep themselves saaif and daon't get bloody caught. At work, Oi maaid it to foreman 'cos Oi'm smarter, fank the Lord 'n Oi didn't moind startin' boi sweepin' the fuckin' floor, for starters—'n I work 'arder van a lot o' people! Some 'ave what it taaikes and 'ave some guts—uvers just 'aven't got noiver and are too fucking lazy to learn. Ya know, some 'v us are laaizy and some 'v us aain't! Some 'v us are smart, and some ain't. No use complaainin', is it? You just 'ave to get on wivvit, and give it what you got. Aain't that right, Flemmin'? That's what Oi saaiy to me own boys ... just get on wivvit! I saaai I'll give you an 'elpin 'and, if Oi can. But in the end it's up to you, son, you can't be the foreman the first daai you gao to work! You 'ave to learn as y' gao! So you 'ave to fend for ya' fuckin' self! That's what Oi tell'm! ... Cheers, old cock!"

My new friend had his own clear understanding of why, given similar opportunities, some people progress while others don't. To him it was obvious that some were better endowed than others, intellectually as well as physically. Alf often alluded to the forces of nature at work "in the bloody jungle" and talked of chiefs and Indians as he mixed his metaphors.

"Vere's got to be a top dog in the jungle. That's just naaichure at work. There aain't no room for us all at the bloody top, now is there, Flemmin'? It's barmy to fink sao! There's got to be some chiefs aroaund, so the Indians don't fuck it all up! But daon't get me wrong—if the chiefs aint no good, Indians get narked and 'ave to send 'em packin'. Get new fucking chiefs! Nuffin wrong wiv that oither once the chiefs and the Indians boaf get the 'ang of the rules."

He openly expressed his appreciation of opportunities given to him and his family by the enterprise and resources of others who were better off. Robert Barlow, who founded the original business at the Hackney factory, was a hero to Alf. He attributed his own progress and his family's modest comforts in life to the opportunities created for him and others by Mr. Barlow's business. Alf knew how Barlow, with a poor education, had himself worked and taken risks to emerge from poverty and deprivation. Working hand in hand with his wife who also had a job, Alf had made sure their boys applied themselves and worked hard to get into grammar school, a step up from the regular public school attended by the majority of local children. Had Alf lived in the USA thirty-five years later, he might have been a Reagan Democrat.

Although I never saw him, it was obvious that the Hackney branch manager made sure I spent time in all the factory's manufacturing and administrative departments. Depending on the particular foreman or supervisor, I was either given some interesting odd jobs, which challenged me at some level, or the most trivial of tasks, which were pure boredom. One department made ingenious, complicated coffee cans with a convenient built-in opening device. The foreman told me I had the week to work out the mechanics of manufacturing and assembly before writing an illustrated manual explaining the whole process for the next trainee to come through. I worked as hard to master that challenge as I ever had for any supervision paper at Cambridge.

One October evening, in 1957, the Soviets sent Sputnik into orbit. The announcement caused the whole western world, including Hackney, to come to a halt. It escaped nobody that our cold war opponents had accomplished something pivotal in the heavens above us. We all left our workstations and stood in the streets, gaping with head in air, trying to catch a glimpse of the little prick of bright light traversing London's night sky, for once clear and lit by only a sliver of a moon. Alf understood:

> "Straaike a fuckin' laaight!" exclaimed Alf, mouth agape with unlit cigarette still clinging to his lower lip as he pointed into the sky. "Crikey Moses! They're bloody clevah, those Ruskies, aren't thaaiy, Flemmin'? I reelly 'ope them Yanks can catch up wiv 'em. If not, we're all fucked. All them Europeens on the continent will become bloody commies, and we'll 'ave no 'ope in poor Ol' Smokey oither! It'll maaike the Battle o' Britain look like a lark-in-the-park on Sundai aah'ternoon! Our London bobbies and the guards at Buck 'Ouse will all be wearin' Ruskie fur caps wiff fuckin' earmuffs—no more 'elmets and busbies."

The three-month assignment raced its way to Christmas. No contrast to life at Cambridge could have been more immediate or stark. The lesson was startling because of its glaring illumination of so many social, cultural, and demographic issues. It highlighted the differences and likenesses in people of all society's strata. It demonstrated the common characteristics of good people and bad, who either contribute to or impede sustainable society. The Cockneys, given half a chance, generally persevered, even in the face of adversity; and they loved to do things well, taking enormous pride in personal accomplishment at any level. These East Enders didn't whine, they hated being dependent, they despised self-pity, took little for granted and they never stopped looking for opportunity and grasping it whenever and wherever it appeared. It was quite clear how they had survived and then recovered from Hitler's devastating blitzkrieg on London. Attitudes in Hackney and Walthamstow were overwhelmingly positive. The glass was half-full. They would have given short shrift to Denmark's *Jantelov*, had they ever come across it.

On the last day of the Hackney stint, the branch manager finally called me into his office and gave me a full fifteen minutes of his time, sending me on my way most thoughtfully. Mr. Brownley told me, in very deliberate terms, that no management books could teach me how to be an effective manager or how to lead people. He said it was all about listening, learning from experience and the mistakes you are bound to make, paying attention to detail and getting the respect of people around you. He told me how his predecessor, Mr. Robert Barlow, had thirty years earlier thrown a telephone set at him (one of the heavy old Bakelite machines) in a fit of rage, right there in that very office, to make his point in correcting some serious mistake Brownley had made as a plant superintendent. He pointed to a patch in the plastered wall to one side of his desk, where a hole had been clumsily repaired, plastered over and painted after the phone set had left its distinct mark.

"Not quoite the participative management style Mr. Barlow naow loikes to talk abaout ... but 'e maaide his fucking point, didn't 'e? I never maaide the saaime mistake agin, that's the truth," said Mr Brownley. "Son, Oi'm sort o' hopin' you've learned a lesson or two whoile you were 'ere in 'ackney. You must've made a mistake or two along the way. I knaow we don't frow no telephaones at people no more, but you moight've 'ad a few other remoinders that you bloody well don't knaow everythin'. I dare saaiy we brought you daown to earth a litt'l bit ... just loike that litt'l ol' Sputnik the other noight 'ad to come daown sometoime, somewhere ... wiv a bit of a thud, eh?"

He chuckled and showed real warmth as he patted me on the shoulder, wishing me well with the hint of a smile and a fleeting twinkle in his eye. I felt I might have passed muster.

When telling Alf about my exit interview, I learned that the Mr. Barlow, who threw the telephone, did so in the days of the small, single factory family firm, Barlow & Sons. I already knew Sir Robert (by this time knighted by the Queen) had not attended any university and had no academic qualifications of note; but it was news to me that he had cut his management teeth in this old Hackney factory of his family firm. It was the company's mother plant back in the 1920s before Barlow had assembled the group that became Metal Box Company. By 1957, he had become an acclaimed captain of British industry. Knowing more about his background, it made it easier to appreciate his national reputation for ridiculing bluster and hubris, behavior so often associated with more pompous members of his peer group in the UK.

For the next eighteen months, the trainee program imposed an itinerary through all corners of the UK except Northern Ireland. The company had 42 plants mainly converting steel and aluminum, but also alternative raw materials such as plastics and paper. In addition, many sales offices and customer service workshops, research centers and machinery building plants were included. The program exposed trainees to all company operations, its highly automated mass production of metal food and beverage cans, its engineering and machinery building organizations and, very importantly, its ground-breaking food science, microbiology and bacteriological research laboratories supporting customers in food processing and the production of an infinite array of packaged consumer goods. The training also covered functional activities from sales to personnel, from cost accounting to quality control. At the modern Wisbech food can plant in the heart of the East Anglian fens and farmlands, the young manager challenged me to seek and define a 10 percent reduction in current costs associated with all procurement, inventory management, warehousing, logistics and delivery functions. My recommendations and implementation plan were to be on his desk six weeks later. This enlightened approach to training was a contrast to the initiation in Hackney: the manager in question, Bob King, was a Cambridge rugby *Blue*, who had graduated from Pembroke College less than ten years earlier.

Metal Box's 1957 trainee intake consisted of 12 men from different universities, five of us from Cambridge or Oxford. The class of '57 was only assembled as a group for the first few days of initiation in October and then sent on individual assignments around the country. A common lesson taught was that you would quickly run into difficulties if you did not relate to the people around you. Trainees could be put into limbo, completely isolated in the organization, which would mean losing every chance of learning from the assignment.

Most of the plants were in and around the UK's murkiest industrial cities like Birmingham, Liverpool, Manchester, Neath, Glasgow or Huddersfield. However, many of these urban hellholes gave quick and easy access to some of the most attractive of England's green and pleasant land. The marvels of the English countryside were there for the asking, an easy escape from grimy-grey factories, dreary accounting offices and smog-blackened assisted housing projects. Often, our digs in depressing soot-coated row-houses were only a short bus ride from lush, verdant landscapes, hedged country lanes, and enchanting villages. The British Isles are rarely given full credit for the breathtaking variety of their countryside or grandeur of their wilderness areas of untouched nature. Intimate views of cattle browsing in carefully groomed parklands here and imposing vistas of craggy highlands there. The velvet-green, softly undulating Downs; the rugged wilderness of the Moors; the majesty of the Lake District; the mystical lochs and mountainscapes of the Highlands; the manicured parks of Buckinghamshire's estates; the bucolic coziness of the Cotswolds and the Chilterns; or the idyllic riparian villages of the Upper Thames.

Four winter months were spent in an East Yorkshire regional sales office located in Hull, on the Humber River, hard by its North Sea mouth. It is a bracing corner of the county known as the East Riding. The wind howling around my digs and their proximity to the barren Yorkshire moors invoked snowed-in *Wuthering Heights* and the wretched Heathcliff. Home was a small apartment in a riverside village called Hessle, shared with two newly hatched graduates training with other large British companies in the area. One of them was an effete fellow *Cantab*, evidently en route to a career in public relations or advertising. The other was a very bright *Oxonian* metallurgist with eclectic interests from opera to blue water sailing. Both of them spent highly social weekends chasing Yorkshire county skirts, often at fox hunts, point-to-point races or grouse-shooting parties. My own social life was predictably built around the respected Hull & East Riding Rugby Union Football Club, where I managed to make the first team. There were three evening training sessions a week, and weekends were devoted to competition and postgame entertainment of visiting teams when not playing away games all over northern England.

The generally drab city of Hull, and its even drabber climate, was home to several major paint manufacturers, fish canners drawing from the large Humberside fishing fleet, and a huge food and household products plant of the Reckitt & Colman Company. These manufacturing companies were big consumers of packaging products. Metal Box had good reason to have a major base there.

The rugby experience in the East Riding taught another series of lessons in life. The season's highlight was a tour of Scotland's Border Country to play against the then renowned Galashiels, Howick, and Kelso clubs over a long New Year's weekend. The little town of Howick extended a very special welcome. It was not only a strong rugby club, but also home to the fabulous Peel's and Pringle's cashmere knitwear factories, where hundreds of Scottish lassies worked, producing luxurious twin sets, sweaters, cardigans and jerseys. The employed girls often wore the company's own products on a daily basis, many filling them exquisitely. Scores of sweater-girls welcomed our team with literally open arms. I had just been to Copenhagen for a two day visit over Christmas, which marked an emotional, yet not traumatic, end to my long and tender romance with

Helle. So a robust New Year celebration in the Border Country tradition was to provide welcome respite and cheer, if not a sense of liberation. It was also to cause a positive change in the tenor of a social relationship, as had the experience in the Hackney factory press shop a month or two before.

Over the first couple of months at the club back in early autumn, despite the after game camaraderie and hospitality of Yorkshire rugby, there had been just the slightest sense of reserve or apprehension in the demeanor of my new teammates in their acceptance of me as a newcomer. Making direct eye contact required a little extra effort on my part. It bothered me, and I could not help pondering as to why. Was it the way I spoke? My manners? Was it my relatively privileged background and education, which had to be obvious in the East Riding? And yet some of my teammates were unabashedly free-spending, well-to-do young farmers or professionals with resources way beyond my own; so it was puzzling.

Happily, this awkwardness totally disappeared like the morning mist, in a matter of a few minutes, because of a serendipitous episode on that Scottish tour, almost three months after my arrival in Yorkshire. Our carefree, jolly post game social with the Howick team and their sweater-girl fan club took us well into the evening, involving some drinking and singing around an old, ill-tuned piano played by a burly front-row forward. The guys took it in turns to make individual vocal contributions, mostly rugby drinking songs varying in degrees of indecency, with everyone joining in the choruses. Multiple Scottish and Yorkshire toasts. Including one from East Riding's rich public house tradition.

> "Through the teeth
> And over the gums
> Look out stomach!
> 'Ere it cums!"

Eventually, there was a pause as eyes turned on me. It was my turn to step up.

My nervous and totally unanticipated solo debut before my teammates was a Danish drinking song in the mother tongue. I explained the song was about a farmer, who lost the affections of his pretty young wife to a randy, fresh-faced student while he was briefly out of the house buying beer for the evening.

> "Der var en go' gammel bondemand—
> Og han gik ud efter oel.—og han gik ud efter oel ...
> Hopsa-sa, tra-la, la-la ...
> Til konen kom der en ung student" ... and so on ...
> Hopsa-sa, tra-la, la-la"

The crowd immediately caught onto the refrain of *hopsa-sa, tra-la, la-la*, with great gusto.

Another song was about two young friends, regularly rivals for the affections of the same girl, one of whom—Jim—would always get lucky and walk off with the girl, while the other again drew the short straw. The audience understood not a word, but got the drift as both tunes had a lilt to them, so the burly pianist picked them up and everybody joined in full-throated refrains of *hop-sa-sa, hop-sa-sa - tra-la!* And that refrain was applied to every song for the rest of the evening, whether it was Danish, Scottish or from Yorkshire.

That little performance snapped whatever underlying chords of apprehension there might have been between me and the East Riding boys. Slaps on the back, arms around my shoulders—no high fives in those days. Inebriated toasts and cheers all around. The relationship was transformed for the duration. The Cambridge rookie, now seen to have let his hair down, promptly became a kindred spirit. As the evening waned, further embrace and reward was warmly bestowed by a sweet Scottish thing sheathed in cashmere.

The next trainee assignment was to industrial Merseyside, a Liverpool suburb named Speke, deep in the land of new English Skiffle, where John Lennon was cutting his teeth on a rhythm guitar. It was soon to be known as the home of the Beatles. It was a very new and different Liverpool compared with the rubble heap encountered when the *Dominion Monarch* docked there thirteen years earlier. The rebuilt city, however, was still grey, sooty and smog bound without the rubble.

With me on this assignment, there was a fellow trainee, a history graduate of Bristol University, who was to focus on the personnel department because of his stated preference for a career in human resources. The plant produced flexible plastic packaging in the form of sachets and sleeves for meat and cheese products, as well as plastic cosmetic bottles and jars. Mike Whitcher was married, personally ambitious to a fault, strangely humorless and uncommunicative; but he had an eye for the girls, which quickly earned him a reputation in his peer group. He was sexually supercharged. Our shared digs were in a modern but modest blue collar semi-detached home, where the host family was blessed with an exceptionally well endowed, nubile daughter of about seventeen. She was proud to be thus blessed. The juxtaposition of supercharged Mike and the girl strutting her perky stuff in this house of intimate dimensions was a ticking time bomb. Mike immediately grasped the opportunity, removed his wedding band the moment he set eyes on her and hid it in a closet above the sink in our shared bathroom.

Mike was tall, slim, athletic and physically all male. He was not handsome, but had strong angular features dominated by a black mop of hair, close-set eyes of ice blue like those of a Siberian husky. His intense stare could melt the armor plate of a tank, so he had little trouble with the girl's blouse. Whether striving to be a budding captain of industry or stalking his female prey, he pursued his plans with telling effect, so expectations were met within twelve hours of arrival. It was fortunate for all in the house that the edifying training assignment in Speke was unusually short.

At the plant, I quickly grasped the essentials of testing incoming raw materials such as low-density polyethylene, polystyrene and polypropylene for container production. Processes such as extrusion, injection—and blow-molding were observed and explained. Meanwhile, Mike spent his time with employee benefits people and the training staff in the plant. Back in our digs for the evening, Mike accelerated the social education of our hosts' daughter upstairs in his bedroom. Later, Michael Whitcher left Metal Box before his traineeship was completed, to join a very fashionable management consultancy where he was to specialize in "inter-personal skill development." What the girl in Speke did with her accelerated education in inter-personal skills is not known.

Other training assignments took me to steel and tinplate processing plants in South Wales where I again connected with the rugby community, and to paper and plastics plants in Portsmouth, where my local hosts took me sailing on the Solent's waters.

The final segment of the programmed traineeship was spent over three months at a giant food and beverage can complex at the very heart of the company in Acton, alongside research laboratories, technical service and machinery design facilities just west of London. Sophisticated science, operations management and strategic planning came together here in this remarkable confluence of industrial initiative. The assignment made a lasting impression on me, as it illuminated the dynamism of the enormous enterprise that was the Metal Box Company and its response to advancing technology and to ever changing consumer needs in ever-evolving global demographics. It was a gem of technological and industrial accomplishment. The company employed nearly 100,000 people in the UK and around the British Commonwealth of Nations as it helped preserve and distribute food, put thousands of branded consumer goods on retail shelves and in street stalls in every corner of the world.

Following that period in Acton, I was tested in an entry level job at the company's headquarters on Baker Street in London's West End, right next to the headquarters of Marks & Spencers. This allowed freedom of residential choice for the very first time. The choice was a shared apartment in Wetherby Gardens, near the South Kensington tube station. Despite modest means, the apartment was nothing short of newfound bliss, a far cry from those first digs in Walthamstow and life in the East End or complete social isolation in grimy row houses in the industrial North. The easy commute and routine office hours meant that, for the first time, a social life in London was within reach. A modestly improved salary also allowed a little bit more discretionary spending. The tight communal life in the apartment was shared with four other impecunious young men embarking on their respective careers. The flat on the second floor of a red brick Victorian townhouse offered a huge living cum dining room, a minute kitchen, a tiny bathroom, and three bedrooms. Quite unfairly, the senior tenant had the largest room all to himself, and yet he only used it when he was not sleeping over with his latest dishy number picked up from behind the counter at some department store, or a curvy nurse from a nearby hospital. The two smaller bedrooms were shared. Wetherby Gardens imposed an introduction to aspects of housekeeping, mainly in the category of basic hygiene, kitchen, bathroom and window cleaning. All my flat mates had their families in the home counties to which they would retreat directly from work on Friday, only to reappear at Wetherby Gardens on Monday evening after work. As lowest man on the totem pole with no home county refuge, I served as cleaning service, supplies manager and chief washerupper. This burden fell upon in-house immigrant labor, unappreciated and unpaid.

One Saturday evening with household chores long done, while taking a shower before joining friends at the nearby *Grenadier's Arms*, I heard loud knocks on the front door. Draped in a towel, I found two tall uniformed London *bobbies*, complete with helmets and nightsticks in the hallway.

> "Good evenin', sir," said the front officer looking vaguely discomforted by my state of undress. "Please 'scuse us, but would Mr Christian Flemmin' Hoilmann be resident and present 'ere, at this address?"

"Yes, in fact that's me, but what's going on? Why would you be asking?" I asked

"Well, sir, if you daon't moind, sir, I'll tell ya, you're about to be put under arrest! It's moi given duty to inform you that you are—and 'ave for some toime bin—in breach of the Aailiens Registraishun Act of 1939 as Ammended, and Oi 'ave to ask you to get dressed, sir, and come wiv'us to Chelsea police staishun, roight awaaiy. If you please, sir, you've got jus' foive minutes," the taller *bobby* declared, "so, you better get to it, sir!"

It immediately dawned on me that as an alien I had, for once, forgotten to comply with the UK rule calling for registration of any address change lasting more than 72 hours. This was the law applied to anybody holding an *Alien's Registration Certificate*. After all those years at school, at Cambridge and then while training with Metal Box all over the country, I had finally slipped up. Dressed and ready to go in two minutes flat, registration certificate in hand, I was gently marched all the way to Chelsea Police Station, with each bobby's hand gently cupping my elbow on either side.

"Very sorry, sir! … Jus' doin' our job, sir! … Yer know wot Oi mean?" explained the lead officer, "Nuffin' personal, of course! Nuffin' personal at all!"

As we marched towards Old King's Road, soon chatting quite comfortably, it turned out that both officers were rugby fans, so before we had reached the station on Pavilion Road, England's chances of winning the season's *Triple Crown* had been thoroughly reviewed.

"Oi weelly wish we could, but fat chance, sir," said the second bobby, struggling with his R's. "Boaf Oirland and Waails will kweam us! We'll scupper Scotland, thaaough ... naaoo pwoblem there, 'cos thaaiy've got nuffin' up fwont."

"My money's on Ireland," I confessed and explained my relationship with Andy Mulligan, which greatly impressed the two policemen.

Chelsea's Police Captain chuckled quietly as I was ushered into his office. He told me I did not sound very alien to him and asked where I went to school. He then shook his head in blank ignorance, perhaps disappointed at the answer. He told me he could see that I had gone up to Cambridge, and that I had a clean record over eight years as an alien UK resident. Frowning, he proceeded to stamp my registration paper with a heavy thud.

"Just remember the rules, old boy!" he said. "Stick to the law and keep your nose clean! As you know, it's not that bloody difficult. You've been around long enough." The captain paused. "I see you were born in Penang—a crown colony, you know, so you could have been one of us, had you chosen to. Why the hell not?" Without waiting for an answer he dismissed me. "I wish you continued joy and success in this land of hope and glory! Good luck and good night to you!"

"A pompous prick, you are, Captain," I whispered to myself after bidding the two *bobbies* goodbye on the way out the station's granite portal.

This incident came to mind time repeatedly over many years in South Africa where the pass laws were so controversial, and later when the proof of ID for voting rights in the United States caused such hysteria. Documentation and privacy issues kindled an international firestorm among left wingers and a feeding frenzy in the ACLU. For all the evil legislation the *Nats* enacted in apartheid South Africa, the pass laws were the wrong focus of indignation when there was so much more evil invasion of Blacks' rights to be addressed. The really wicked aspects of the pass laws were their discriminatory use by the police to terrorize, while the worst of the population's white scum did not have to carry any identification. In the USA, there has always been cause for monitoring of suspects' international communications, a sensible precaution to counter terrorist threats, especially after 9/11. Given my own experience as an alien in dozens of countries, I have always felt that if you behave yourself, you need have no concern about the Special Branch, MI6, CIA or FBI checking you out. It is ironical that today's loudest "lost privacy" protesters are among the quickest to spill the sordid details of their private lives all over social media. In the UK of the 1950s, I simply appreciated my great privilege of free access to a wonderful British education and all the social and cultural treasures of that great nation. It was quite logical and sensible to me that as an alien visitor, my movements should be checked by my hosts.

Evenings and weekends in London rekindled old friendships and spawned some new. Andy Mulligan, when he wasn't playing rugby for London Irish or touring the antipodes with Ireland or the British Lions, was again among my closest pals. He had an ill-defined job with Thomas de la Rue, whom he had chosen to join because, he claimed, his work would be mainly about organizing "cocktail parties and PR stuff." Not the industrial Midlands for our Andy, nor the long hours of banking in the city. It was during this time that I introduced him to my attractive Danish-Eurasian cousins, Birgitte Bramsen and then Pia Schioeler. He married the latter a couple of years later.

Life in London revolved around chums from school and university days, colleagues at work and new acquaintances struck in neighborhood pubs or at a smarter SW3 party. Life was fun and the pleasures simple. Personal finances were limiting, but not prohibitively so. The occasional trip to Cambridge, the regatta at Henley-on-Thames or a weekend in the country at the family home of friends—all were within the budget.

Sophistication was largely beyond our means. Pub suppers, walks in Hyde Park, St James or along the Thames embankment. Exhibitions, museums, concerts—even the Royal Festival Hall—and all manner of sporting events were affordable. Conversations were lighthearted, but not unaware of the real world around us. Social issues and politics were engaged, frequently with someone in the group being well informed on the given subject. The fluid group of young people harbored some bright minds.

UK and Commonwealth politics at the time were dominated by Harold Macmillan's regime. He had taken over the Tory government from Anthony Eden. The new prime minister presented a dramatic contrast to the elegantly dapper but weak Anthony Eden, whose kneejerk reaction to the Suez situation briefly set Britain on its heels and cost him his job. His sartorially scruffy successor, of droopy eyelids, walrus mustache and gravelly voice restored Britain's role abroad in the late 1950s. Macmillan's giant intellect led to international appreciation of the *Winds of Change* sweeping through Africa. His prescient view of the continent's political climate change caught the attention of the world. He was to redraw the map as he spearheaded the decolonization of Africa south of the Sahara. Macmillan's grasp of the implications of the nuclear age drove his abolition of the UK's national service draft, eliminating the waste of millions of man-years spent in an obsolete, irrelevant army. While the Soviets rattled sabers, Macmillan was in no mood for appeasement as he rebuilt the UK's special relationship with the USA. This prompted France to veto Britain's initial entry into the EU because Macmillan would not share classified American nuclear secrets with them! His pro-business policies supporting development of the UK's domestic market managed "to fuel the engine of growth." His premature retirement caused by a medical misdiagnosis was criminal and most unfortunate; but happily he was no longer at the helm when Defense Minister Profumo's tryst with a pretty call girl, Christine Keeler, toppled the Tory government.

At this time, Bertrand Russell was busy leading his anti-nuclear campaign, including the impressive 50-mile protest march from London to Aldermaston in western Berkshire—with a lot more impact than modern protest strolls. The medical journal *Lancet* described the first use of ultrasound as a diagnostic tool. Blacks and whites battled and beat each other up in west London's Notting Hill, while Cliff Richards' song *Move It* gave birth to British rock 'n roll. West End audiences flocked to see Rex Harrison and Audrey Hepburn in the opening run of *My Fair Lady*, and Ian Fleming brought *Dr. No* to his James Bond series.

It was during these lighthearted London months that I met Marilyn Harter. She had gone to Runton Hill, a small bluestocking boarding school in Norfolk for upper crust county girls. She must have excelled as she won an *exhibition*, a financially valuable and most competitive scholarship at prestigious Lady Margaret Hall at Oxford University in 1953. It was the most sought after of Oxford's very few female colleges at the time. Gaining admission to *LMH*, let alone winning a scholarship is still the most coveted academic accomplishment of ambitious British schoolgirls. Nothing short of Mensa-level IQ and lots of hard work could get a girl to that point. By 1958, Marilyn was private secretary to an upmarket City solicitor called Freddy Berkley, having trained at secretarial school in Oxford after being sent down after only a few months at LMH. She had failed prelims (the very first round of early spring time exams for freshman students at Oxford). Marilyn had blown it horribly, yet did not want to lose access to her rarefied Oxford social life to which she had become addicted.

"I was just—well, overwhelmed," she explained with forthright honesty, "by the fab social life and all the parties.

I was in denial, ignoring the polite warnings from my tutor and supervisors. Little thought was given to the once-in-a-lifetime opportunity I had been given. Everything had been handed to me on a silver platter. I just took it all for granted. Runton Hill's Miss Vernon-Harcourt wasn't there to stand over my shoulder and crack the whip. I was just having so much fun, Flemming! Nobody reminding me how damned lucky I was. Then, all of a sudden it was too late. I totally buggered up the prelims and was suddenly a goner! It was all over! Just like that!"

I was impressed by her unreserved admission, confessing to laxity and irresponsibility—an approach she did not always take later in life. She was clearly holding down a demanding and responsible job in the city working for her lubricious, silver-haired Freddie. We developed a warm relationship, which over a period of months was to go all the way. She was one of three girls sharing a tiny basement flat in Bina Gardens, round the corner from Wetherby Gardens in South Kensington. They shared a flutter-by, quasi-socialite lifestyle of aspirations beyond their budgets. Penny was dating the heir to the renowned Symington dynasty of Port wine fame, while Phoebe, a colonial farmer's daughter from Kenya's highlands, was recovering from an aborted bush romance with a district officer in Nakuru. The third was Marilyn. To judge by the feminine banter in the apartment, she was somehow romantically linked to someone named Johnny, to whom they never referred without conspiratorial giggles. Her family had seen more privileged times and frivolous living in the Dedham Vale district on the River Stour in Suffolk, where Constable, Gainsborough, and Paul Nash did some of their best work. Again, according to Marilyn's forthright telling, *Daddy*, as a gadabout of the roaring twenties, had frittered away a small fortune, living it up and dashing around the county at high speed in his Bugatti convertibles, giving little attention to making a living before he died prematurely. Widowed mother,

Doris, a pianist raised in Rhodesia, lived quite modestly in fashionable Frinton-on-Sea on the Essex coast. All three Bina Gardens girls were very English, very *county*. Rosy cheeks, upper crust accents, pastel twin sets with strings of pearls, tweed skirts and sensible shoes.

My entry level job was that of research clerk in Metal Box's highly professional consumer and industrial market research department at Baker Street headquarters. It was edifying work, which opened the eye to a vast, intriguing world of branded consumer goods, retailing, and graphic design, as well as industrial processes and equipment. A world that spanned products from Unilever's Pepsodent toothpaste, Watney's Pale Ale, Shell's lubricating oil and International Paints' marine coatings to tinplate, or coated steel coil produced by the Steel Company of Wales and polyethylene made by ICI. The lateral dynamics of competitive marketing at retail level were as intriguing as the vertical value-adding conversion of raw materials into consumer goods—all part of a worldwide economy, ultimately to the benefit of man. It was an extraordinary perch from which to learn. Coupled with the months spent at the front line on factory floors with the labor force, the market research experience was an invaluable extension of academic education.

Before long it was announced that Metal Box South Africa Ltd. in Johannesburg had decided to establish a market research capability de novo. MBSA was the parent company's largest and most successful subsidiary, a public company listed on the Johannesburg Stock Exchange. John Baxter, MBSA's chairman and CEO, had signaled that I was offered a real job, with real responsibilities, with a budget and defined objectives: Establish a market research capability in Johannesburg to serve the company and its customers and retailers throughout the sub-continent. The offer included a one-way ticket aboard the *Pretoria Castle*, flagship of the Union Castle shipping line, departing at the end of November 1958, and a trip on the Blue Train from the Cape to Johannesburg. There was more than a hint of finality behind the one-way characterization of the paid passage; there was also a premonition of the cost of failure. A new and distant environment was now presented, where I had no connections beyond my parents and a brother, all of whom were still in South Africa— but no chums, no extensive network of friends and associates, and so far from familiar England and comfortable Denmark. In the context of launching a career, nailing a job, and starting a new life in a society fraught with some alien aspects and civic notions, it meant taking a plunge. A bad decision or failure could have significant consequences.

There was time for a quick but emotional last trip to Denmark to say goodbye to the extended family and many dear friends, returning to London for a last minute round of farewell parties. Departing Tammestrup, longtime home away from home, was especially heart-breaking after the years of intimate relationships and warmth in that beau-tiful old and very Danish homestead. Cozy candlelit dinner parties with Copenhagen family and friends were wrenching, too. Denmark and the familiar traditions of childhood would be with me for life, so it made little difference that my parents and brother with his family were, for the time being, in South Africa. What mattered was the realization that my home base was about to be moved six thousand miles. (John and his wife had left the Philippines for South Africa because they had been unsettled by the escalating conflict over Formosa as Mao and Chiang Kai Shek faced off. *Mor* and *Far* were approaching retirement to Denmark.) Never again was I to spend more than a couple of unbroken weeks in Denmark, where personal roots were so deep and still remain.

The world in which a career was to be launched and an education finally put to work was again marked by turbulence and change. Batista's Cuban dictatorship ended with his departure and the recognition of Castro's revolutionary regime. Alaska and Hawaii became the 49th and 50th American states respectively. Desegregation was introduced in Little Rock, Arkansas. The first Barbie dolls went on sale and Singapore installed its first freely elected government as Lee Kuan Yew took the city state out of newly independent Malaysia. The Dalai Lama fled from the Chinese in Tibet to seek asylum in India while China moved troops across the border and killed a number of Indians. The USSR signed a contract to construct a nuclear reactor for Iraq. In Britain the traditional Empire Day was renamed Commonwealth Day, reflecting Harold Macmillan's prescience and his winds of change. The South African Nationalist government was feeling its oats, steadily legislating its apartheid policies into place after a full decade in power. It was actually a time of significant change in South Africa, the implications of which certainly escaped a lot of people at the time, including me.

Militant Black *Africanist* members of Nelson Mandela's African National Congress were objecting to the latter's inclusive co-operation with sister organizations representing *Coloureds*—people of mixed race, by South African nomenclature—and ethnic Indians. The *Africanists* also protested ANC's resulting *Freedom Charter*. It was Robert Subukwe who led the formation of the Pan-African Congress, which broke away from the ANC to become a rival organization promoting more extreme positions in *The Struggle*.

The white opposition United Party experienced a parallel development, as Helen Suzman and a group of followers became frustrated with the United Party's feeble and ineffective resistance to the Nationalists' march to apartheid. She led the formation of the Progressive Party to fight for a plat-form, which included a qualified franchise for Blacks based on minimum education and property ownership requirements. Eleven Progressive Party colleagues ran with her in the following election, but only she kept her seat. As the sole female member of parliament for decades she was an unswerving opponent of apartheid. Her phone was wire-tapped and she was harassed by police. She famously discouraged the wire-tapping by blowing a loud, shrill whistle into the receiver. Charles Robberts Swart was appointed South Africa's last Governor General (the head of state under the British Commonwealth arrangement), later to become the country's first State President of the new republic outside the British Commonwealth. Swart's personal history was a microcosm of the country's history. Born of Afrikaaner farming parents in the Orange Free State under British rule, he was the third of six children. He was interned with his mother and siblings by the British during the Boer War, which only three of the children survived. A brilliant student, he went to a *CNO School* specifically created for Afrikaans children as a result of Lord Alfred Milner's program for enforcing anglicized education. He completed his *matric*, preparing him for university education when he was thirteen, proceeding to qualify as a lawyer and then taking a master's degree in journalism at Columbia University in New York.

The winds of change were not yet at gale force in the southern tip of Africa, but they were blowing at 180 degrees to the direction prevailing further north on the continent.

Having visited South Africa twice, once as a schoolboy and later as an undergraduate, I was conscious of the villainy and vile inequities of the Nationalist dogma, but like the complacent United Party opposition, and in fact most observers around the world, I believed it was only a matter of time before the insanity would be reversed. The immense resources—mineral, agricultural, and marine—of the country and its enterprising business leaders would as a matter of course turn back this craziness. The country would continue to lead the African continent as the winds of progress and prosperity blew through it. I concluded it was a good and exciting place to be launching a career. Fifty-five years later I am still not sure whether I would have chosen differently, knowing what I know today. I did have a small role to play in that scenario, as things turned out.

The night before leaving London to embark in Southampton, I gave an intimate party for my closest friends in London, amongst whom were Andy and my beautiful cousins from Copenhagen, Marilyn and her roommates, my own flat mates in Wetherby Gardens and peer group friends at Metal Box. Andrew played his guitar and sang Irish ditties with my cousin Pia sitting at his feet. The Metal Box fellows were envious of the glamour of the South African job and the chance to take some real responsibility. My flat mates joked about the need to find housecleaners to do their chores for them, now that I was leaving. Everyone piled into my

Danish herring, meat balls, liver pate and cheeses as the once ample stock of Carlsberg and Aalborg Akvavit vanished. It was a relaxed gathering, which spawned songs, jokes and anecdotes, long soul-searching debates deep into the early hours. Several warm relationships fostered that evening were to enjoy unexpected longevity. Other bonds withered with the passage of time, falling prey to geography. The evening marked some terminal changes and some unforeseen beginnings. Like the one-way passage to Cape Town, the evening had an element of finality about it.

The next day, the boat train from Victoria Station delivered hundreds of passengers to the great docks of Southampton by late afternoon, leaving time to settle into our cabins before dark. On the promenade deck of the *Pretoria Castle*, with all earthly possessions in a single trunk stowed in the hold and a smaller suitcase under the bunk in my steerage berth, I watched the shores of England melt into the gray gloom as the liner slipped stealthily down Solent Waters, heading into the English Channel, bound for the south Atlantic via Biscay.

The moment marked another melancholy break with a country, which had for over ten years enveloped me in its rich culture and had extended the privilege of its brilliant educational opportunities. I had sunk roots here, too, soaked up England's green and pleasant land, gaining treasured friendships. I had been nurtured by Britain's endearing traditions, values, and its people. The sterling character of the nation so heroically exhibited in the Battle of Britain and through the devastation of the Blitz, had made its mark. So had its rich culture—its flare for ceremony, its unmatched ecclesiastical and choral music, its literature and architecture. The British sense of fair play and sportsmanship is also unique. For better or worse, these cherished years had endowed me with a life-enduring English accent, which prompts even Brits to take me for English. I was happily to return to England regularly for the rest of my life, but the country was never again my operating base in the sense it was during the formative years.

By the time darkness fell, the ship was cruising, gently heaving and sighing as she cut into the swell of open waters in the English Channel. A young crowd lined the railings, drinks in hand, watching the pinpoint coastal lights extinguished one by one as distance grew and night descended. The two-week party in tourist class aboard Union Castle Line's flagship was about to enjoy lift off. Many in the excited group sensed they were on their way to a new life in Southern Africa; others were happily returning home from sundry British schools and universities, or from job assignments "overseas," as the South Africans call any destination north of the Limpopo or beyond their own shores. The celebrations began.

After skirting the grey, unavoidably choppy Bay of Biscay, came carefree sunny days on the recreation deck reading, chatting by the pool or playing deck tennis. As the latitude declined the temperature rose, and the Atlantic's indigo blue deepened to the delight of all passengers, pasty pale from the persistent gloom of autumnal England.

Warmer climes brought a one-day stop at Madeira, a lonely Portuguese rock leaping nearly 6,000 feet out of the vast ocean, lush greenery clinging to its precipitous volcanic cliffs. Funchal's narrow streets, stucco red-roofed houses and tiny gardens were smothered in the scents and primary colors of subtropical flora, tumbling vines, citrus trees straining under the weight of oranges, lemons, and limes. Captain's Dinner, a fancy dress ball, tournaments for every deck sport, opportunistic romances and one-night stands, laughing banter, dolphins at play at the ship's bows and a single ominous sighting of a triangular dorsal fin breaking the water's surface. Standard British fare of John Collins, Bucks Fizz, Pimm's No. 1 through No. 3, torrents of draft Castle Lager and pale golden rivers of fruity-fresh Nederburg Riesling. Despite the brevity of voyage, daring affairs and superficial rivalries created gossip and little tensions, especially among the girls. A number of the men hardly left the bar and its liars' dice, poker and rummy games for the fourteen days; so beyond the bar's confines an imbalance of gender arose. This in turn sparked some feline, feminine competition—a welcome reversal of the problem that had plagued Cambridge—especially when deck sports and the fancy dress party required pairing off.

Quite early on my partner for the voyage was to be Georgina Milner, the epitome of an English rose. A lithe and lissome creature made for the 1920s society in England, she had a lily-petal complexion, wide-set hazel eyes under arched brows, a big mischievous mouth with a gummy smile and a bobbed auburn hairdo. In seductive masquerade costume she was Lady Hamilton for my own Lord Nelson. On other nights of dancing she enhanced my best shot at the Charleston in her above-the-knee chiffon frock, cloche hat, feather boa, and 15-inch cigarette holder. Georgina fiercely disclaimed any lineage, legitimate or otherwise, linking her to the famous Lord Alfred Milner of British South Africa fame. However, upon landing in Cape Town, she was nevertheless headed for a part of Constantia's historical real estate, which challenged her denials. The two-week voyage had been a bubble of lighthearted banter and abandonment, divested of all anxiety or concern about the unknown world waiting ahead.

Almost the same crowd as that which had lined the promenade deck of the *Pretoria Castle* as we said goodbye to the *Solent* two weeks earlier, was again assembled as grey eastern light turned pale pink, and dawn then broke on a southern summer's morning at the swirling convergence of the Indian Ocean and the South Atlantic. The horizon was still a clean uninterrupted line, but then as a huge orange sun breached it, the sea to the east suddenly exploded into a million twinkling flashes of fluid white, yellow, pink, and orange. As the incandescent sun climbed, it grew smaller and blinding white while the ocean's liquid fireworks were extinguished and the sea quickly turned from gray to azure, reflecting a deepening, clear blue sky. Meanwhile, the distant purple mesa-like silhouette of Table Mountain also poked through the horizon to extend continental Africa's early welcome from its antipodal extremity. The fairest cape of all was about to reveal its astonishing, unmatched glory.

Vancouver, Hong Kong, Rio de Janeiro, Stockholm, Sydney and San Francisco can all, with some justification, lay claim to being the crown jewel of all the world's spectacular coastal cities, but that accolade is in-disputably earned by glorious, captivating Cape Town. Painters of global repute have been painting the mountain from every angle for five hundred years, usually from some point along Bloubergstrand across Table Bay.

As the rhythmic muscular throb from the liner's engine room slowed to an almost musical murmur and its bow-wave shrank to a ripple, the huge ship almost seemed to drift, magically drawn by the pull of the stunning deep purple mass that was the silhouette of Table Mountain, which then steadily turned mauve and light lavender as dawn brightened. The sun soon struck and illuminated the great mountain's sheer rock face and its much smaller sisters, *Lion's Head* and *Signal Hill* and the craggy *Twelve Apostles,* a dozen rocky promontories ranging southward down Cape Peninsular toward distant Cape Point. The landmarks of Table Bay's sweeping crescent dropped into their place, one by one, in this magnificent vista as the sunlight strengthened, as if it were a panoramic video projected onto a screen by the sun as the mountain's long, dark shadow to the west retreated. A forest of cranes hovering over heavyweight freighters in the busy harbor; Robben Island, shunned and lonely, sulking in the middle of the bay to the west; glorious luminescent miles of brilliant white beach stretching to distant Bloubergstrand; office high-rises and hotels of the harbor-side city; urban residential blocks, giving way to the colorful Malay quarter further up hill, and nearby suburban houses and gardens creeping up onto the steep slopes of the iconic mountain's base and towards *Lion's Head.* Cape Peninsula to the east, like a great igneous dagger cleaving the two oceans as it plunged southward to Cape Point itself, where the oceans crashed into each other and onto the jagged promontory sending columns of white salty spume hundreds of feet into the air.

By mid-morning, the *Pretoria Castle* was expertly eased into her berth in the docks catering to passenger traffic in Cape Town's hectic harbor, which had served 75 seafaring and colonizing generations since Jan van Riebeck first anchored in Table Bay. A small crowd was assembled dockside to greet arriving friends and returning family members. An army of mostly *Coloured* longshoremen waited discretely to one side, ready for disembarkation.

In the almost exclusively white crowd on the dock was an attractive young couple specifically waiting to welcome me, an unknown new employee of Metal Box Company of South Africa arriving from "overseas" to do an undisclosed job at the company's headquarters in Johannesburg. John Baxter, the company's chairman had sent word to Cape Town that a new young employee en route to Johannesburg was to be met and given a quick tour of the company's operations in the Western Cape province before continuing inland on *The Blue Train* two days after arrival. Andy and Maureen Page-Wood made me feel as if all of Africa had been awaiting my arrival since the Union was declared by the Brits in 1910. He was a regional sales manager for the company, looking after its efforts to serve the packaging and processing needs of the Cape's fabulous food canning industry, which encompassed enormous deciduous fruit, vegetable and fish canning industries. Andy was my local conduit to a real job, a career in South Africa after nearly two decades of education and training. Nobody could have made it easier or less nerve-racking than this warm and attractive couple, who immediately invited me to their home. The South African welcome lived up to the country's deserved, indelible reputation for generous and warm hospitality.

About ten years earlier a voyage from Malaya to England had been the opening of my young life's British chapter. It had been the prelude to ten years of tutelage, experiential maturing and new understanding. This voyage just completed had been somewhat akin to rolling onto a launching pad before blastoff. In between the frivolities aboard the *Pretoria Castle* there had been time to pause for thought and contemplate what was happening. Ten years of new and changing perceptions, education and training had placed me at a threshold through which I was about to plunge. A new and very real world with which I was, in fact, unfamiliar—a world of unknowns. It was clear that the chosen but uncharted path ahead would bring with it real consequences, some of them irreversible, and that the responsibility for the choice and those consequences were solely mine. I was at a point where the consequences, more than ever before, would affect not only me and my aspirations, but also many people around me.

The last page of the English chapter was turned as the *Pretoria Castle* docked in Cape Town harbor. The tutorial was behind me, the training period in England was over, so the curtain had fallen on the dress rehearsal. It was time to plunge, time for immersion in the realities and challenges still to be defined. Success or failure, frustration or fulfillment, progress or stagnation—the realities ahead were mine to manage in a brand new world.

Photo Gallery
1950 to 1957

These were Flemming's schoolboy years at Gresham's School,
the undergraduate time at Downing College, Cambridge, and then his
industrial training with Metal Box Company in the UK before his first job
in South Africa, starting in January 1959.

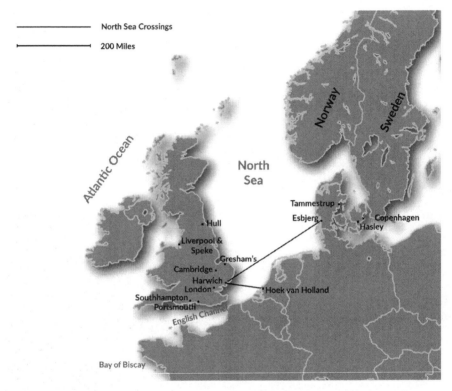

European "ports of call" on my Odyssey.

Tammestrup, residential north range, Jutland, Denmark
Circa 1950s

Mor on the hood of *Far's* Buick, "Passe Partout," Transvaal roadside,
South Africa, 1953

New citrus plantings, Ngonini Estate, with Swaziland hills in background
Circa 1950s

"Big School" assembly hall and classrooms, Gresham's School, Holt,
Norfolk, England, Circa 1950s

Gresham's 1st XV (varsity) rugby team.
Sitting at front right are rookies Flemming and Andy Mulligan aged 15
1951

M J Olivier, center, with school prefects.
Standing: L to R Andy Mulligan, Brian Johnson,
Tom Whittle, Richard Tilson.
Seated: Flemming and Napier Russell
1954

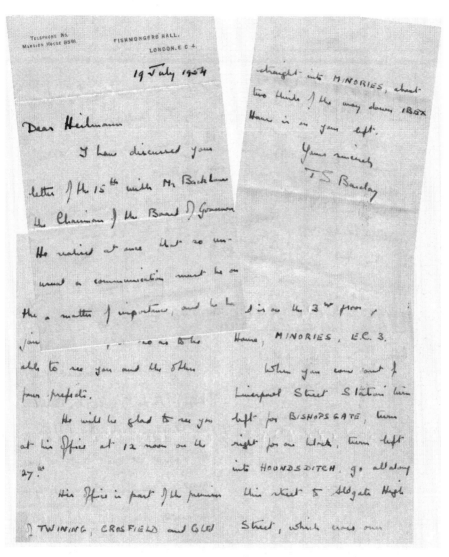

Letter from Fishmonger's Hall, finally granting a hearing
1954

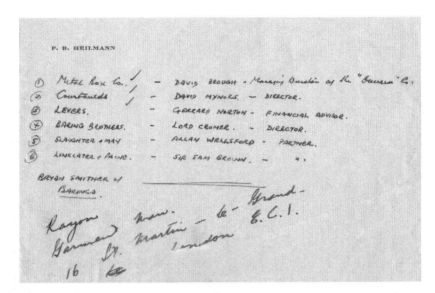

Brian Smither's suggestions for Flemming's job search upon graduation
from Cambridge a year later
1956

My room on staircase M5 in Downing College residence
1955

My study room at Gresham's School. Note the stereo equipment
1953

Fatimas' wedding in full traditional Malaya matrimonial dress
1955

Summer croquet on Downing College lawns
1956

C Flemming Heilmann, BA Hons. (Cantab)
1957

Clare College and King's College Chapel, on the Cambridge "Backs"
1957

Downing College Chapel seen from the quad
Circa 1950s

Epilogue

"The dangers of life are infinite, and among them is safety."
Goethe

THE LANDING IN Cape Town at the age of 23, marked the end of an itinerant childhood and education during seismic geopolitical convulsions, family upheavals, encounters with mortal danger, immersion in diverse cultures and exposure to the world's major religions on three different continents. Interrupted family life and associated anxieties had been managed by two loving, pragmatic and decisive parents who took personal responsibility—occasionally flinching, but never shrinking from risk. The glue holding the family structure together was stronger than any test to which it was put; that glue had been formulated and the structure built steadfastly since 1930 when *Far* and *Mor* joined forces. The formula and structure had sensibly undergone refinement and modification as the challenge of life's realities evolved. We, like most other strong families, learned many lessons and came through them even stronger. Lacking such a case-hardened family structure, too many children and parents sadly succumbed to the trials and torments of war, while others survived with troubling symptoms and after-effects. Many, however, gained strength of character along with qualities of flexibility, tolerance and understanding.

We were fortunate in avoiding the brutality of Japanese internment suffered by many women and children in Malaya, where hundreds were captured; but refugee women with no financial means, caring for their children while fretting over the fate of their husbands also endured the real wartime trauma that accompanies fear of the unknown. Our family avoided some of that because PB, looking down the Japanese gun barrel, considered the risks and took personal responsibility by acting proactively. The turmoil of that turbulent childhood did little more than accelerate the maturing process for John and me, robbing us of only very few childhood joys that really mattered. Perhaps the most significant deprivation was never getting to know our grandparents, all four of whom died during the Nazi occupation of Denmark. On the whole we were unscathed, if not strengthened, by our experience. We certainly learned a bit about facing realities, adapting to change and navigating the unfamiliar. Paucity of options can even strengthen the human capacity to cope with realities. Twenty-first century psychologists, pediatric counselors and family therapists would have had a field day addressing patient histories half as complex as ours. Every circumstance, every decision and every action would be minutely analyzed. Psychiatric speculation would trigger a cascade of diagnostic acronyms, each calling for prescriptions of stimulants, depressants, therapies or special needs counseling and teaching.

Collectively these experiences had a positive effect. We learned fundamental lessons that are never taught in classrooms—or even brought to the attention of 21st century schoolchildren. Horizons were widened and young eyes were opened to realities never contemplated by children raised in more coddled, sedentary circumstances. One overriding consequence of my childhood and education was an enduring questioning of religion and dogma, popular preconceptions and conventional wisdom. Diversity of culture and ethnicity along with differing styles of governance had encouraged tolerance of the unfamiliar, if not a real curiosity and appetite to learn how other people think and do things, leading to a liberal respect and appreciation of disparate creeds and ideas. Today's youth is generally raised on far too much conventional wisdom offered in a narrow setting of political correctness and parochial constraints. Society today so often has no stomach for candid conversation. Western academia and the media, despite their unctuous pretensions, far too rarely engage in honest and open debate in search of truth. Their audiences, alas, swallow information or apply filters according to their pre-existing mindsets. Thus we live in a world excessively ruled by unchallenged predilections and prejudgments— political, social, philosophical and religious.

Religious dogma is probably history's most influential source of prejudice, exploitation and abuse of the underprivileged, the intellectually lazy and the less endowed.

Without doubt, civic order, societal structure, education, welfare of the poor and even human health have for thousands of years benefited from all manner of religious teaching, rules and practices; religious values and precepts have indeed often been a positive influence on social progress. However, religion has forever been exploited by overweening, self-serving clerics, from pontiff to prophet, patriarch to proselytizer and from parish priest to protestant pontificator—all making judgments and claiming authority over the morals of mankind. With very rare exceptions, the leaders and elite of any given religion live high on the hog's back, in nothing short of luxurious settings, in great physical comfort, usually enjoyed at the expense of their unquestioning faithful. London's Lambeth Palace and the excesses of the Vatican and its Papal Penthouse apartment provide nice illustrations (India's Mahatma Gandhi was an exception as is the 21st century Pope Francis, who was quick to forsake the papal penthouse for truly modest quarters). For many centuries, the endeavors of religious leaders have been driven by territorial greed, avaricious gain and self-indulgence at the expense of other humans—often the feckless, the intellectually bankrupt and the defenseless, including young boys—almost invariably unpunished. Untold hundreds of millions of people have been slaughtered and persecuted in the name of God, Christ, Allah and other deities. Religious bigotry has often been a principal obstacle to social progress, science and technology, and so continues to this day. Respect for logic, science and the observed realities of life on four continents led me to a carefully considered view: that the role of religion in life is grossly overvalued, and that religion too often plays a role in politics and public affairs where it does not belong. On a more personal basis, the conclusion is that religion demands more leaps of faith and intellectual gymnastics than my flexibility allowed.

Wartime illuminated the essential role of leadership whenever countries, communities or a group of people are threatened by overwhelming force or confronted with the uncontrollable and even the unfamiliar. Effective leadership expands the ability of groups or affiliations of people to accomplish things they would not be able to do as individuals. However, the notion of "leadership ability" is commonly scorned in Denmark, for example, by the Danes who would embrace the egalitarian fallacies of *Janteloven*, because their particular dogma will not allow anyone to dare think they may have individual skills, knowledge or talent that can assist the collective! I have heard a Danish visitor to the Jacob Riis Settlement House in New York's inner city express surprise that underserved youth were offered courses in leadership.

> "You actually try to teach these kids leadership?" she asked in astonishment. "in Denmark we couldn't do that! America's society was built on individual enterprise and initiative, but Denmark's was established by the collective effort and participation. The collective approach doesn't permit people to think they could in any significant way be different or better than anybody else."

That was in 2017, believe it or not.

The answer is, of course, that ad hoc individual activity and effort can rarely serve the common cause as well as coordinated initiative, activity and effort guided by leadership at some level. (A society totally committed to the collectivist egalitarian dogma could not in the long run prevent chaos or anarchy without some form of leadership and coordination). World War

II taught the value of leadership qualities in the civilian population, where an individual's contribution of talent, experience or knowledge—even courage and determination—could and did save thousands of lives. This civilian concept of leadership is far removed from the military context, where designated rank comes into the leadership mix.

The corollary is that the wartime experience taught recognition and appreciation of other people's ability to provide leadership, especially in situations (some dangerous) in which there would otherwise be a shortfall of the expertise, capacity or even understanding needed. That lesson demands a level of humility that is not always present in those with excessively egalitarian views of the world.

In parallel, wartime circumstances called upon the individual's duty to be a team player, putting personal entitlement and preference aside for the good of the group or community of which one was a part. It became obvious at a young age that individual people have varying capacities, different levels of experience to draw from, and disparate talents.

Claims that we are all equal or equally endowed simply did not stand the reality test—this egalitarian notion was exposed as fundamentally false. The fallacy is the product of the pervasive and persistent muddling and confusion of universal, all-encompassing *equality of man* on the one hand, and equal opportunity, equal access and equal treatment before the law on the other. Ideas of mankind's equality—intellectual or physical—are abundantly debunked by nature and history. Yet the egalitarian creed lives on and drives flawed social theories, politics, policy and conjecture. It is equality of opportunity, access to the tools of citizenship and equal treatment before the law that are the imperatives. Billions of people, generation after generation, have suffered at the hand of this counterproductive confusion, despite the demonstrated collapse of Marxism or Leninism, the generally discarded preaching of Engels and the failure of every variation of socialism. Witness Cuba, Venezuela, and the erstwhile Soviet satellites (where the egalitarian political dogma succumbed to totalitarian dictatorships). Western European countries like Denmark were also seduced by egalitarian dogma to a point where they nearly self-destructed before they turned to individual responsibility, free market economics and democratic capitalism, while maintaining a sustainable safety net for the truly needy—that is where social progress still requires a radical adjustment of approach to governance and politics in the west.

Fascist totalitarianism, wartime challenges, family crises, childhood in bustling Southeast Asia, experience of sadly stagnant sub-Saharan Africa and the failures of socialism in Europe—were all the source of lessons not taught by today's classroom pedagogues.

Those who will dispute this position on egalitarianism vs. equality of opportunity should contemplate and compare the plight of Africa's enormous sub-Saharan population today with the ancient, incredibly sophisticated civilizations of Mesopotamia, China, Egypt, Greece and Rome, or the Inca and Mayan cultures. Had all men been born equal and undifferentiated, there would have been nobody to lead those very first migrants northward, out of Kenya's Rift Valley; there would have been nobody to drive for improvement upon the subsistence living standards endured by the East African hunters-and-gatherers descended from Homo Erectus and Homo Sapiens. It took later Semitic, Hamitic and European migrations back into sub-Saharan Africa, several thousands of years later, to introduce the utility of the wheel and the use of script or hieroglyphics to communicate and record. Sub-Saharan Africans had not ventured beyond some primitive cave drawings. Those left behind on the sub-continent by more venturesome leader-migrants barely advanced from being hunters-and-gatherers to living as warrior-herdsmen, thousands of years later. Encountering Caucasian settlement from the Cape triggered an acceleration of cultural development. Our greatest and most urgent challenge in today's international development agenda is to promote equal opportunity and equal access to these millions of potentially contributing world citizens, so those so endowed and capable can be empowered to make positive change. Legislation and omnibus asset redistribution as tools to mandate equality, uniformity or homogeneity for billions of human beings are nothing short of futile. Anybody heard of Darwin?

There are plenty of potential leaders in Sub-Saharan Africa, who could help forge a pathway out of destitution for hundreds of millions, but their emergence and empowerment requires an international and disciplined focus on just a few prerequisites and imperatives; first, a massive and effective investment in education and vocational training; second, an equally massive and unforgiving prosecution of corruption in each country's public and private sectors; third, equality of treatment before the law; fourth, the creation of an adequately attractive investment environment where employment opportunity and jobs can support growth to keep pace with population and, fifth, universal access to clean water. Other conditions are also called for, but without prioritized focus on these imperatives, the world will never get to them. It is the lack of this focus and discipline that after more than half a century the efforts of the UN, its multiple agencies, thousands of NGO's have been so pathetically ineffective in causing positive and enduring change. Setting priorities involves choices as to how finite resources are put to use or squandered. Consider the choice between NGO's concerned with feeling good about "cultural exchange and mutual understanding between Congolese and Ruandans" on the one hand, and lazer-focused investment in providing access to clean water to villages in South Sudan!

If all people were equal, why do we need any process of selection in government? Why do we have elections? Why have athletic competition? Why would we revere the art of Rembrandt or Manet? Is Placido Domingo no more talented than the lead tenor in St. Luke's church choir? Why did Orwell write about some pigs being more equal than others? Ask New England soccer moms to address these questions as they pathetically struggle to ensure that no team can lose a game? The fatuous answer is that they don't want their little darling to consider herself a loser, so they give all the little darlings a nice chrome-coated-plastic "winner's" trophy made in China. The name of the real game is creating more equal access to the tools needed for success, access to the development of attributes required for success—such as study, training, practice, tenacity, dedication and patience, knowing that not all can be winners, and even winners can't win 'em all. There's no instant gratification. The little darlings have to learn that success has to be attained in a measure proportionate to the effort invested and the level of available talent. The unswerving political and social commitment of mankind has to be focused on improving equality of access to opportunity, not fatuous attempts to improve upon or reverse evolution by prescribing unattainable egality.

A deep revulsion for waste was generated by seeing many millions of poor people deprived of adequate nourishment in Asia and Africa, along with personal experience of wartime deprivations and their slow remediation. It was only in my freshman year at Cambridge, nine years after the World War II ended, that strict rationing of meat, sugar, eggs and butter was finally lifted in the UK. Knowing that the world today wastes one-third of global food production, one can but abhor the repulsive western habits and mindsets regarding waste of food and other finite resources. In the 21st century, Europe and North America lose 40 percent of their food production post-harvest and post-processing, with Americans wasting about the same percentage, or 20 pounds of nourishing food per person per month! At least 800-million people on this planet in 2015 were under-nourished. That encompasses 13 percent of the population in many developing countries. Meanwhile our western attitudes and practices actually encourage disgusting waste, especially of food. Literally hundreds of millions of half-eaten servings of good food regularly get scraped off plates and tossed into the trashcans of restaurants, cafeterias and, yes, home kitchens! Mindlessly, doting American mothers at every level of society, including many on welfare and food stamps, insanely overload their kids' plates, only to have criminal amounts of valuable nourishment scraped off those same plates and consigned directly to the garbage bin.

Our schools and our parents don't even care about it. Our children grow up unappreciative, picky and wasteful, everywhere from inner city housing projects to the starter castles in Montecito, California, and Greenwich, Connecticut.

As for other forms of unchecked waste, just think of the world's private and public bureaucracies wasting financial and human resources. The United Nations organization with its sinfully elastic budgets thrives as history's largest, legitimized waste of money and human resources—persistently unaccountable for sixty years and counting. Think of the scores of office towers in Los Angeles and San Francisco burning every bright light in each office, through the night, while California's governor apologizes for power outages leaving hundreds of thousands in the dark; or think of Hollywood's fossil fuel divestment activists driving around solo in their cavernous black, shiny SUVs and 12-cylinder Ferraris or Aston Martins. Waste of financial and human resources pervades the western world. Some of our resources require more cautious stewardship and husbandry than others; but ultimately all resources are finite. Westerners at all levels of society tend to be careless and wasteful, partly because so few have ever known deprivation.

In contrast, decades of observing industrious Asians in tenacious pursuit of progress illustrated for me their focus on saving and avoiding waste. Their attitudes are based on individual and independent effort in quest of opportunity rather than entitlement. By extension, this tireless Asian determination and patience confounds our typical western insistence on instant gratification, which plagues our cloyed society and distorts the raising of our children. My Chinese *amah* in Malaya was the first to teach me this lesson 75 years ago:

> "You keep work hard long time 'nough, Flemmin', so you make lucky, you make money, and you make happy. You make Mummy and Daddy happy too!"

> Note *amah's* reminder: I had an obligation of gratitude to my parents, too!

The unpredictability of a migratory childhood also meant repeatedly confronting unknowns and the unexpected, which in turn meant making choices with imperfect information. That experience forced an early appreciation of risk and its role in life. A secure, more controlled and predictable childhood and adolescent setting tends to insulate the young, preventing them from appreciating, let alone addressing the role of risk and dealing with it in plotting life's course. Lack of experience in coping with the unknown spawns inertia in varying degrees, depending on individual character and the level of comfort with the status quo. Dangers lurk in the avoidance and fear of risk. Aversion to risk is a common enemy of progress—personal or societal.

In every setting, in wartime or in peace, I watched my parents define their options, weigh the range of potential risks and rewards, and then make decisions, knowing that complacency and inaction would levy a heavy toll. Their decision-making process taught me lessons that few children learn. They provided real time, real life illustrations of need to make cost/benefit assessments in life. The role of risk in life was brightly illuminated by upheavals and ever-changing circumstances through my early years. I learned to admit, respect and face realities and to reject wishful thinking. That called for frequent challenge of conventional wisdom. My childhood and student years left me better equipped than some to make my own choices, regularly having to set a course without a chart.

45811473R00214

Made in the USA
Middletown, DE
14 July 2017